Copyright © 2020 Eric L. Green, TG Publishing

All rights reserved. No part of this publication may be reproduced, distributed, or transmitted in any form or by any means, including photocopying, recording, or other electronic or mechanical methods, without the prior written permission of the publisher, except in the case of brief quotations embodied in critical reviews and certain other non-commercial uses permitted by copyright law. for permission request, right to the publisher, addressed "Attention: Permissions Coordinator," at the address below.

TG Publishing
One Audubon Street, Third Floor
New Haven, CT 06511
(203) 285-8545

Table of Contents

About the Author 6

Why Businesses Get Into Trouble With Payroll Taxes 8

How Payroll Taxes Work 9

    EFTPS: The Electronic Federal Tax Payment System 12

    Payroll Tax Penalties 12

Third-Party Liability 14

    The Willfulness Requirement 15

    Hochstein v. United States 15

    The 100% Penalty 16

    The Statute of Limitations 17

    The Purpose of IRC § 6672 and IRC § 3505 18

    Personal Liability: A Functional Test 19

    Purcell vs. United States 20

    So Who May Be A Responsible Person? 22

    Family Relationships and Dominance 24

    Edward Goodick v. United States of America 92-1 USTC ¶50,279 (E.D. La. 1992) .. 24

Assessment & Collection Against the Company 26

    The IRS Collection Division 27

    Collection Appeals 29

    The Statute of Limitations 31

    Federal Tax Liens 32

    Federal Tax Levies 33

    The Viability of the Company 34

Collection Alternatives 35

Installment Agreements 36

In-Business Trust Fund Express Installment Agreement 37

Regular Installment Agreement 37

Partial-Pay Installment Agreements 38

Defaulted Installment Agreements 39

Uncollectible Status 39

Offers-in-Compromise 40

Issues Concerning Business Assets 41

The Offer-in-Compromise Program 42

Lump-Sum Offers 43

Deferred Offer-in-Compromise 44

Reasonable Collection Potential (RCP) 44

Bankruptcy 45

The Automatic Stay 46

Discharging Taxes 46

Payment Plans 47

Tax Liens 48

Tax Compliance 49

Injunctions by the IRS Against Employers 50

Assessment Against the Responsible Party 53

The Trust Fund Recovery Penalty (IRC § 6672) 54

The Trust Fund Recovery Penalty (IRC § 3505) 55

The Assessment Process 55

Making the TFRP Determination 56

The Trust Fund Interview – Form 4180 57

Raising Collectability 58

The Proposed Trust Fund Assessment: Letter 1153 and Form 2751 59

So, Should the Taxpayer Sign the 2751 Waiver or Not Sign? 59

So, When Do I Have My Clients Sign the Form 2751 Waiver? 60

Challenging the Trust Fund Assessment 62

Protest 63

The FOIA Request 65

Copies of the Payroll Tax Returns 66

Bank Signature Card 66

Copies of Cancelled Checks 66

Speaking with Potential Witnesses 67

Doubt-as-to-Liability Offers ("DATL") 67

Refund 68

Strategies for Minimizing Personal Liability 70

Voluntary Payments – Revenue Procedure 2002-26 71

Shut-Down the Company 72

Criminal Aspects of Payroll Taxes 75

IRC § 7202 - Willful Failure to Collect or Pay Over Tax 76

The Duty to Collect and/or Truthfully Account and Pay Over 77

Failure to Collect, or Truthfully Account For and Pay Over 77

Willfulness 78

Statute of Limitations for Prosecution 79

IRC § 7215 - Offenses with Respect to Collected Taxes 79

Willfulness 80

Defense: Circumstances Beyond the Taxpayer's Control 80

The Non-Trust Portion - IRC § 7201: Attempt to Evade or Defeat Tax 81

Case Studies 82

Case Study 1 84

Case Study 2 86

Case Study 3 87

Case Study 4 89

Checklist: Payroll Tax Case 91

Exhibits 94

About the Author

Eric Green is a partner with the law firm of Green & Sklarz LLC in Connecticut & New York. The focus of Attorney Eric L. Green's practice is taxpayer representation before the Internal Revenue Service, Department of Justice Tax Division, Connecticut Department of Revenue Services as well as handling tax and estate planning for individuals and closely held businesses. He is a frequent lecturer on tax topics, including civil and criminal tax controversies. Eric was the creator, author and lecturer for CCH's Certificate Program in IRS Representation, which trained other tax professionals to handle IRS matters on behalf of clients. Attorney Green has also been quoted in The Wall Street Journal, USA Today, CreditCard.com, Consumer Reports Financial News, and is an advisor and columnist for CCH's Journal of Tax Practice & Procedure.

Eric is a past chair of the American Bar Association's Closely Held Businesses Committee, and has served as the chair of the subcommittees on Business Succession Planning and Estate Planning. Attorney Green is a past chair of the Connecticut Bar Association's Tax Section Executive Committee. Eric is also a Fellow of the American College of Tax Counsel, an organization in which membership is an honor reserved for those at the top of their chosen profession. The College's members, called "Fellows," are recognized for their extraordinary accomplishments and professional achievements and for their dedication to improving the practice of tax law. Fellows must be nominated by their peers for this honor. Self-nomination is not permitted. Each nominee must satisfy the established criteria and pass a rigorous screening process before he or she becomes a Fellow

Attorney Green has served as adjunct faculty at the University of Connecticut School of Law where he taught law students to handle taxpayer representation matters in the low income taxpayer clinic. Eric is also the founder of the New England IRS Representation Conference, an annual conference that brings practitioners and IRS personnel together from all 50 states and several countries for a full-day in IRS training and updates.

Attorney Green is admitted to practice in Connecticut, Massachusetts and New York, and admitted to practice before the United States Tax Court, the Federal Court of Claims and the Federal District of Connecticut. Attorney Green is also a member of the Connecticut and Massachusetts Bar Associations, as well as the American Bar Association. Attorney Green received his Bachelor of Business administration degree in Accounting with a minor in International Business from Hofstra University and is an honors graduate from New England School of Law. He earned a Masters of Laws in Taxation from Boston University School of Law.

Why Businesses Get Into Trouble With Payroll Taxes

Payroll taxes are the number one reason why businesses and their owners end up in our office. The issue is why?

Given that most businesses fail due to cash-flow issues, it should not be surprising that taxes collected and withheld by the business also get spent when the business starts to struggle. Add to that most businesses start their life cycle under-capitalized, and it is easy to see why payroll tax debt can become a problem.

Payroll taxes are the easiest loan to take and the hardest to pay back. Easy because there are no loan documents to fill out or permission to ask. Just keep and spend the money. It is the hardest loan to pay back because with all the various penalties and interest, the struggling business soon finds itself in a financial hole it has no hope of getting out from.

The worst part about payroll tax debts is the personal liability to the owners and, even, certain employees. Because of the potential personal liability, not making payroll tax deposits has the potential to destroy the owner's personal finances. Because of the devastation that can be wrought by not paying the payroll taxes, resolution of such claims makes the knowledgeable tax practitioner extremely valuable.

This guide will explain in detail how payroll tax debts are assessed, what can be done to save a business saddled with them, and how to resolve the owner/employee's personal liability. I hope you find it useful and educational.

Eric L. Green, Esq.

How Payroll Taxes Work

Payroll taxes are a significant stream of revenue for the United States Government. In 2018 more than $1.13 trillion were collected in federal employment taxes and more than $1.34 trillion collected in income taxes withheld by employers. The total taxes paid over by employers on behalf of employees totaled more than $2.48 trillion, representing more than 71% of all the taxes collected by the United States Government.[1]

Income tax and Federal Insurance Contributions Act ("FICA") taxes are withheld from each employee's paycheck by the employer and paid over to the United States Government on either a weekly, monthly, quarterly or annual basis depending upon the size of the employer's payroll. These taxes are reported using the following forms:

- Form CT-1: Employer's Annual Railroad Retirement Tax Plan
- Form 720: Quarterly Federal Excise Tax Return
- Form 941: Employer's Quarterly Federal Tax Return
- Form 943: Employer's Annual Federal Tax Return for Agricultural Employees
- Form 944: Employer's Annual Federal Tax Return
- Form 945: Annual Return of Withheld Federal Income Tax
- Form 1042: Annual Withholding Tax Return for U.S. Source Income of Foreign Persons

FICA consists of a 6.2% tax for Social Security[2] and a 1.45% tax for Medicare withheld from an employee's gross pay, with a corresponding match from the employer. The amounts withheld by an employer from the employees for the employee's share of the FICA taxes and federal income tax are referred to as "Trust Funds" because the employer is holding these funds in trust for the United States Government.

In an effort to protect this revenue source, Congress created Internal Revenue Code ("IRC") § 6672 to allow the Commissioner of the Internal Revenue Service, when payroll taxes are not paid over to the government, to assess a penalty against individuals and/or businesses whom it deems to be responsible for accounting for and paying over the payroll taxes and who willfully failed to do so. The penalty is equal to 100% of those

---

[1] See IRS Databook for 2018: https://www.irs.gov/statistics/soi-tax-stats-irs-data-book
[2] For 2020, the maximum limit on earnings for withholding of Social Security tax is $137,700.00.

trust funds taxes not properly accounted for and paid over to the United States Government by the employer.

In addition to IRC § 6672, the IRS also has available IRC § 3505, which allows it to collect unpaid Trust Fund taxes from third party lenders who knowingly loaned funds to cover a company's net payroll knowing that the company either could not or would not deposit the payroll taxes.

There are also criminal aspects of failing to withhold and/or pay over payroll taxes. IRC § 7202 makes it a crime punishable by both fine and/or incarceration for those parties that willfully try to evade or defeat the accounting and payment of the trust funds to the United States Government. In light of the difficulty of proving intent, Congress later created IRC § 7215 making it a misdemeanor when individuals and/or businesses fail to account and pay over the Trust Fund taxes. IRC § 7215 reduced the fines and potential time for incarceration from those allowed under IRC § 7202 but, because it is a misdemeanor, there is no requirement for the Government to prove intent to obtain a conviction.

Though the Government has historically found it difficult to prove criminal intent where the payroll taxes were spent to sustain business operations, recently the IRS and United States Department of Justice have increased their enforcement in the payroll tax arena, both civilly and criminally. Now, the Department of Justice more frequently seeks injunctions against employers who fail to deposit properly and the prosecution of employers who violate IRC § 7202 and/or IRC § 7215.

The increased enforcement and focus on payroll tax issues creates opportunities for practitioners to help taxpayers and make money resolving these cases. These types of payroll tax cases tend to be more lucrative than the routine income tax collection case: the practitioner needs to resolve the issues for the employer, then often deals with the individual responsibility for the owners and officers. Practitioners will need to focus on compliance for the business, resolving the outstanding debt for both the business and individuals, and take a larger retainer than usual.

EFTPS: The Electronic Federal Tax Payment System

The Electronic Federal Tax Payment System, or EFTPS, is an online method for businesses and individuals to pay their employment taxes. Once enrolled in EFTPS, a business can use EFTPS to make tax payments electronically for the following taxes:

- Form 720 Quarterly Federal Excise Tax Return
- Form 940 Employer's Annual Federal Unemployment Tax (FUTA) Return
- Form 941 Employer's Quarterly Federal Tax Return
- Form 943 Employer's Annual Tax Return for Agriculture Employees
- Form 945 Annual Return of Withheld Federal Income Tax
- Form 990-C Farmer's Cooperative Association Income Tax Return
- Form 990-PF Return of Private Foundation
- Form 990-T Exempt Organization Business Income Tax Return
- Section 4947(a)(1) Charitable Trust Treated as a Private Foundation
- Form 1041 Fiduciary Income Tax Return
- Form 1042 Annual Withholding Tax Return for U.S. Sources of Income of
- Foreign Persons
- Form 1120 U.S. Corporation Income Tax Return
- Form CT-1 Employer's Annual Railroad Retirement Tax Return
- Section 4947(a)(1) Charitable Trust Treated as a Private Foundation

In addition, EFTPS can be used to make non-depository payments of Federal income, Department of the Treasury estimated, estate and gift, employment, and various specified excise taxes.

Payroll Tax Penalties

There are a number of penalties that generally apply when an employer fails to properly account and pay over the payroll taxes. These penalties are significant, and include the following:

- Failure to File: The failure to file a Form 941 or Form 940 is 5% per month, limited to 25%;
- Failure to Pay: The penalty for failing to pay over payroll taxes is .5% per month, limited to 25%;
- Failure to Deposit Penalties: the penalty for failing to make federal payroll tax deposits depends upon the number of days late that the deposit is ultimately made:
    - 2% Deposits made 1 to 5 days late.
    - 5% Deposits made 6 to 15 days late.
    - 10% Deposits made 16 or more days late, but before 10 days from the date of the first notice the IRS sent asking for the tax due.
    - 10% Amounts that should have been deposited, but instead were paid directly to the IRS, or paid with your tax return.
    - 15% Amounts still unpaid more than 10 days after the date of the first notice the IRS sent asking for the tax due or the day on which you received notice and demand for immediate payment, whichever is earlier.
- Dishonored payment penalty: a penalty of 2 percent of the amount of the check or other commercial payment instrument generally applies if the check does not clear the bank. However, if the amount of the check or other commercial payment instrument is less than $1,250, the penalty is $25 or the amount of the check or other commercial payment instrument, whichever is less.

The reason why payroll tax issues become so difficult to overcome is because the failure to withhold and pay-over the moneys properly adds up, but then the application of the penalties and interest piles up. Often business owners believe they can make up the shortfall "soon". However, they do not appreciate how severe the penalties are. Eventually they show up in our office where the liability is now so large the business has almost no hope of climbing out of the financial hole.

Third-Party Liability

IRC § 6672 allows the Internal Revenue Service to recover "trust funds" withheld from employee's pay from "any person required to collect, truthfully account for, and pay over any tax imposed" and "who willfully fails to collect such tax, or truthfully account for and pay over such tax, or willfully attempts in any manner to evade or defeat any such tax or the payment thereof"

There are two key elements required for an individual or business to be held responsible for the Trust Fund Recovery Penalty under IRC § 6672:

1. The person had to be required to collect, account and pay-over the payroll taxes, and
2. The person's failure to do so must have been willful.

The Willfulness Requirement

For purposes of IRC § 6672 the failure to account and pay over the payroll taxes must have been willful.

The IRS' stated position is that willfulness exists where "money withheld from employees as taxes, in lieu of being paid over to the Government, was knowingly and intentionally used to pay the operating expenses of the business, or for other purposes."[3] The fact that there are insufficient funds to pay both employees and taxes is not a defense. In such a case, employers are expected to prorate the payments so that the employees get a portion of their pay and the IRS obtains the proper amount of withholding for the pay distributed. Individuals with sufficient control over the payroll process will be deemed responsible when the company fails to pay-over the payroll taxes, even if they are not the ultimate decision maker. Thus bookkeepers, finance personnel, and even third-parties such as accountants and bankers, can be held liable.

Hochstein v. United States

In *Hochstein v. United States*[4] the taxpayer was the controller of a corporation that was in financial trouble. An outside lender agreed to advance the money for operations in

---

[3] Revenue Ruling 54-158
[4] 900 F.2d 543 (2nd Circuit, 1990)

exchange for the company's receivables and equipment. As the company wound down operations, the outside lender reduced its advances, allowing the taxpayer to only pay for the bare essentials, including fuel and net payroll, despite repeated requests to the lender for more money to pay the payroll taxes.

When the IRS pursued Mr. Hochstein as a responsible party for the unpaid payroll taxes the taxpayer argued that he did not have the ultimate authority to determine whether the funds advanced could be used for the payroll deposits. The court determined that the taxpayer was responsible, holding that for a taxpayer to be subject to the trust fund recovery penalty, it is not necessary for such individual to have ultimate decision-making authority, but rather just have "significant control" over the disbursements.[5] As the controller for the company, Mr. Hochstein had control over the disbursements and was in a position to see that the taxes were paid over to the United States properly.

As Mr. Hochstein discovered, simply taking orders is not a defense to the Trust Fund Recovery Penalty. For taxpayers in Mr. Hochstein's position, withdrawing from his or her employment may be the only way to avoid personal liability for unpaid Trust Fund taxes.

The 100% Penalty

The "penalty" authorized by IRC § 6672, referred to as the 100% penalty, is a penalty in lieu of the taxes that were not withheld, meaning that the penalty is used to collect the actual tax itself, not an addition to the tax.[6] Practitioners frequently confuse this issue, believing that the penalty effectively doubles the tax, i.e. what will be collected are both the tax and an additional penalty equal to 100% of the tax. The reality is that the IRS policy is only to collect the tax once, and the penalty is used to collect the equivalent of the tax that should have been paid over by the employer.[7]

Example: XYZ Corp. fails to pay over three quarters of federal payroll taxes totaling $95,000 in taxes, plus $22,000 in penalties and $8,500 in interest. The Trust Fund portion of the payroll tax liability is $57,000. Corporate Officer A is deemed by the IRS to be responsible for the failure of XYZ Corp's failure to pay over the payroll taxes.

---

[5] Id.
[6] IRS Policy Statement P-5-60 (2/2/1993), at IRM 1.2.1.5.14
[7] Id.

Pursuant to IRC § 6672 Officer A would be subject to a penalty equal to 100% of the trust fund taxes that XYZ Corp failed to pay over to the IRS, or $57,000. Officer A would not be personally responsible for the non-trust fund portion of the payroll taxes (the employer's match), the penalties or the interest.

The Statute of Limitations

Once a tax is assessed against either an individual or business the IRS has ten years to collect the tax.[8] A separate ten-year collection statute will start for the Trust Fund Recovery Penalty once it is assessed against the responsible parties pursuant to IRC § 6672. The ten-year collection statute against the parties assessed pursuant to the Trust Fund Recovery Penalty will continue until either the ten-year statute lapses or until the Trust Fund taxes are collected. This is true even after the ten-year collection statute to collect the taxes from the company has lapsed.

There are a number of events that toll the ten-year collection statute, meaning that the statute will cease to run while the event occurs, and such time must be added to the original ten-year collection period. These events include the following:

a) Issuance of a statutory notice of deficiency;[9]
b) Assets of the taxpayer are in control or custody of a court;[10]
c) The taxpayer is outside of the United States for a continuous period of 6 months;[11]
d) An extension exists for the payment of the estate tax;[12]
e) A wrongful seizure of property or a wrongful lien on property;[13]
f) Taxpayer files bankruptcy, which not only tolls the statute but adds an additional six months;[14]
g) Filing of a Collection Due Process (CDP) hearing request;[15]
h) Filing an Offer in Compromise;[16]

---

[8] IRC § 6502
[9] IRC § 6503(a)
[10] IRC § 6503(b)
[11] IRC § 6503(c)
[12] IRC § 6503(d)
[13] IRC § 6503(f)
[14] IRC § 6503(h)
[15] Regulation § 301.6330-1(g)
[16] Regulation § 301.7122-1(i)

i) Pending Installment Agreement: CSED is tolled from the date of the request for an installment agreement, plus appeals, plus 30 days.

The occurrence of any of the events listed above will add additional time to the ten-year collection statute.

Example. Taxpayer A, a former controller for a failed corporation with a payroll tax liability is formally assessed by the IRS as a responsible person for the Trust Fund Recovery Penalty on December 1, 2009. Pursuant to IRC § 6502 the IRS will have ten years to collect the Trust Fund taxes from Taxpayer A, or until November 30, 2019. Taxpayer A is forced to file personal bankruptcy on January 1, 2010 and is discharged from bankruptcy on June 30, 2010. The ten-year collection statute would be extended for an additional twelve months until November 30, 2020: six months for the time Taxpayer A was in bankruptcy and an additional six months pursuant to IRC § 6503(h).

IRC § 3505

In addition to IRC § 6672, the IRS also has available IRC § 3505, which allows it to collect unpaid Trust Fund taxes from third party lenders who knowingly loaned funds to cover a company's net payroll knowing that the company either could not or would not deposit the payroll taxes. The lender is potentially liable for the amount of the unpaid payroll taxes, limited to 25% of what the lender loaned to the employer. Though IRC § 3505 does not come up often, the parties usually involved are family and friends of the owner/employer. Most banks will not lend for net payroll, but rather extend a line of credit that the employer can use for whatever they need. It is the friend or family member that is asked for a loan to cover the workers payroll that gets dragged in as liable pursuant to IRC § 3505.

The Purpose of IRC § 6672 and IRC § 3505

So why does the IRS get so cranky when an employer fails to pay-over the payroll taxes? The reason is because the unpaid payroll taxes act as a double-hit to the government fisk:

- The government will be required to issue refunds to the employees who file their 1040 income tax returns despite the fact the IRS never received the funds, and
- The employees will need to be credited for their social security earnings, again, despite the fact the IRS never received the money.

Given that withholding accounts for more than 70% of the revenue into the United States government, it is easy to see why the IRS is aggressive about trying to protect this critical source of funds.

Personal Liability: A Functional Test

Many times, companies have many owners and key officers and employees. Can they all be responsible, or can the IRS only pursue one key employee? The answer is it depends upon who functionally was responsible. Though a person's title may be an indicator that he or she was responsible, the IRS will pursue those they believe were involved in the decision to willfully not pay the payroll taxes. The analysis is therefore a functional test.

Example: When XYZ corporation fails to pay its payroll taxes, a Revenue Officer from the IRS is assigned to do the investigation and enforcement follow-up to try and collect the unpaid taxes from the company and/or responsible individuals. The IRS Revenue Officer interviews three individuals:

- Mr. X, the President of the Corporation, who is generally absent from the home office and relies on the finance staff to handle the company finances,
- Ms. M., the Executive Vice-President of Sales, who oversees the field sales force but does not have signature authority for the company and is not involved in the finances of the company, and
- Ms. T., the Staff Accountant, who prepares all checks and pays the invoices for the company.

After a review of all the facts and circumstances the IRS ultimately deems both Mr. X and Ms. T as responsible for the unpaid payroll taxes. Mr. X is assessed because as President he is responsible for the oversight of the entire company, and disregarding that duty is generally not an excuse, as he had the power to make sure the taxes were paid but failed to properly manage the finances. Ms. T is also responsible because she had the power to pay the taxes but chose to pay other vendors and creditors instead. The fact that her title is "staff accountant" is not determinative, as the test is a functional test. This is the same reason Ms. M was cleared of any responsibility: though she is a senior executive she has no involvement in the financial functions of the company, and without signature authority, had no power to make sure the taxes were paid, which means her failure to make sure the taxes were properly paid was not willful (unlike Mr. X's).

Purcell vs. United States

In the case *Purcell vs. United States*, 1 F.3d 932 (9th Cir. 1993), the court reviewed the issue of whether a corporate president may be held personally liable for his corporation's failure to pay over federal withholding taxes to the Internal Revenue Service when he had delegated responsibility for all financial matters to his chief financial officer.

Joseph Purcell ("Purcell") was president and sole shareholder of Purcell Temporaries, Incorporated (the "Company"). From the time he founded the Company in 1978 until February 1980, Purcell also served as its chief financial officer ("CFO"). At that point, however, Purcell decided to devote more of his energies to sales and promotional activities, and so hired Lester Hatchard ("Hatchard") as CFO. This was not a good decision. Hatchard embezzled over $450,000 from the Company during his tenure, using a signature stamp bearing Purcell's signature to issue Company checks payable to himself.[17] Eventually, Purcell learned that Hatchard had a prior criminal record; confronted with this discovery, Hatchard resigned his position in July 1981.[18]

After Hatchard left the Company, Purcell reassumed control over its financial affairs. He quickly discovered that, contrary to what he had been led to believe, the Company was

---

[17] NEVER allow a client to use a signature stamp – this is asking to be embezzled!
[18] Hatchard later pled guilty to charges of embezzlement and served a prison term. In the same litigation which is the subject of this appeal, a default judgment was entered against Hatchard as a responsible person under § 6672 with respect to the Company's unpaid withholding taxes for the first two quarters of 1981.

in terrible financial shape, with a negative net worth, and a substantial bank overdraft. He also learned that Hatchard had failed to file federal employment tax returns for the first two quarters of 1981 (the "Hatchard Period"), and that the withheld taxes had not been paid over to the Internal Revenue Service.

There followed a number of meetings between Purcell and the IRS regarding the Company's tax situation. During the second and third quarters of 1982 (the "post-Hatchard Period"), returns were properly filed, but not all the withheld taxes were paid over. In 1983, the Company filed for bankruptcy protection.

On March 27, 1985, the IRS assessed Purcell in the amount of the unpaid withholding taxes for 1981 and 1982. Purcell eventually brought suit in federal district court, seeking refund of certain amounts transferred to the IRS in partial satisfaction of those liabilities, as well as other relief. The United States filed a counterclaim seeking judgment for the balance of the assessment. In January 1991, a three-day jury trial was held. At the close of the evidence both sides made motions for directed verdicts. A series of hearings was held over several days, after which the government's motion was granted, and Purcell's denied. Purcell appealed the decision to the 9th Circuit Court of Appeals.

At the 9th Circuit Mr. Purcell argued that he was not a responsible person during the Hatchard Period, and that he did not willfully fail to pay over taxes withheld during that period. In upholding the lower court's decision, the Appeals Court concluded that Mr. Purcell was a responsible person within the meaning of IRC § 6672, and he had the authority required to exercise significant control over the corporation's financial affairs, regardless of whether he exercised such control in fact. The authority that permits control carries with it a nondelegable duty to ensure that withholding taxes are duly collected and paid over to the government. The court also found that after Mr. Purcell reassumed control of the Company's finances and knowing that the Company had not remitted to the government the taxes withheld during the Hatchard Period, he paid out corporate funds to numerous other creditors while the company operated. Every such payment was an intentional act to prefer other creditors over the United States.[19]

---

[19] *Purcell vs. United States*, 1 F.3d 932 (9th Cir. 1993).

So Who May Be A Responsible Person?

As you have probably noticed, anyone who is involved in the finances of the employer and who has the ability to determine which creditors are paid may be deemed responsible for any unpaid taxes. The list of the usual employees deemed responsible include:

- Sole Proprietors
- Partners
- Bookkeepers
- Lenders/creditors
- Accounting firms
- Parent companies
- Purchasing companies

Whether someone will be held liable is based on the specific facts and circumstances.

Example 1: Taxpayer is a Senior Vice-President of sales for a chain of automobile dealerships. She is in charge of all the sales force and makes constant trips to each dealership to check on sales numbers. Taxpayer has neither signature authority over the bank accounts nor is she involved in the finances of the company. Taxpayer should not be deemed responsible for any unpaid payroll taxes for the dealerships given she is not functionally responsible for the finances of the company, despite her impressive title.

Example 2: Staff accountant works for a construction company. She is a long-time friend of the owner and comes in one day a week to do the books and pay the bills, as Joe the owner is busy on job sites. Each Friday she signs the checks and mails them to the various vendors. For those weeks that she does not have enough money to cover all the bills she pays the vendors (because without supplies the company will close) and simply assumes they will make up the unpaid payroll taxes later when things improve. A year later, when the IRS does catch up with the company, she will most likely be held responsible for the unpaid trust fund portion of the payroll taxes. Despite not being an owner and only working part-time, she was responsible for payment, had check signing authority, and made the decision to pay other vendors instead of the payroll taxes. Thus, she was responsible, acted willfully, and is liable for the TFRP.

Example 3: Similar to the staff accountant in number 2, here our bookkeeper arrives each week and prepares the checks for the owner. Upon updating the books, the bookkeeper calls the owner and discusses which vendors should be paid. She then signs those checks and mails them, with the rest left in the safe for the owner to mail later when he has the money. Here, the bookkeeper is potentially liable for the TFRP – she can sign checks: But she could avoid liability if she can show she was acting at the owner's direction, her signature authority was merely for his convenience, and she did not actually have authority to decide which bills to pay.[20]

As the examples above show, the facts are critical. Practitioners need to make sure they completely understand the chronology of events and obtain backup to support their client's position. Generally speaking, taxpayers who do not have signature authority cannot be held liable for unpaid taxes that they themselves had no ability to assure were paid. The one notable exception is where one taxpayer wields so much influence over another that they can be held responsible even though they had no signature authority over the bank accounts.

---

[20] In the actual case, we managed to find several worksite supervisors who signed affidavits that they were present when the owner instructed her who to pay and which bills/taxes to not pay. The IRS Appeals Office eventually cleared her of any responsibility.

Family Relationships and Dominance

When it comes to family members who work in the company, the courts have taken in account such family relationships in determining responsible person status where one member of the family is domineering and assertive.[21]

Edward Goodick v. United States of America 92-1 USTC ¶50,279 (E.D. La. 1992)

Plaintiff Edward D. Goodick is the son of Randall G. Goodick, who was president of Northwood Cuisine, Inc. ("Northwood") from its inception in 1979 until its liquidation in Chapter 7 bankruptcy proceedings in 1982. During its corporate existence, Northwood operated on the Gulf Coast of Mississippi as a franchisee of Popeye's Fried Chicken ("Popeye's").

The uncontradicted evidence also shows that Randall Goodick dominated Edward Goodick in all of his affairs. Even though he managed some of the company's restaurants and was authorized to sign checks, he could not disburse funds except in emergency situations, and he did not have authority to pay creditors. In addition, although he held the office of Secretary/Treasurer and technically owned 10 percent of the stock of the corporation, he did not control that interest, had no authority to sell the stock, and was completely accountable to his father. Finally, even if it had been determined that he was a responsible person, he lacked authority to pay the taxes and other debts of the corporation and, therefore, could not be found to have willfully failed to carry out that responsibility.

When Edward Goodick got married in September of 1979, his father insisted that he execute a prenuptial agreement so that he could insulate his ten percent (10%) Northwood stock from his wife's potential control. Edward Goodick testified that he

---

[21] McCullough v. U.S., 462 F.2d 588 (5th Cir. 1972) (Son not responsible person where father had sole and dominating control of the corporation); Barrett v. U.S., 580 F.2d 449 (Ct. Cl. 1978) (No responsible person status where wife did not act willfully, was dominated by husband, and was powerless to write company checks without husband's specific authorization). See Williams v. U.S., 25 Cl. Ct. 682 (1992) (Officer who prepared and signed tax returns not responsible person because he lacked independent authority and was kept on a "short leash" by his father); Goodick v. U.S., 92-1 USTC ¶50,279 (E.D. La. 1992) (Son not responsible person because his father dominated son's decisions such that he had no significant control over company).

believed that if he did not execute the agreement, his father would have taken his ten percent (10%) stock interest away. Even as late as September 1992, when Edward Goodick completed Internal Revenue Service Form 4180[22], he did so at his father's instructions. It was his father who told him to write "About 2 weeks before the Co. filed Chapter 11" in response to the question "When did you first become aware that the tax liability was not paid?" Edward Goodick testified that he and his father jointly filled out the 4180 forms and his father wanted to make sure that everything agreed.

The court found that Edward Goodick was not liable for the unpaid employee withholding taxes of the corporation because he was not a responsible person obligated to withhold and pay over taxes. Accordingly, he was entitled to a refund of civil penalties assessed for the willful failure to pay taxes.

---

[22] Form 4180 *Report of Interview with Individual Relative to Trust Fund Recovery Penalty or Personal Liability for Excise Taxes* is discussed in detail in Chapter 4 of this book.

Assessment & Collection Against the Company

When a company fails to either file its employment tax returns or make its employment tax deposits, the IRS Collection process will start. It is the IRS's Collection Division that is responsible for obtaining missing tax returns, making sure the tax liability is assessed and then attempt to collect the outstanding balance.

The IRS Collection Division

This is the official mission statement of the IRS Collection Division:

> *The mission of Field Collection is to provide SB/SE [Small Business/Self-Employed] taxpayers with top quality post-filing services by helping them understand and comply with all applicable tax laws and by applying the tax laws with integrity and fairness.*

Our experience is that most clients don't find the IRS "post-filing services" to be either top quality or educational. They find them to be abusive, scary, and financially devastating. Clients often don't understand what is expected of them and how to work with collection division personnel, and the government employees of the Collection Division don't bother to explain the process to the taxpayer.

In order to properly represent the company and its owner you will need an executed IRS Power of Attorney Form 2848, one for the company (see Exhibit 1) and one for the owner (see Exhibit 2).

Once the tax is assessed, a billing notice is mailed to the taxpayer requesting payment (see Exhibit 3). If the tax is paid in full, including interest and penalties, then the deficiency for that tax period is closed.

If the tax due continues to go unpaid, then additional notices are sent to the taxpayer. These include:

Types of Additional Notices	
CP-501	You have a balance due (money you owe the IRS) on one of your tax accounts.
CP-503	We have not heard from you, and you still have an unpaid balance on one of your tax accounts.
CP-504	Intent to Levy. You have an unpaid amount due on your account. If you do not pay the amount due immediately, the IRS will seize your assets in an attempt to pay the balance due.

After these notices have been sent, another notice will arrive: "Final Notice of Intent to Levy and Your Right to a Hearing," ("Final Notice", see Exhibit 6). With the Final Notice also comes a blank Form 12153, "Request for a Collection Due Process or Equivalent Hearing,"[23] also referred to as "CDP." (see Exhibit 7). The Final Notice is a critical notice, because 30 days after the date of this notice, levy action may commence against the taxpayer. The way you stop the levy action is by requesting the hearing with the Form 12153.

At any time during the process, the taxpayers can establish a resolution to their tax problems. Some critical points to consider:

- Get any missing employment tax returns filed as soon as possible.

---

[23] There are three versions of the "Final Notice": Letter 1058, which is sent from IRS Headquarters Collections, a letter CP-90 utilized by the field collection force (Revenue Officers), and a Letter 11 comes from the Automated Collection Service area of Collections ("ACS").

- Open the mail! Opening the mail is critical to understanding the tax situation and knowing when to call the IRS, or more critical, when to seek professional tax help.
- Respond to IRS requests in a timely fashion.
- Every response should be sent in a way that the taxpayers can prove when they sent it: fax with a fax receipt, certified or registered mail, or overnight service that can be tracked. It may become critical for the taxpayers later to have to prove they sent in something by a particular date, so this is no time to get cheap! They should spend the extra money and send the filing by certified mail.

Collection Appeals

It is critical that the Form 12153 be filed within 30 days of the date on the Final Notice. In fact, with the exception of certain circumstances discussed later (under the Statute of Limitations section), it is (in the author's opinion) essential to file the CDP request. By filing the CDP request, a number of things will happen in the taxpayer's case:

- The IRS ceases all collection action against the taxpayer for the tax periods in question,[24] with notable exception (see the section on Disqualified Employment Tax Levies later in this Chapter);
- The taxpayer's case is forwarded to Appeals;
- The taxpayer has the right to go to the Tax Court if the taxpayer cannot work out an arrangement with Appeals; and
- The taxpayer has additional time to prepare any missing returns and sort out the proposal for resolving the outstanding tax debt.

Unfortunately, many taxpayers (and their equally clueless practitioners) don't realize the seriousness of the need to file the appeal. The National Taxpayer Advocate reports that only about 3% of taxpayers ever take advantage of their appeal rights!

---

[24] Collection action will cease for a CDP filed on a Final Notice of Intent to Levy. It does NOT stop when the CDP is filed for the filing of a Notice of Federal Tax Lien.

What if the taxpayer misses the 30-day deadline to request the CDP hearing? On page 2 of Form 12153 there is a box, line item 7, that if the request is late, the taxpayer would like a hearing equivalent to a CDP hearing (see Exhibit 7). The taxpayer has up to one year to request an equivalent hearing in this manner, that is, by filing the Form 12153 and checking line item 7. This still gets the case to Appeals. However, by requesting an equivalent hearing (having missed their 30-day CDP request deadline) the taxpayer has lost some significant rights:

- Collection action does not stop for an equivalent hearing, so the taxpayers or their representative still have to continue dealing with the collection division while they await their appeal;
- There is no right to go to the United States Tax Court, as anything the appeals officer decides at the equivalent hearing is final.

> **HOT TIP**
>
> If the Final Notice is received, the taxpayer must file the CDP request! It is critical for the taxpayers to file their request for a CDP within 30-days from the date on the letter. In doing so they stop any enforced collection action against them and preserve their right to go to Appeals and the Tax Court.

The IRS cannot extend more time to the taxpayer. The CDP right is statutory, created by Congress, and IRS personnel have no authority to grant the taxpayer more time. Many times taxpayers call the IRS, and the IRS tells the taxpayers they will give them more time to get information. This additional time is the IRS agreeing to voluntarily hold off on levy action. If later the IRS Collection Division and the taxpayer do not come to terms, the taxpayer has lost the right to a CDP hearing and an appeal to the Tax Court.

The Statute of Limitations

The IRS has 10 years from the date of assessment to collect a tax debt. In most cases, after 10 years the debt becomes unenforceable. For example, if the fourth quarter Form 941 is electronically filed and assessed on January 25, 2015, then the 10-year statute would begin on that date and run until January 24, 2025. If the balance went unpaid and an IRS Revenue Officer began collection action and assessed the owner as a responsible person under IRC § 6672 on May 1, 2015, then the individual owner would have their own 10-year collection statute running for the unpaid trust fund portion of the payroll taxes from May 1, 2015 until April 30, 2025.

How does a practitioner know the date of assessment? Practitioners should obtain what are called "Account Transcripts" from the IRS that list everything that has occurred with that particular tax year for the taxpayer, including when the return was received, when the tax was assessed, the penalty and interest charged, and payments received. If you have never seen an Account Transcript there is one at the end of this chapter (see Exhibit 8). It is usually best to obtain the Account Transcripts for both the Form 1040 as well as Civil Penalties when dealing with an individual taxpayer.

The reason the statute of limitations is so important is that the amount of time remaining on the collection statute determines which solution the practitioner should select to resolve the client's tax liability.

The other key point about the statute of limitations is that certain actions on a client's part will toll, or freeze, the statute, preventing it from running. Such actions include the filing of an Offer-in-Compromise, filing a CDP request, requesting an installment agreement, and filing for bankruptcy.[25] These actions prevent the IRS from taking collection action, and, therefore, stop the 10-year collection statute from running. The rationale is that it would be unfair to allow the statute to run against the government while it is prevented from taking collection action.

For instance, if the liability is recent and most of the 10-year limitations period remains, an Offer-in-Compromise may make the most sense, as clients don't want the liability

---

[25] The filing of a bankruptcy by statute not only tolls the statute from running but adds an additional six months. So for example, a bankruptcy filed on January 1 that was discharged on May 31 would add 11 months to the collection statute: the five for the bankruptcy plus the extra six-months by statute.

Page 31

hanging over their head for years to come. If, however, the tax liability is already older and not much more time remains on the limitations period, perhaps having the taxpayer deemed currently-not-collectable makes sense, as this would allow you to hold the IRS Collection Division at bay while the 10-year statute continues running on the old tax debt.

The tolling of the collection statute is why filing Offers-in-Compromise that have no chance of success accomplishes nothing but wasting the practitioner's valuable time and the client's limited resources.

Federal Tax Liens

The federal tax lien arises automatically by law. The IRS doesn't have to file anything for the statutory lien to come into being. However, in an effort to put other potential creditors on notice, the IRS files a Notice of Federal Tax Lien (NFTL) if the taxpayer owes more than $10,000 and fails to pay it upon demand (the billing notice). This filing is not only embarrassing, but it could impact the client's credit and starts an avalanche of junk mail from those national tax-help companies.[26] Why?

Those national tax-help companies that have not yet been put out of business for deceptive marketing purchase lists of new tax liens that are filed and send all sorts of mail to the taxpayer promising "pennies on the dollar" settlements. Sometimes it's even worse. They send letters that are designed to look like formal IRS notices, misleading the taxpayer into calling and hiring them, believing they are actually dealing with the IRS.

Though the Notice of Federal Tax Lien filing can be upsetting to taxpayers, it generally is not the biggest concern. Tax levies have a far more destructive impact!

---

[26] The IRS ceased reporting tax debts directly to the credit reporting agencies several years ago. However, it is still possible for the credit reporting agencies to find the tax debts through public filings or information provided voluntarily by the taxpayer on a financial statement or credit application.

Federal Tax Levies

A tax levy is the seizing of a taxpayer's assets to pay the back tax debt. This can include a garnishment of wages, a seizure of everything in the taxpayer's bank account at a given moment in time, and a seizure of money owed to the taxpayer by third parties. Levies, unlike liens, can cause not only embarrassment but immediate economic devastation. I frequently get new clients after the IRS has issued levies. The conversation generally goes like this:

> *"Attorney Green, I need to see you right away!"*
>
> *"Why?"*
>
> *"The IRS just cleaned out our company's bank accounts."*

Thankfully, the IRS has a process that it must follow before it gets to the point of issuing levies (see the notices listed previously). However, it is all too often that clients ignore the IRS notices and then seem shocked when the levies are served. Worse, now they have to borrow the money to hire the professional to help them. And, when it comes to payroll taxes, the IRS could levy both the company's bank accounts and those accounts and wages of the responsible individuals in an attempt to recover the unpaid payroll taxes (assuming the TFRP has been assessed).

Once a levy has been issued there is an opportunity to have it released and the money put back if the taxpayer's representative moves quickly (banks hold the money taken for 21 days before sending it to the IRS in case your client can get a release). These steps include the following:

1. Call the IRS.
2. Find out what the IRS is missing as far as business returns (entity and employment tax).
3. Explain that the missing returns and collection documentation will be provided to them within 30 days.

4. Ask to have the levy released because it is causing an economic hardship. It's amazing how often this works, and the IRS releases the levy if it's the first time in contact with the taxpayer.

Think about what just happened: The professional contacted the IRS and told them the taxpayer will get into compliance and send paperwork with a proposed resolution for the back taxes. This is exactly what the IRS wanted to hear, and this is how to start the process of getting the client's issue resolved.

Of course, when the client shows up in our office, we have a big issue to deal with first: is this company worth saving?

The Viability of the Company

So, the client comes to our office and starts off with,

"I have a great little company..."

(Listen, if the taxpayer had a great little company, he or she would probably not be in my office, but let's continue.)

"I have a great company. My dad started it and I am hoping my daughter will take it over. Unfortunately, we have fallen a bit behind on our payroll taxes. And then this woman from the IRS shows up, looked around like she was seeing what she could seize from us and is threatening to close us down."

"I bet she did, and yes, she will seize the assets if we do not address this issue. Okay Mr. Owner, can I see the notices she dropped off?"

After I scan the notices, doing some quick math, I ask him how much the company is netting each year. He shows me a cash basis profit and loss with a profit of $97,000.

"We net about $100,000 per year," he tells me proudly.

> "Great," I respond, "and you have been running up about $70,000 a year in taxes, plus penalties and interest. So in reality this company is netting about $30,000, right?"

His stunned look tells me all I need to know.

> "You see," I continue, "if you had paid you taxes properly and on-time you would have netted around $27,000. I am not sure how much income personally you need to live on but after your personal expenses are allowed, I do not see how this company is viable in its current condition. Meaning I do not see how this company can afford to start repaying this debt. Something tells me that the friendly neighborhood IRS Revenue Officer knows this too."

The first critical decision is whether the company is worth saving. We need to walk through with the client what is causing the tax problem and whether it can be changed and fixed. If the company is viable, restructuring options can be discussed. Otherwise, the company should be closed.

Business people love their business. Taxpayers need to understand that the company is an asset no different than any other asset, like a stock or a bond. The only difference is that when the business goes bad it has the potential to destroy the taxpayer's other assets as well (see Chapter 4 about personal liability).

Collection Alternatives

Assuming we have determined that the company is viable and is worth saving, then there are four options for resolving the business's tax debt, three of which you can propose to the IRS:

- An Installment Agreement
- Uncollectable Status
- An Offer-in-Compromise

The fourth option is bankruptcy, which is not actually something you do with the IRS. Bankruptcy is a legal proceeding that attorneys can handle. We touch on bankruptcy later on in this chapter, but the detailed scope and analysis for a taxpayer to make the decision to use bankruptcy to resolve the tax issue, and the many variables that must be considered when deciding, is beyond the scope of this Guide.

Installment Agreements

An installment agreement is an agreement between the IRS and a taxpayer to allow the taxpayer to pay the back-tax debt in monthly payments. There are various forms of installment agreement, each of which has special rules.

There is something practitioners and taxpayers need to understand when setting out to negotiate an agreement with the IRS: the IRS knows that installment agreements historically default within 48 months, and, therefore, the IRS is told to collect as much as it can as fast as it can. This is an issue when taxpayers try to negotiate smaller payments for longer periods of time.

When determining what a business can afford to pay monthly through an installment agreement a practitioner needs to consider the owners as well. The reason for factoring in the owner's financial needs is that without doing so, the business may, or may not, end up paying an amount it can afford.

Example: ABC is an Subchapter S Corporation and owes $100,000 to the IRS for unpaid payroll taxes. ABC's sole shareholder and employee is Dave. ABC pays Dave a salary of $60,000 and has net profit distributions to Dave of an additional $70,000. The IRS should obtain a Collection Information Statement on ABC Corp (Form 433-B) and one on Dave personally (Form 433-A). If the collection analysis of Dave shows he needs $80,000 a year to cover his allowable expenses, the IRS should seek an installment agreement of the $50,000 remaining after Dave's necessary salary and distributions ($60,000 of salary plus $70,000 of profit means ABC has $130,000 available less the $80,000 Dave needs to live).

When it comes to installment agreements for businesses there are three variations:

1. In-Business Trust Fund Express installment agreements (if the business owes less than $25,000).[27]
2. Regular.
3. Partial Pay

The IRS charges fees for setting up an installment agreement. The current fee structure (as of 2019) is: $105 for non-direct debit agreements, $52 for direct debit agreements, and $45 for reinstatements.

In-Business Trust Fund Express Installment Agreement

A streamlined installment agreement is a payment plan where, if the taxpayers meet the following criteria, they can either make a phone call to the IRS and arrange an installment agreement or do so online through the IRS website:

- The business owes less than $25,000.
- The taxpayer has not had a back-tax debt or an installment agreement in the last five years.
- The taxpayer agrees to pay the liability in full within 24 months in equal, level payments.

With a streamlined agreement the taxpayer doesn't have to provide any financial information.

Regular Installment Agreement

When a business can't meet the requirements of a streamlined installment agreement either because it owes more than $25,000 or because it is unable to repay the amount back at the rate required by a streamlined installment agreement (that is, within 24 months), then the taxpayer will be required to complete a Collection Information

---

[27] IRM 5.14.5.1.

Statement (IRS Form 433). The IRS uses Form 433-B for a business (see Exhibit 9). Generally speaking, the IRS will want the net income from the business used to repay the back taxes. I say 'generally' because the owners personal expenses do need to be considered when setting up a payment plan with the IRS.

For individuals, the IRS will use Form 433-A to determine the individual's necessary expenses (see Exhibit 10). When an employer has a payroll tax liability the IRS will request a 433-B for the business and a 433-A for the owner or owners. The reason for the 433-A is that, without knowing how much money the owner needs to live, it is impossible to properly set-up the business's installment agreement.

Example: ABC company has net income of $125,000 before salaries to the owner and any profits. After a 433-A analysis we determine the owner needs $75,000 to cover his or her allowable living expenses. That would leave $50,000 a year available for the company to use toward paying the back tax debt.

The benefit of a regular installment agreement is that, so long as the taxpayers remain in tax compliance and makes their installment agreement payments on-time, they won't have to revisit their payment plan. A default of the agreement results in the IRS cancelling the payment plan and beginning the process all over again. Also, unlike a streamlined installment agreement which requires equal level payments, a regular installment agreement can have a step up or step down in the monthly payment based on the reasonable circumstances of the taxpayer.

Partial-Pay Installment Agreements

A partial-pay installment agreement, known as a PPIA, is exactly the same as a regular installment agreement, with one exception. Here the taxpayer doesn't show the ability to pay the balance due in full over the time remaining on the statute. Just like the regular installment agreement, the IRS agrees to set up the payment plan based upon the taxpayer's ability to pay. Unlike the regular agreement, the IRS will revisit the taxpayer's ability to pay. Hence, taxpayers who enter into PPIAs can expect to be contacted by the

IRS again to revisit their financial condition (usually within two years) and see whether the taxpayer can afford to increase their monthly payment.

Defaulted Installment Agreements

Taxpayers default on their installment agreement by doing any of the following:

- Failing to make employment tax deposits timely
- Incurring a new employment tax penalty
- Failing to file a tax return timely
- Failing to make their installment payments

When taxpayers default on their installment agreement the IRS will send them a letter (CP 523) "Intent to Terminate your Installment Agreement" (see Exhibit 11). The taxpayer will have to either pay the balance due in full, request an Appeal under the Collection Appeal Process (see IRS Form 9423, Exhibit 12), or contact collections to begin renegotiating for a new installment agreement.

Uncollectible Status

What happens when taxpayers have no equity in available assets and their income is not sufficient to cover their IRS allowable expenses? The taxpayers will be deemed "uncollectible," also referred to as "CNC." (see Exhibit 13) Both individuals and businesses may have their accounts deemed uncollectible.

When taxpayers are deemed uncollectable, it means that the taxpayers' accounts are coded so that the IRS doesn't take any levy action against them. Being uncollectable doesn't actually resolve the outstanding tax issue, but it does do a number of things for the taxpayer:

- The 10-year collection statute continues to run, and

- The IRS will not take enforcement action against either the taxpayer's assets or income.

The taxpayer still owes the money, so interest continues to run on the outstanding debt, and the IRS may still file a Notice of Federal Tax Lien to secure its interest in anything the taxpayer owns or after-acquires.

So if having a taxpayer deemed uncollectable doesn't really resolve the issue, why consider this as a collection alternative?

There are times when an Offer-in-Compromise simply will not work, such as when the owner has equity in assets that he or she cannot tap to fund an Offer. Though the IRS generally does not like making an ongoing company uncollectible, it will do so where the company is necessary to create an income stream for the taxpayer and their family.

Offers-in-Compromise

One of the most popular yet misunderstood programs the IRS has for settling an outstanding tax debt is the Offer-in-Compromise, or "OIC", or "Offer", in practitioner speak.

An Offer-in-Compromise is a proposal for the IRS to accept less than the total owed by a taxpayer to settle the taxpayer's outstanding tax debt. What many taxpayers don't understand is that the OIC program, at its core, is a formula. Hence, many offers filed by taxpayers and practitioners are not accepted because they fail to consider the formula and make offers that stand no chance of success from the moment they are filed with the IRS.

The IRS does accept many offers. But to be accepted, the Offer must meet the requirements established by the IRS. In this section we review the Offer-in-Compromise program, discuss the various forms of offers that can be pursued, and review common issues that arise when you are preparing offers. Finally, we discuss appealing a denied offer, that is, how to prepare the appeal and file it.

When an Offer is filed it uses its own special financial forms: Form 433-A (OIC) for individual taxpayers, Form 433-B (OIC) for business entities, and the Offer-in-Compromise itself, Form 656. All of these forms are found in the IRS Offer Booklet, 656-B. (See Exhibit 14)

How does the IRS determine what a taxpayer should offer? It's called "Reasonable Collection Potential," or RCP. As long as the taxpayer's offer meets or exceeds the IRS calculated RCP, then the offer should be accepted.

Active companies seeking an Offer-in-Compromise raise particular issues, such as going-concern value and the assets of the business that may have equity but also are necessary for the production of income.

Issues Concerning Business Assets

The IRS will look at business assets when considering an Offer-in-Compromise. When investigating the RCP for an offer that includes business assets, an analysis is necessary to determine if certain assets are essential for the production of income. When it has been identified that an asset or a portion of an asset is necessary for the production of income, it is appropriate to adjust the income or expense calculation for that taxpayer to account for the loss of income stream if the asset was either liquidated or used as collateral to secure a loan to fund the offer.

As a general rule, equity in income producing assets will not be added to the RCP of a viable, ongoing business; unless it is determined the assets are not critical to business operations. The bigger issue is what to do when the business is losing money.

The way the IRS will look at the assets therefore is as follows:

IF	THEN
There is no equity in the assets	There is no adjustment necessary to the income stream.

There is equity in the assets and no available income stream (i.e. profit) produced by those assets	There is no adjustment necessary to the income stream. Consider including the equity in the asset in the RCP.
There are both equity in assets that are determined to be necessary for the production of income and an available income stream produced by those assets	Determine if an adjustment to income or expenses is appropriate.
An asset used in the production of income will be liquidated to help fund an offer	Adjusting the income to account for the loss of the asset may be appropriate.
The asset owned by the business is real estate and has equity	Include the equity in the RCP and adjust the income for any loan that needs to be repaid to tap the equity

If the business is generating income for the taxpayer, the IRS will generally not include the equity in the RCP calculation for an Offer given the assets are necessary for the family to produce income to live. If, however, the business is not generating income, or there are excess assets, then the equity in those assets will be included in the RCP calculation, and any repayment for loans taken will be allowed as an expense.

The Offer-in-Compromise Program

The Offer-in-Compromise program allows taxpayers to settle their back tax debt for less than the amount owed under certain circumstances. In order for taxpayers to obtain an OIC, the taxpayers must be in tax compliance, meaning that at least the last six years of tax returns must be on file, and they must have made their current tax payments.

There are two types of Offers-in-Compromise:

1. Doubt-as-to-Collectability Offer: The taxpayers don't dispute the amount owed in back taxes, but they can't afford to pay the tax debt back in full. The taxpayers

make an offer to the IRS based upon their particular financial circumstances and provide back-up documentation to support their proposal.
2. Doubt-as-to-Liability Offer: The taxpayers offer to settle the debt based upon being able to show they don't actually owe all of the underlying tax. In many ways a Doubt-as-to-Liability Offer is similar to audit reconsideration. Here, the taxpayers provide documentation as to why they don't owe the money the IRS claims they do. We discuss this more in Chapter 7, "Challenging an Assessed Tax."

For doubt-as-to-collectability offers there are two forms the offer can take: lump sum and short-term deferred.

Lump-Sum Offers

A Lump-Sum Offer is one in which the taxpayer agrees to pay the offered amount in less than six months upon acceptance. Once the taxpayer and practitioner calculate the taxpayer's RCP, then the following steps occur:

1. The taxpayer files the offer based upon two components to calculate RCP:
    a. Net Equity in Assets
    b. 12 months of Future Income
2. The taxpayer sends in two checks that accompany the offer:
    a. $205 for the offer application fee[28]
    b. Twenty percent (20%) of the amount offered (for instance, if a taxpayer offered $10,000 he would send in a check for 20% of the amount offered, or $2,000)
3. Upon acceptance of the offer the taxpayer would have five months to pay the balance of the amount offered

---

[28] Practitioners are warned to always check and make sure they have the latest fee schedule. The IRS does update the filing fees from time-to-time, and Offers filed with the wrong fee will be returned, the fee and deposit being kept. Clients in tough financial straits do not appreciate being told they just wasted money because you used the wrong application fee amount!

Deferred Offer-in-Compromise

A deferred offer is one in which the taxpayer begins making monthly payments while the offer is pending and pays the balance of the offer in more than six months but not more than 24 months. It operates exactly the same as a lump-sum offer, except that the taxpayer must begin making monthly payments and continue making the monthly payments while the offer is being considered, just like an installment agreement. The other difference is that the IRS calculates the RCP using 24 months of future income instead of 12 months.

Here is a comparison of the two types of offers:

	Lump-Sum	Short-Term Deferred
Application Fee	$205	$205
Initial Payment	20% of Offer	1st Monthly Payment
Monthly Payments	No	Yes
Length of Time to Pay	Up to 5 months	6 – 24 months
Future Income Included	12 months	24 months
Balloon Payment Allowed	Yes	Yes

How does the IRS calculate how much a taxpayer needs to offer? Let's discuss Reasonable Collection Potential as it pertains to Offers-in-Compromise.

Reasonable Collection Potential (RCP)

The IRS calculates the Reasonable Collection Potential based upon its financial guidelines: net equity in assets and future income.

For net equity in assets, the IRS seeks the equity in all assets. For an installment agreement the IRS generally does not seek the equity in a taxpayer's vehicle (unless it is a collectable or extremely expensive). With an offer the IRS adds in all the equity of all assets. The way we generally approach offers (and explain them to clients) is to think about what the IRS would get if it foreclosed its lien, sold everything at quicksale value (80%), paid off any loan ahead of its lien and took the net equity. That is the RCP from the assets the IRS would expect to be included in the taxpayer's OIC.

Bankruptcy

There are many myths and rumors concerning the issue of bankruptcy when it comes to tax debts. Most practitioners tell clients that payroll taxes are not dischargeable in bankruptcy. While this is true, bankruptcy can still be used very effectively to assist taxpayers in resolving their financial issues, including the payroll taxes. It's critical that practitioners understand when to use bankruptcy and what may and may not be dischargeable. Obviously, these decisions need to be made by a knowledgeable bankruptcy attorney, but it is useful to understand when bankruptcy should be considered as an option.

There are many benefits to using bankruptcy to resolve back tax issues. These include the automatic stay on collection activities, possibly the discharge of tax penalties, discharging other debts owed by the business, challenging the underlying tax liability, and forcing the government to accept payment agreements it otherwise may not be interested in accepting.

The first thing to understand is the basics of the various forms of bankruptcy. In a Chapter 7 bankruptcy, the taxpayers seek to have their debts simply discharged. If a Chapter 7 bankruptcy is filed for a business, it will be immediately closed and liquidated. Businesses do not require discharges in Chapter 7.

Chapter 13 is a plan of reorganization for individuals who need to restructure their debts in order to pay back their creditors. There may be some discharged debts through Chapter 13, but otherwise it is a forced plan of repayment to creditors, usually lasting no longer than 60 months, that is overseen by a bankruptcy trustee.

Chapter 11 is for reorganizing business debts, although some individuals do use Chapter 11 to reorganize their personal debts as well. Similar to Chapter 13, it allows the filer to discharge those debts that can be discharged, and then reorganizes the remaining debts into a plan of repayment that is overseen by a bankruptcy trustee. Tax debts must be repaid within 60 months of filing.

With that as a quick overview of the various forms of bankruptcy, let's review the potential benefits of using the bankruptcy code to resolve our client's outstanding tax debts.

The Automatic Stay

Section 362 of the Bankruptcy Code provides that, with few exceptions, all collection activity by creditors must cease once the client files for bankruptcy.[29] This includes the IRS and its efforts to pursue collection of back taxes. So, one of the immediate benefits of filing a bankruptcy is that it can put a stop to all IRS and state revenue departments' collection efforts against the taxpayers and their property. The bankruptcy effectively removes the case from the IRS Collection Division and moves it to the IRS's Insolvency Unit, which deals with bankruptcy cases. This can give a taxpayer immediate relief to work out a plan through a bankruptcy when the IRS may have otherwise been unwilling to work with the taxpayer.

Discharging Taxes

The issue of discharging taxes can be complicated. It depends upon a number of factors, including the type of tax, how old the tax year is, when it was filed, and what the taxpayer has done since filing the return. What we focus on here are employment taxes, which are never dischargeable. Also, never dischargeable is the trust fund recovery penalty that is applied to the responsible individuals for the employers failure to pay the payroll taxes.

Non-Discharge-ability of Payments of a Non-Dischargeable Tax. If you pay a non-dischargeable tax with what would otherwise be a dischargeable method of payment

---

[29] 11 U.S.C. § 362.

(that is, a credit card), the credit card balance for the tax paid would also be non-dischargeable in bankruptcy. Taxpayers are not going to be permitted to turn otherwise non-dischargeable debts into a dischargeable one because they used a credit card to pay the debt. So no paying the Trust Fund taxes with a credit card and then trying to discharge the credit card debt!

Discharge-ability of Penalties. The rule is that penalties that are designed to repay the government are non-dischargeable in bankruptcy; however, penalties designed to punish the taxpayer may be dischargeable. For income tax penalties (accuracy, failure-to-file, and failure-to-pay) the government is already collecting the tax and interest, so the penalty is purely to punish the taxpayer's behavior, and, therefore, may be discharged. The penalty is treated as a non-priority, unsecured debt (like a credit card) and may be discharged through the bankruptcy.[30] The Trust Fund Recovery Penalty assessed against responsible individuals who failed to pay over the company's payroll taxes are non-dischargeable, as they relate to a non-dischargeable debt (a Trust Tax).

Discharge-ability of Interest. Interest on tax debts follows the underlying tax: If the tax is dischargeable then the interest is also dischargeable.[31] If the tax is not dischargeable, then the interest will not be either. The government is entitled to interest on its money, and is allowed to collect the money owed and the interest that accumulates during the bankruptcy.

Payment Plans

One of the other major benefits of using a Chapter 11 or Chapter 13 bankruptcy filing is that the taxpayers can create an installment agreement with the government to repay their taxes over time (generally up to 60 months). We have used this in cases in which a taxpayer had a valuable business but just could not get out from under some old tax debt and the IRS would not work with the taxpayer any longer.

---

[30] 11 U.S.C. § 523(a)(7). See Roberts v. United States (In re Roberts), 906 F.2d 1440 (10th Cir. 1990); Polston v. United States (In re Polston), 239 B.R. 277 (Bankr. M.D. Pa. 1999).
[31] Jones v. United States (In re Garcia), 955 F.2d 16 (5th Cir. 1992).

Example: Taxpayers had a childcare business with nearly 400 children. They owed $275,000 in payroll taxes, plus $30,000 in interest, and $85,000 in penalties from several years back when the company owner became sick and the business faltered. The company had already defaulted on two installment agreements. The taxpayer came to us, and we offered the IRS $7,500 a month through a new installment agreement to repay the debt based upon the company's current Collection Information Statements. The Revenue Officer refused because the taxpayers had already defaulted on prior agreements. The clients filed a Chapter 11 bankruptcy. All collection action by the IRS against the company stopped. We were able to discharge the penalties ($85,000) and credit card debt ($50,000) and create a monthly payment plan for the tax and interest of $5,500, much better than the $7,500 required by the IRS RCP calculation. Guaranteed payment arrangement, $135,000 in savings (credit cards and tax penalties), and a lower monthly payment plan.

Tax Liens

It is often said that bankruptcy can't disturb liens and that security interests pass through bankruptcy. This is particularly important in the context of a federal tax lien because the federal tax lien passes through bankruptcy and attaches to the debtor's future interests. Thus, while the underlying tax debt may be sufficiently old to be discharged in bankruptcy, if the federal tax lien remains and the debtor owns or later acquires lienable property (that is, real estate) the IRS is still able to execute on its tax lien.[32]

The impact is that, when clients have a federal tax lien, they can use bankruptcy to discharge tax debts; however, those assets they have that the lien attached to are still subject to collection, and other resolution options may be considered for dealing with those, such as an Offer-in-Compromise.

---

[32] *IRS v. Orr (In re Orr)*, 180 F.3d 656 (5th Cir 1999).

HOT TIP

Payroll taxes, including the civil penalties assessed against the responsible individuals, are never dischargeable in bankruptcy. However, a bankruptcy reorganization (i.e. Chapter 11 or Chapter 13) can be extremely useful for helping companies create an installment agreement with an otherwise unwilling IRS. In addition, penalties are treated as unsecured debt, and therefore may be able to be partially or entirely discharged as part of the bankruptcy reorganization. Taxpayers need to be aware that these plans are generally limited to 60 months from the date of the bankruptcy filing, and often include a trustee's fee of 10% of the monthly payment. Taxpayers and practitioners who believe bankruptcy may be an option should see representation from an experienced bankruptcy attorney to evaluate the bankruptcy option properly before any bankruptcy filing should be made.

Tax Compliance

Tax compliance generally means that the company has filed all tax returns that are due and owing as of that moment and is making its current quarter's payroll tax deposits. So, for instance, if a company comes to you in November, to be in compliance it would have had to have filed its first 3 quarterly tax returns for that year and have made its 4th quarter deposits. Once all 941s and 940s are filed that are past due and the current quarters deposits are caught up then the company is in compliance and can now seek a collection alternative from the IRS, including uncollectable status, installment agreement, or Offer-in-Compromise. It is worth noting that compliance is required both to get into an arrangement with the IRS but also to maintain that arrangement or risk default.

With a company, compliance becomes a big deal, often a bigger deal than with individual taxpayers. With individual taxpayers the IRS has no choice but to deal with them. If the individual taxpayer is unable to get into compliance, the IRS would still need to work with them, even if it won't accept an Offer-in-Compromise. This is not the case with a business. When a business fails to either get into compliance or maintain compliance, the IRS does NOT need to deal with it. The IRS can move to force it out of business. First will come the IRS Letter 903 threatening such action (see Exhibit 15). If that fails to get the business owner to maintain the business's compliance, then the IRS will move to seek an injunction, putting the company out of business.

Injunctions by the IRS Against Employers

An injunction is a court order that requires a party either to refrain from certain actions or to perform certain actions. Federal district courts have jurisdiction to issue injunctions under IRC § 7402(a). Injunctions can be obtained to restrain the future conduct of any person or business when necessary or appropriate to enforce the tax laws.[33] Suits for injunctions may be appropriate against employers and their responsible officers who have a history of non-compliance. Repeatedly running up payroll tax debt is commonly referred to as "pyramiding". Pyramiding can lead to criminal charges as well.[34]

When the IRS, through the Department of Justice, seeks an injunction against an employer, the court will focus on two critical factors: first, the defendant's persistent failure to comply with employment tax laws after repeated administrative efforts to effect voluntary compliance; and second, the reasonable likelihood that the defendant will continue to pyramid trust fund liabilities.[35] Accordingly, requests for injunctions against a trust fund violator should show:

1. the violation is not an isolated occurrence, but part of a pattern of past violations including, where applicable, evidence of prior assessments and penalties;

---

[33] United States v. Ernst & Whinney, 735 F.2d 1296, 1300–1301 (11th Cir. 1984), cert. den., 470 U.S. 1050 (1985); United States v. Hart, 701 F.2d 749 (8th Cir. 1983); and United States v. Ekblad, 732 F.2d 562 (7th Cir. 1984).
[34] IRM 5.17.4.17
[35] United States v. Buttorff, 761 F.2d 1056, 1062 (5th Cir. 1985) and United States v. Kaun, 827 F.2d 1144, 1149–50 (7th Cir. 1987).

2. the defendant is clearly a "responsible person" with respect to the pyramided taxes;
3. the defendant's activities place him in a position where continued violations can be anticipated, and
4. the anticipated violations jeopardize the effective enforcement of the employment tax laws.

In the past when it came to employers pyramiding their trust fund taxes, the Internal Revenue Service has first sought a preliminary injunction against in-business taxpayers preventing them from:

- failing to timely pay their future corporate income tax, FUTA tax, and withholding and FICA tax liabilities;
- transferring any money or property to any other entity to have that entity pay the salaries or wages of the defendants' employees; and
- assigning any property or making any payments after the preliminary injunction is issued until the trust fund liabilities, accruing after the preliminary injunction, are first paid to the Service.

The individual defendants and other persons authorized to disperse company funds have been required monthly to sign and deliver to the Service statements that they have read the court's preliminary injunction order and will obey it.

Beyond just seeking to assure deposits are made, the Justice Department has also asked district courts to issue preliminary injunctions authorizing the Service to enter an employer's business premises and seize and sell corporate property if the defendants violate the injunction. Such violations may result in further court proceedings against the violator for civil or criminal contempt, including the possibility of imprisonment. If a district court judge is initially unwilling to imprison the principals of a failing business for violating a preliminary injunction, the court cal also appoint a receiver to take over and liquidate the business.

There is a sample Injunction at Exhibit 16.

What is critical to know is that the IRS and Department of Justice takes the failure to pay over the trust funds withheld from the employees very seriously, and not only have injunctions been on the upswing, but criminal tax prosecutions for payroll taxes have also increased significantly.

Assessment Against the Responsible Party

4

If an employer owes money to the IRS and can pay that liability back in full in short order, then the IRS will resolve the case that way. If, however, the employer will be unable to repay the liability back quickly then the IRS will begin trying to determine which owners and/or employees were responsible for the company's failure to pay over the payroll taxes. Once the IRS determines who it believes is responsible for the company's failure to collect and remit the payroll taxes, it will begin the procedures to assess those individuals for the unpaid trust fund portion of the payroll taxes.

The Trust Fund Recovery Penalty (IRC § 6672)

IRC § 6672 allows the IRS to assess a penalty against either individuals or third-party companies that it believes was responsible for the employers failure to account and pay over the payroll taxes:

> *Any person required to collect, truthfully account for, and pay over any tax imposed by this title who willfully fails to collect such tax, or truthfully account for and pay over such tax, or willfully attempts in any manner to evade or defeat any such tax or the payment thereof, shall, in addition to other penalties provided by law, be liable to a penalty equal to the total amount of the tax evaded, or not collected, or not accounted for and paid over. No penalty shall be imposed under section 6653 or part II of subchapter A of chapter 68 for any offense to which this section is applicable.*[36]

The goal of IRC § 6672 is to allow the government to recover the trust fund portion of the taxes from those responsible for the employer's failure to properly account and pay-over the employment taxes. As noted in the Internal Revenue Manual, IRC § 6672 accomplished three things:

1. It encourages prompt payment of income and employment taxes withheld from employees and other collected taxes;
2. It makes the responsible person liable for 100% of the unpaid trust fund taxes; and

---

[36] 26 U.S.C. § 6672

3. It facilitates collection of trust fund taxes from secondary sources.[37]

The Trust Fund Recovery Penalty (IRC § 3505)

IRC § 3505 creates liability for third parties that lend moneys to pay the net payroll of the employer's workers. Under IRC § 3505 a lender, surety, or other person who supplies funds to or for the account of an employer for the specific purpose of paying wages of the employees of such employer may be personally liable for any unpaid withholding taxes, whether this person did or did not directly pay the employees' wages.

In our experience it is usually family and friends that get dragged into liability through IRC § 3505. Liability under IRC § 3505 is limited to the lessor of either the trust fund liability or 25% of the amount loaned.

Example: Son is a contractor and is short of funds when payday arrives. He asks his father to help him cover the checks to his employees, and dad dutifully lends son the exact amount necessary to cover the net checks: $5,600. There is another $2,400 due for FICA taxes to the IRS that goes unpaid. Later, the Revenue Officer who is handling the son's collection case sees the deposit come in and go out to cover the checks, and assesses dad for liability under IRC § 3505. Dad's liability would be limited to $1,400, the lessor of 25% of the amount he loaned ($5,600) or the unpaid trust taxes ($2,400).

The Assessment Process

Once a business fails to account and pay over the employment taxes, the IRS will begin a duel-track process to collect the employment taxes from both the company and the responsible individuals.

The IRS process for identifying and pursuing the responsible individuals for the unpaid payroll taxes is:[38]

---

[37] IRM 5.17.7.1(3)
[38] Unless collection of TFRP is in jeopardy, the taxpayer must be given a preliminary notice at least 60 days before the date of notice and demand for payment of the TFRP. *See* IRM 5.19.14.1.

1. Summons bank record and bank signature cards and review them to see who signed the checks,
2. Review the filed returns and determine who authorized and signed the payroll returns and business returns,
3. Interview employees, officers and owners (Form 4180 will be used to conduct the interviews),
4. Make the determination as to which parties are responsible for the employers failure to collect, account for and pay over the payroll taxes,
5. Send the proposed assessments to those responsible individuals, done with IRS Letter 1153,
6. IRS Form 2751 will be included so those responsible can waive their right to protest the proposed assessment if they wish,
7. The protest by those parties who wish to challenge the IRS assessment of the trust fund liability will be filed within 60 days of the date of the Letter 1153,
8. Appeals will hear the taxpayer's protest and make its determination,
9. If the taxpayer is deemed to not be responsible then the proposed assessment will be vacated/abated,
10. If Appeals determines that the proposed assessment is correct then it will uphold the assessment against the taxpayer, and
11. For those parties deemed responsible bills will go out to the taxpayer to either pay or seek a collection alternative with the IRS Collection Division.

Making the TFRP Determination

The IRS Revenue Officer will begin the process of determining which owners and/or employees are responsible for the business's failure to pay the payroll taxes to the IRS. That process will include obtaining information about who was running the business and signing returns and checks. The Revenue Officer will request copies of all the bank statements, the bank signature card and organization documents (by-laws, corporate minutes, partnership or LLC agreements, etc). The Revenue Officer will also review the state website to see who officially owns the entity.

Based upon the information they receive, the Revenue Officer can make some preliminary determinations as to responsibility, which will generally include:

- Listed owners,
- Those individuals listed on the bank signature card,
- Those individuals who signed checks, and
- Those individuals who signed tax returns.

After obtaining the information above, the Revenue Officer will start interviewing persons they believe necessary to determine who is liable for the TFRP. In cases where the company is no longer in business, and the owners and employees are no longer around, the IRS will obtain the above information through administrative summonses issued on the banks. Once the IRS has the information it needs, the IRS will issue proposed assessments against anyone it finds who was either an owner or an employee involved with the returns and banking.

The Trust Fund Interview – Form 4180

The Revenue Officer will often seek interviews with those individuals it believes are responsible for the unpaid payroll taxes. The reason is that it helps the IRS determine if there were other individuals who should be considered as responsible parties and pursued for the Trust Fund assessments. The Revenue Officer will conduct the interview utilizing its Form 4180, Report of Interview with Individual Relative to Trust Fund Recovery Penalty or Personal Liability for Excise Taxes. See Exhibit 17.

There are issues with the IRS Form 4180. If you review the sample, we have given you (see Exhibit 17) then you might notice the questions are broad, very broad. In fact, this Form used to be eight pages long in 2003. It is now three pages long. In an effort to reduce the paper used in forms this form had its questions combined into broader ones, reducing the amount of print and therefore the number of pages. The problem is that the questions have become very broad and encompassing, allowing the IRS to potential claim people are responsible who should not be.

Example: Mike is a staff accountant for a small, closely held corporation. Mike prepares the payroll tax returns, which he then sends on to the controller Ms. Smith. Mike does not have signature authority, is not an owner of the company and has no authority over financial policy. Yet when the corporation failed to pay its payroll taxes Mike was interviewed by an IRS Revenue Officer who checked the box for Section 2, Line 1.(c) "yes" because Mike answered that he did prepare the payroll tax returns.

HOT TIP

Do not allow the client to be interviewed for the 4180 with the Revenue Officer without representation present. The client should hand the prepared 4180 Form to the agent.

As a practice point, we generally have the client do the Form 4180 with us so that we can answer the questions and add further explanation on notes page at the end (page 4 of the Form 4180) to make sure that the information gets into the administrative record. Hence, for the question in Section 2, line 1.(c) we would answer "No – see attached" and then explain the situation. If the question is simply answered yes the taxpayer may find they are later assessed by a supervisor and now have an uphill battle to challenge the proposed assessment at Appeals.

Raising Collectability

When dealing with a Revenue Officer during the Trust Fund investigation taxpayers are allowed to raise collectability, meaning the taxpayer can provide evidence that they have no means of paying the liability. Pursuant to the Interval Revenue Manual, the

IRS Revenue officer is allowed to consider the ability of the IRS to collect the debt when making the decision to propose the Trust Fund assessment.[39]

Taxpayers and their representatives who wish to raise collectability and argue to avoid the trust fund assessment should prepare a Collection Information Statement IRS Form 433-A (see Exhibit 10) and provide it and supporting documentation to the Revenue Officer. If it supports that the taxpayer has equity or future income available to pay the trust fund liability then the revenue Officer may decide to not assess the taxpayer personally for the trust fund penalty.

The Proposed Trust Fund Assessment: Letter 1153 and Form 2751

Once the IRS Revenue Officer identifies the persons responsible for the employer's failure to pay the payroll taxes, the agent will propose an assessment against those individuals. The taxpayers will receive IRS Letter 1153 (see Exhibit 18) which will tell them that the IRS believes that they are responsible. Along with Letter 1553 will be a waiver Form, Form 2751, that provides a breakdown of the proposed trust fund Liability (see Exhibit 19). To accept responsibility for the trust fund liability that taxpayer just needs to sign Form 2751 and return it to the IRS.

If the taxpayer does not agree that they should be held responsible than the Letter 1153 lays out how to file the protest to challenge the proposed assessment. To challenge the assessment, the taxpayer must file their protest within 60 days of the date on the Letter 1153.

So, Should the Taxpayer Sign the 2751 Waiver or Not Sign?

Great question! In general, I do NOT have my client sign the 2751, either because we do not agree with the proposed assessment or, even if we do agree, I want the 60 days to work on a game plan for resolving the tax debt. By not signing the Form 2751 waiver and allowing the 60 days to run, I have effectively bought myself 4-6 months before a

---

[39] IRM 5.7.5.1.1

potential levy, and possibly as much as a year. How do I calculate this? The timeline for enforcement before a levy can be issued by the IRS is as follows:

1. 60 days for the taxpayer to protest the proposed assessment;
2. Billing Notice is issued 2 weeks after the assessment goes final
3. Threat to levy is issued 30-45 days after the billing notice
4. Final Notice of threat to levy is issued 30-45 days after the Threat to Levy
5. IRS will wait 45 days to see of a Collection Due Process hearing is requested by the taxpayer to issue its first levy.

So, at this point the IRS has been forced to wait almost 6 months before it can start levy action to try and collect the outstanding trust fund balance against the responsible taxpayer. Now, if we file for a Collection Due Process hearing, it could be another 3-6 months before we have our hearing with an Appeals Officer. So, we do have time to work on a game plan:

- Can the company pay the balance?
- If the company cannot pay the balance is it worth saving or can it be reorganized so, it's worth saving?
- If the Company is not worth saving, how do we best wind down the Company to minimize the liability and try and get the debt paid down or off?
- Can my client full-pay the trust fund liability?
- What resolution options work for my client: Installment agreement, offer-in-compromise or uncollectible status?

These questions are complicated and will take time to work through. Hence the need for not rushing the assessment by simply signing the Form 2751. Let's take the 60 days plus and work through this with the client, who often does not understand all the issues and needs guidance through this process.

So, When Do I Have My Clients Sign the Form 2751 Waiver?

I have my client sign the Form 2751 when we need to have everything assessed to go forward with a resolution. If you were not aware, once an installment agreement is established or an Offer-in-Compromise is filed, any new liability that gets assessed will void the plan and send the case back to collection to start over. Therefore I do not want to start trying to resolve the issue until all the assessments are done.

For example, when the Taxpayer's business is closed and gone I will need all the assessments to all be made so we can file an Offer-in-Compromise for the owner to resolve the trust fund tax problem he or she has. In that case, I often will contact the Revenue Officer and ask them to hurry up and send us the Forms 2751 so we can sign them and get everything assessed. Once the assessments are done, I can move forward with filing the Offer.

Challenging the Trust Fund Assessment

5

For taxpayers faced with a proposed assessment for the unpaid payroll taxes, there are several ways for them to challenge the assessment. The method chosen will depend upon where the taxpayer is in the process:

- If the Taxpayer is within the 60 days to protest the Letter 1153 (which proposed the trust fund assessment), then putting together and filing a protest to get the case to Appeals is the best way to challenge the assessment;
- If the Taxpayer no longer has the right to an administrative protest because the 60 day window to do so has passed, and the taxpayer has neither paid any of the tax nor been levied by the IRS, then the taxpayer has the option to file a Doubt-as-to-Liability Offer ("DATL") and challenge the assessment; or
- If the taxpayer did not challenge the proposed assessment within the 60-day window to do so and has made payments, then a refund claim may be brought to force a review of the assessment.

So, to challenge the assessment, which option you choose really depends upon where the taxpayer is in the process at that time.

Protest

If the taxpayer is within the 60 days of the date of the date on the Letter 1153 proposing the trust fund assessment, than it makes the most sense to file a protest with the IRS. The letter 1153 describes in detail what needs to be included in the protest.

The protest must include the following information:

1. The taxpayer's name, address, and social security number;
2. A statement that the taxpayer wants a conference;
3. A copy of the Letter 1153, or the date and number of the letter;
4. The tax periods involved (which should be listed on the attached Form 2751);
5. A list of the findings the Taxpayer disagrees with;
6. A statement of fact, signed under penalties of perjury, that explains why the taxpayer disagrees and why the taxpayer believes that he or she shouldn't be charged with the penalty. Include specific dates, names, amounts, and locations

which support their position. Usually, penalty cases like this one involve issues of responsibility and willfulness. Willfulness means that an action was intentional, deliberate or voluntary and not an accident or mistake. Therefore, the statement should include a clear explanation of the client's duties and responsibilities; and specifically, the client's duty and authority to collect, account for, and pay the trust fund taxes. If the taxpayer disagrees with how the IRS calculated the penalty, the statement should identify the dates and amounts of payments that they believe were not considered and/or any computation errors they think were made;

This statement of fact needs a declaration that it is true under penalties of perjury, you must add the following to the taxpayer's statement and sign it:

"Under penalties of perjury, I declare that I have examined the facts presented in this statement and any accompanying information, and, to the best of my knowledge and belief, they are true, correct, and complete."

If you rely on a law or other authority to support your arguments, explain what it is and how it applies.

There is a sample of a protest attached as Exhibit 20 as an example of what our written protests look like when we submit them to the IRS. Sometimes, after receiving the protest the Revenue Officer has contacted us and requests a meeting, usually when the taxpayer was not interviewed and the Revenue Officer. Upon receiving the protest, the Revenue Officer can decide to drop the proposed assessment. Usually, however, they do not, in which case the protest will be sent on to the Office of Appeals to schedule a hearing on the matter.

The key to a successful protest is to build your client's case by gathering sufficient evidence that they were not responsible. Some of this information will take time to put together and gather, more time than the 60-day protest deadline allows. It is perfectly fine to file the protest in advance of having all the information, just make sure to have the client review the statements and protest and confirm they believe they are accurate.

To build a case to defeat a proposed TFRP assessment you should do the following:

- Making a Freedom of Information Act (FOIA) request for the administrative file,
- Getting copies of the payroll tax returns,
- Seeking copies of the bank signature card,
- Obtain copies of the actual checks during the periods in question, and
- Interview witnesses and obtain affidavits from those witnesses that support the client's story.

The FOIA Request

Whenever dealing with the IRS it usually makes sense to have as much information about what the IRS knows as possible. One of the ways to do this is obtain a copy of the IRS's administrative file. The administrative file is the file the IRS agent put together and it will have copies of their notes, returns, and other information the agent gathered in making their determination for liability. The way to obtain the file is to make a FOIA request for the administrative file pertaining to the trust fund investigation. The IRS will send the file on a CD with a password in one mailing and will send the password to unlock the CD in a separate mailing. This is to try and maintain client confidentiality. A sample FOIA request and the letters received in response are at Exhibit 21.

You will want to review the administrative file in detail. There could be thousands of pages of information, including copies of tax returns, bank records, interview forms, etc. In doing this on our cases we often find interesting information and notes where revenue officers did not believe the client was responsible but were overruled by a supervisor, etc. These are great facts to bring up at the Appeals hearing on your protest.

Copies of the Payroll Tax Returns

If the client does not know if they reviewed and sign the Form 941s and 940s for the company, try and obtain copies if they are not included in the administrative file received through the FOIA request. This can be critical information to show whether the client had some knowledge of the tax problem or not.

Bank Signature Card

If the client claims that either they did not have bank signature authority or does not know if they had authority, the bank signature card is critical. A copy of the bank signature card may be in the FOIA information you receive, but if not, have the client go to the bank to obtain a copy. If the bank refuses because they do not have signature authority, you can raise this in your protest or at the Appeals hearing. One of the best defenses to a trust fund assessment is to show the taxpayer could not have been responsible because they did not have signature authority. This means they could not have paid the taxes even if they wanted to as they could not direct payment for taxes, thus rebutting a claim of willfulness.

Copies of Cancelled Checks

Just because someone had signature authority does not mean they ever used that authority or had any knowledge of the tax problems. A critical piece of information to support a client's defense that they did not sign payroll checks or even other checks would be copies of the cancelled checks. Like the bank signature card, a copy of these checks may be in the administrative file you obtain through the FOIA request. If they are not, the client may need to obtain copies from the bank. You need to review cancelled checks to determine that the client:

    A. did not sign checks, or
    B. if they did sign checks, that they did not sign payroll checks.

Speaking with Potential Witnesses

It is often helpful to a taxpayer's case if they have other employees who can bear witness to the fact that they were not the decision makers. We often have clients ask other employees or former employees to speak with us and, if they support the client's story, we ask if they are willing to sign an affidavit (see Exhibit 22). We have used affidavits from other employees for:

1. Supporting our client's story that despite being the owner's wife she was never on premises or involved in her husband's business when the IRS proposed an assessment against her purely for having signature authority;
2. For explaining that the bookkeeper asked the owner each week which checks she should mail to creditors and which ones he wanted her to hold in the safe, proving that the bookkeeper (our client) did not have the functional responsibility for making the decisions over the finances despite signing all the checks; and
3. For supporting our client that the signatures on the payroll tax returns were not his but rather they witnessed the owner forging our client's name.

A signed affidavit from another employee (or former employee) who witnessed the behavior can be very powerful and it sends a clear message to IRS Appeals: if we litigate this issue, we have witnesses that will take the stand under oath and support our client's story. This shows the government it has real hazards of litigation and should settle.

We have found that affidavits are given serious weight by Appeals and usually do help get the matter settled in our client's favor, so if you do have witnesses this is a defense strategy that should be employed.

Doubt-as-to-Liability Offers ("DATL")

A DATL is an Offer-in-Compromise that is not based upon a taxpayer's ability to pay but rather is based upon the fact that the taxpayer can prove they do not owe this money. The form itself is fairly straightforward, though there are some things practitioners need to be aware of when completing it:

You must offer some amount of money. So even if the taxpayer believes they can prove they owe nothing, they must offer at least $1, and

The most critical aspect is the evidence you supply, which must be filed with the Offer form 656-L (see Exhibit 23). When we submit these packages to the IRS they are often several inches thick and include copies of the original tax return, the amended return or audit adjustments (if the Offer is being made to challenge audit adjustments), and all supporting documents and receipts that back-up the taxpayer's claimed numbers. These must be submitted with the Offer.

Once the Offer is received by the IRS it will often be routed to the original auditor (if the taxpayer was audited) or to an examiner to review. If they agree with the Taxpayer they can either accept the Offer, or contact the taxpayer and ask them to withdraw the offer so they can simply abate the inaccurate numbers in their system. If the examiner does not agree then the case will be forwarded to the Appeals Division for an Appeals review.

> **HOT TIP**
>
> There is no application fee or deposit required for a Doubt as to Liability Offer.

The reason for the withdrawal request is that neither the IRS Revenue Agent nor Appeals Officer can abate taxes or penalties if the taxpayer's account is coded for an OIC. An abatement will allow the Taxpayer to avoid the liability and also get any refunds they are owed once the adjustments go through.

Refund

Another method to challenge the liability is for the Taxpayer to pay the trust taxes for one employee for each of the quarters they wish to challenge and then seek a refund of the amounts paid. Once the refund claim is made, the Taxpayer must wait until the refund is rejected or until six-months has passed, at which point the taxpayer can file a refund suit in either their local United States District Court or the United States Federal Court of Claims. If the Taxpayer does plan on suing, the suit cannot be brought before

> **HOT TIP**
>
> Taxpayers who make a refund claim must wait at least six months or until the claim is rejected to bring a refund suit against the government but cannot wait more than two years from the date of the payment. If the two years passes, the money is lost if the Taxpayer does not ultimately succeed administratively. An attorney should be involved in this process and dates "calendered" so the right to bring suit is not missed.

the rejection, or six months after the refund claim is made, and MUST be brought no later than two-years after the payment is made.[40]

Mechanically, the Taxpayer makes the payments, one for each quarter. We usually do this at an IRS walk-in center so we can get copies time stamped immediately. Once the payments are made the Taxpayer files the Form 843, Request for Abatement or Refund (see Exhibit 24), one for each quarter. This starts the refund claim and the six-month clock running. These payments also begin the two-year clock for a refund as well.

If the taxpayer is not in a rush to bring suit they can wait to see if the refund claim is acted upon or rejected. If it is rejected than the Taxpayer will be given the opportunity to file an administrative appeal with the IRS Appeals Division. Practitioners and Taxpayers must be aware though that the filing of the Appeal does not extend the time to bring suit. Once two-years has passed from the payment the money will be gone if the taxpayer loses their appeal. See Exhibit 25 for a sample refund suit.

---

[40] IRM 34.5.2.2

Strategies for Minimizing Personal Liability

6

When it becomes obvious that the company cannot expeditiously repay the payroll taxes, the IRS will pursue the responsible individuals. It is up to us, as their tax professional to guide them through the process and how to minimize or even avoid personal liability. These ideas usually involve either:

A. "I will make a payment to show good faith to the IRS so I can get a better deal;" or
B. "My buddy suggested I just shut down and open a new company."

Voluntary Payments – Revenue Procedure 2002-26

It is generally a great idea for those taxpayers who have the means to make a voluntary payment to reduce the taxes to do so, but how they make that payment has a huge impact. Revenue Procedure 2002-26 (see Exhibit 26) allows a taxpayer to designate how his or her voluntary payment is applied. If there is no designation, then the IRS will apply those funds first to penalties for the oldest period, then to the non-trust fund portion of the taxes, then the trust fund portion. See Exhibit 27 for a sample letter designating the payments to the Trust Fund portion of the employment tax liability. This is probably explained best with an example.

Example: Joe's Construction Company

Joe comes to see us with tax bills for unpaid payroll taxes for his subchapter S corporation for 5 quarters totaling $100,000 of taxes, plus $50,000 in interest and penalties. Of the $100,000 of taxes owed, $65,000 of that is the trust fund taxes withheld from the employees' pay. He tells us that the company went through a rough patch but is now doing great and is worth saving. So currently the company owes $150,000, of which Joe is responsible for $65,000 personally for the trust fund portion of the taxes.

Joe knows he can borrow $50,000 from his mother and wants to make a payment to reduce the liability and then get into a payment plan. If Joe just sends the $50,000 to the IRS, the IRS will apply it against penalties, interest and the non-trust fund taxes first.

This would reduce the liability for the Company to $100,000 and leave Joe still responsible for the $65,000 of trust taxes.

If, however, Joe sends that payment, and designates it to be applied against the trust fund portion of the taxes, the Company still owes the $100,000 balance, but now Joe personally would only be responsible for the $15,000 balance of the trust fund portion.

Revenue Procedure 2002-26 allows taxpayers to make the best use of a voluntary payment from the responsible person so that, in the event the business ultimately fails, they have not wasted their money reducing the non-trust fund taxes that he or she is not responsible for paying.

Shut-Down the Company

If the company is unable to maintain compliance and/or the owners see no future for it, the decision to close the business makes sense. Once the business is closed the owners should assume that if he or she has not already been deemed responsible for the unpaid payroll taxes, they soon will be.

> **HOT TIP**
>
> A Voluntary payment against the trust fund portion of the taxes must come from the responsible person, it cannot come directly from the company. The IRS will generally refuse to allow the company to use its resources to clear the responsible owners and officers and not the liability that it is responsible for (ie. the non-trust fund portion, penalties and interest).

The business needs to be wound down in an orderly fashion, the entity liquidated, bank accounts closed, and final returns prepared for both the IRS and any state that the company was registered with for business.

Because only the business is responsible for the non-trust fund taxes, interest and penalties, often owners assume they can walk away, take their assets and start anew. Unfortunately, it is not that simple, and the assets in particular can cause some sticky issues.

1. **The Assets and the IRS Lien.** When a tax debt arises and the IRS makes demand for payment if payment is not forthcoming then a lien arise by statute under IRC § 6321 that attaches to all the business's assets currently owned or after acquired. This means that there is a lien on the assets owned by the business whether the IRS has filed a Notice of Federal Tax Lien or not. This means those assets are the collateral of the IRS.

   Now, the IRS generally does not want the assets, it would rather have the cash, so it is up to us to work out a deal with the IRS to clear the assets from the lien and allow the owner that wants the assets to purchase them and move on. The way we accomplish this is by the following:

   a) Complete a final IRS Form 433-B for the business (Exhibit 9),
   b) Complete an IRS Form 14135, Application for Certificate of Discharge of Property from Federal Tax Lien (Exhibit 28),
   c) Attach any appraisals or statements of value that support the value you are claiming for the assets, and
   d) If real estate is involved, include the title search and draft sales contract.

   The IRS will review the request, and if comfortable that it will receive value, then send a letter approving the release, stating it will send the buyer a lien release upon its receipt of certified funds for the value.

2. **Nominee / Alter-Ego Issues.** Nominee or alter-ego ownership occurs when #1 above is not done. If assets are transferred from the business to the taxpayer or a third-party without the lien being cleared, and the IRS receiving value, then the IRS may, at its discretion, file a nominee lien or alter-ego lien against the third party that now owns the asset. A "Nominee Lien" is filed against an individual that is holding the asset as nominee for the tax debtor. An "Alter Ego" lien is when the owner creates a new business that is substantially the same as the past business that owned the assets and owed the payroll taxes. When this occurs, the IRS will file an "Alter Ego" lien against the new business, claiming it is not a new business but merely the alter-ego of the old business, and all the debts

follow the assets into the new business. Hence, it is best if the liens and assets are dealt with before they are transferred away.

3. **Fraudulent Conveyance Issues.** A fraudulent conveyance is where the tax debtor transfers assets to a third-party with the object or the result of placing the property beyond the reach of the creditor or hindering the creditor's ability to collect a valid debt. A fraudulent transfer also occurs when property is transferred without fair consideration. Taxpayers who attempt to frustrate collection by transferring away assets that the IRS lien has attached to are usually subject to this claim of fraud, and these liens would be filed against the recipient of the assets.

Taxpayers that receive assets fraudulently transferred may find themselves personally liable for the value of the assets so transferred. Also, the transferee will be liable to repay the value of what they received.[41]

---

[41] There is also a 2013 federal case where a family that transferred assets from their corporation to repay family loans and then attempted to walk away from the non-trust fund taxes were held liable for the entire tax balance, including penalties and interest, under the theory that their actions were an attempted fraud on the government. See United States v. Sperry, 2013 WL 1768664 (S.D.Ind. 2013)

Criminal Aspects of Payroll Taxes

7

Recently, the IRS and United States Department of Justice ("DOJ") have been criminally prosecuting more payroll tax cases than ever before. Several years ago the decision was made to focus on payroll tax cases for both civil and criminal enforcement, given the importance of payroll taxes to the federal income stream.

When it comes to charging taxpayers criminally for the failure to account and pay over payroll taxes there are three main statutes the IRS and DOJ use: IRC § 7202 (the felony statute for payroll tax violations), IRC § 7215 (the misdemeanor statute for payroll violations) and IRC § 7201 (Tax Evasion).

IRC § 7202 - Willful Failure to Collect or Pay Over Tax

IRC § 7202 makes the failure of an employer to account and pay over the payroll taxes a felony. The actual statute states:

> *Any person required under this title to collect, account for, and pay over any tax imposed by this title who willfully fails to collect or truthfully account for and pay over such tax shall, in addition to other penalties provided by law, be guilty of a felony and, upon conviction thereof, be fined* not more than $10,000, or imprisoned not more than five years, or both, together with the costs of prosecution.*

This statute describes two offenses:

a) a willful failure to collect; and
b) a willful failure to truthfully account for and pay over tax

IRC § 7202 was designed primarily to assure compliance by third parties obligated to collect excise taxes and to deduct from wages paid to employees the employees' share of Federal Insurance Contribution Act (FICA) taxes and the withholding tax on wages applicable to individual income taxes. The withheld sums are commonly referred to as "trust fund taxes" because the employer is holding those funds in trust for the United States Government.

In order for the IRS and DOJ to establish that a taxpayer violated this criminal statute, it needs to show beyond a reasonable doubt that:

a) There was a duty for the taxpayer to collect, and/or to truthfully account for and pay over taxes; and
b) The taxpayer failed to properly collect, or truthfully account for and pay over those taxes; and
c) That the failure to do so was willful.

The Duty to Collect and/or Truthfully Account and Pay Over

The duty of employers to truthfully account for and pay over is set forth in IRC §§ 3102(s), 3111(a), and 3402 (1986).[42] More specifically, it is the individual responsible for making the payment and filing the returns who is culpable when there is a failure to perform this duty.[43] It is that individual (or individuals) that the IRS and DOJ would seek to prosecute. See Exhibit 29 for a sample indictment for a criminal I.R.C. § 7202 payroll tax charge.

Failure to Collect, or Truthfully Account For and Pay Over

Historically, the Department of Justice Tax Division's position has been that a willful failure to truthfully account for and pay over is a "dual obligation."[44] The position that the government must prove the defendant violated both elements to get a conviction has been rejected by the courts.[45] As an example, in United States vs. Evangelista, the Second Circuit held a violation of § 7202 can result from either a failure to account for

---

[42] See United States v. Porth, 426 F.2d 519, 522 (10th Cir.), cert. denied, 400 U.S. 824 (1970).
[43] For an example of the criteria used to determine the individual with the duty to truthfully account for and pay over, see Datlof v. United States, 252 F. Supp. 11, 32 (E.D. Pa.), aff'd., 370 F.2d 655, 656 (3d Cir. 1966), cert. denied, 387 U.S. 906 (1967).
[44] 2008 Criminal Tax Manual, United States Department of Justice, Tax Division, Criminal Section, p. 9-4.
[45] United States v. Thayer, 201 F.3d 214, 219-22 (3d Cir. 1999), cert. denied, 530 U.S. 1244 (2000); United States v. Evangelista, 122 F.3d 112, 120-22 (2d Cir. 1997); United States v. Brennick, 908 F. Supp. 1004, 1011 (D. Mass. 1995).

withholding taxes and FICA contributions or a failure to pay over such taxes, but the statute does not require both to sustain a conviction.

Thus, the duty of the taxpayer is to both account for (by filing accurate returns) and pay over (remit to the government) the taxes due. Failure to do either may result in criminal prosecution.

Willfulness

The requirement that the violation of IRC § 7202 be willful is the same as all tax offenses: that the government show the defendant voluntarily and intentionally acted in violation of a known legal duty.[46]

The question of whether a taxpayer can be prosecuted for the failure to account and pay over the payroll taxes withheld when the taxpayer did not have the funds available has been raised in court cases. In particular, the 9th circuit dealt with this issue in its decision in *United States v. Poll*.[47]

In reversing the conviction in Poll, the Ninth Circuit held that to establish a willful failure to truthfully account for and pay over taxes, both the failure to truthfully account for and the failure to pay over must be willful. As the Ninth Circuit viewed it, in addition to establishing a willful failure to truthfully account for taxes required to be withheld:

> *[t]he Government must establish beyond a reasonable doubt that at the time payment was due the taxpayer possessed sufficient funds to enable him to meet his obligation or that the lack of sufficient funds on such date was created by (or was the result of) a voluntary and intentional act without justification in view of all the financial circumstances of the taxpayer.*[48]

The government can meet its burden with testimony by employees or suppliers that other creditors were paid during the period in question and that any lack of funds to pay

---

[46] Cheek v. United States, 498 U.S. 192, 201 (1991)
[47] United States v. Poll, 521 F.2d 329, 332-33 (9th Cir. 1975).
[48] Poll, 521 F.2d at 333.

was voluntary and intentional. It should also be noted that Poll had filed false 941s and failed to 'account for' the employment taxes withheld.[49]

Later the Ninth Circuit ruled, without overruling the Poll decision, that paying employees while not remitting employment taxes to the government was a willful act despite a claim of lack of funds.[50]

Statute of Limitations for Prosecution

The statute of limitations in IRC § 7202 prosecutions is six years.[51] The issue is often, however, when does the statute of limitations begin to run? Is it when the IRS Form 941 quarterly payroll tax return and payment are due, or rather on April 15th of the year following the year for which the employment taxes are due? Courts appear to have adopted the more conservative view and accept the date when the Form 941 was due.

IRC § 7215 - Offenses with Respect to Collected Taxes

IRC § 7215 is a misdemeanor offense for the failure of an employer to separately account for collected taxes under IRC § 7512. The actual statute states:

> *Any person who fails to comply with any provision of section 7512(b) shall, in addition to any other penalties provided by law, be guilty of a misdemeanor, and, upon conviction thereof, shall be fined not more than $5,000, or imprisoned not more than one year, or both, together with the costs of prosecution.*

The statute also states the following exceptions where IRC § 7215 will not apply, including:

- to any person, if such person shows that there was reasonable doubt as to (A) whether the law required collection of tax, or (B) who was required by law to collect tax, and

---

[49] It should be noted that Poll did not go free. Following the reversal of Poll's conviction, the government promptly secured a new indictment that did not charge him with a section 7202 violations, but with filing a false return in violation of section 7206(1). His conviction was affirmed on appeal. United States v. Poll, 538 F. 2d 845, 848 (9th Cir.), cert. denied, 429 U.S. 977 (1976).
[50] In United States v. Gilbert, 266 F.3d 1180, 1185 (9th Cir. 2001).
[51] See United States v. Adam, 296 F.3d 327, 330-31 (5th Cir. 2002. Be aware, however, that two district courts have concluded that the statute of limitations for section 7202 prosecutions is three years. United States v. Brennick, 908 F. Supp. 1004, 1018-19 (D. Mass. 1995); United States v. Block, 497 F. Supp. 629, 630-32 (N.D. Ga.), aff'd, 660 F.2d 1086 (5th Cir. 1980).

- to any person, if such person shows that the failure to comply with the provisions of § 7512(b) was due to circumstances beyond his control.

It is worth noting that IRC § 7215 is a misdemeanor statute, and is very rarely used by the government when prosecuting a payroll tax case. The reason, based on conversations with prosecutors (Assistant United States Attorneys) is that the government generally does not want to tempt the jury into giving a sympathetic defendant a lesser sentence so they still get something but not the full felony IRC § 7202 treatment. So though IRC § 7215 does exist and would seem to be easier to prove without any requirement to show willfulness, it is a statute that is rarely used by the government.

Willfulness

Section 7215 is a strict criminal liability provision, which means the government is not required to prove any particular mental state, intent, or willfulness, as it must in other criminal tax violations.[52]

Defense: Circumstances Beyond the Taxpayer's Control

Section 7215(b)(2) provides that there is no violation if the defendant "shows" that the failure to collect, account for, or pay over the tax was "due to circumstances beyond his control." Section 7215(b) also provides that a lack of funds existing immediately after the payment of wages, whether or not caused by the payment of the wages, "shall not be considered to be circumstances beyond the control of a person."

The scope of this "circumstances beyond control" exception to the statute "was intended to be narrow."[53] If one were to search through the legislative history of section 7215 you can find examples of what Congress thought the "circumstances beyond control" which would cause a lack of funds after (but not immediately after) the payment of wages. These include:

- Theft,

---

[52] United States v. Erne, 576 F.2d 212, 213-15 (9th Cir. 1978)
[53] United States v. Randolph, 588 F.2d 931, 932-33 (5th Cir. 1979)

- Embezzlement,
- Destruction of the business by fire or other casualty, and
- The failure of the bank in which the employer had deposited funds prior to transferring them to the trust account for the government.[54]

Conversely, having insufficient funds due to disbursements to other creditors is not considered a circumstance beyond a person's control and is not a viable defense.[55]

The Non-Trust Portion - IRC § 7201: Attempt to Evade or Defeat Tax

IRC § 7202 covers the "trust fund" portion of the payroll tax debt, which includes just those amounts withheld from the employee's pay. It does NOT cover the other portion, which consists of the FICA match by the employer and the federal unemployment taxes. Prosecutors may charge violations of the duty to pay with respect to either just the employer portion of the employment taxes, or may choose to charge both the employee and employer portions of employment tax by charging the employer with tax evasion in violation of IRC § 7201.[56] The point is that the government is generally unwilling to allow the non-trust fund portion to go unpunished. If it is going to prosecute the taxpayer, it might as well go all-in on the prosecution!

---

[54] Id at 933
[55] United States v. Plotkin, 239 F. Supp. 129, 131 (E.D. Wis. 1965).
[56] United States v. McKee, 506 F.3d 225, 233-34 (3d Cir. 2006); United States v. Butler, 297 F.3d 505, 509 (6th Cir. 2002)

Case Studies

8

We have created four case studies to illustrate the concepts and mechanics that we discussed in the book when it comes to resolving the taxpayer's payroll tax issue. Included are the forms completed as we would complete them. We hope you find this illustrative and helpful when handling your own cases.

Our four case studies include:

1	The Taxpayer believes that he is not responsible for the unpaid payroll taxes and we are going to challenge the proposed assessment.
2	The Taxpayer does not believe that he is responsible for the employer's failure to pay the payroll taxes and comes to see us after the assessment is final and is now in IRS Collection.
3	The Taxpayer concedes they are responsible and has decided to shut the business down.
4	The Taxpayer is responsible and wishes to keep the business open and work out an arrangement with the IRS.

Case Study 1

Joe is a manager at Global Construction in New Haven, Connecticut. Joe's job was to manage the job sites for the company. Joe was given signature authority over one of the four bank accounts, which was used to pay for materials and supplies, as Joe often had to run to hardware stores and lumber yards to grab emergency items for job sites. When the company failed three months ago a Revenue Officer set up interviews with many of the owners and executives. Joe did receive a phone message that the Revenue Officer wanted to speak with him. When he called her back he did not get her so left a voicemail message. Two months later Joe received a Letter 1153 proposing an assessment against him for more than $200,000, and a Form 2751 that he can sign if he agrees he is responsible. Joe asks around and gets our name as a professional that helps people with these problems.

When we meet with Joe, we note the following:

- Joe is insistent that he had nothing to do with the finances of the company. When pressed he names Carol D. as the financial staff person who can back him up;
- Joe tells us he never had signature authority on any of the other accounts where the finances of the company or payroll were handled;
- When asked if he knew about the payroll issues Joe explains that when he was asked by employees about bonuses or anything else financial about the Company, he would always have to call Carol D. to find out because he was never given any financial information.

Given the information we receive from Joe we decide to file a protest of the proposed assessment, and support our arguments by having Joe attempt to obtain information about the other bank accounts (he is denied by the bank because he did not have signature authority, which they fax him in writing), and we ask carol D if she would sign an affidavit supporting Joe's story, which does agree to do. We also will file a Freedom of Information Act Request to obtain the administrative file and confirm if the IRS has information we do not have but will need for the Appeal hearing.

As examples, we have included here the following:

1. The retainer agreement
2. The Power of Attorney
3. The 1153 Joe received
4. The Form 2751 Joe received
5. Our protest of the proposed assessment
6. Our Freedom of Information Act ("FOIA") request for the administrative file
7. The affidavit we drafted and Carol D. signed

March 14, 2020

Manager Joseph
Street
City, State, Zip

  Re: **Client Retention Agreement**

Dear Mr. Joseph:

  We are pleased you have requested that Green & Sklarz LLC ("G&S" or "Firm") provide you with representation as set forth below. We would appreciate receiving written acknowledgement of this agreement for our files. The Bar recommends that there be a written fee agreement between attorneys and their clients. Additionally, we feel that it is in the best interest of our clients that they be fully informed of our billing practices. The purpose of this letter, therefore, is to set forth the scope of our engagement as legal counsel to you, to set forth the financial arrangements regarding our engagement and to verify our agreement of the foregoing:

1. **Scope of Engagement**

  Subject to the terms and conditions herein, including without limitation advance payment of the retainer and a signed copy of this agreement G&S will perform those legal services which you requested and, more specifically, to represent you before the Internal Revenue Service in regards to their proposed trust fund assessment against you (the "Engagement").

2. **Fee for Representation**

  Our billing practice is to charge for our services based on the hourly rate of the attorney involved. We bill in increments of no less than 1/10 of one hour. Please note, we bill for all services our office provides, including but not limited to: correspondence, telephone calls, document preparation, legal research, electronic legal research, inter-office conference, depositions, trials, meetings, etc. We use the amount of time devoted to a matter by a particular attorney at that attorney's hourly rate. These hourly rates are based upon experience, expertise and standing. In addition, we try to use associate, paralegal, legal assistant and/or secretarial support on projects whenever possible. All hourly rates are reviewed from time to time and may be adjusted and/or increased without notice. It is likely that all of these hourly rates will be increased annually usually commencing at the beginning of each calendar year and you hereby consent to such increase. My hourly rate is $475/hour. Our firm's rates for staff range from $75 - $275/hour, and for partners from $350 - $550/hour.

  The detail and the monthly statement will inform you not only of the fees and disbursements incurred but also of the nature and progress of the work performed. These statements are due and payable upon receipt, but in any event, no later than thirty days thereafter.

We reserve the right to charge interest at an appropriate rate (currently 1% per month) calculated monthly starting forty-five days after issuance of the statement and continuing until fully paid. You will be sent monthly billing statements as to work performed. We generally bill clients on either the 1st or 15th of the month. If you have a preference as to when you receive a bill, please let me know.

We do our best to see that our clients are satisfied not only with our services but also with the reasonableness of the fees and disbursements charged for these services. Therefore, if you have any questions about or objection to a statement or the basis for our fees to you, you should raise it promptly and not more than thirty (30) days after you receive a bill for discussion. If you object only to a portion of the statement, we ask you pay the remainder, which will not constitute a waiver of your objections.

3.   **Disbursements**

The performance of legal services involves costs and expenses, some of which must be paid to third parties. These expenses include, but are not limited to, filing fees, court reporters, deposition fees, travel costs, copying costs, telecopier costs, messenger services, long distance telephone charges, computerized research expenses and expenses of experts whom we deem appropriate to assist in our representation of you. We do not charge for internal copying costs, but if a production job is large and must be sent out we will charge you the actual expense. We expect that you will either pay directly or reimburse us for such costs. If such costs may be calculated beforehand and appear to be substantial, we may ask you to advance us those sums before we expend them or to reimburse the vendor directly.

4.   **Retainer**

We will require a payment of $5,000.00 prior to commencement of work on Your behalf, the amount to be determined at that time depending upon the scope of the work you require. Should the Engagement require work beyond the anticipated scope, we may require an additional retainer be paid. If the retainer is exhausted and you receive a bill, please pay the amount due. At the conclusion of the Firm's representation of You, any remaining positive retainer balance will be returned to You. You also agree that the retainer payment may be deposited in the Firm's general operating account and comingled with other funds.

Please note, we have tried to keep the retainer amount as low as possible, however, given the nature and complexity of the Engagement, it is possible that the retainer amount may be exceeded.

5.   **Withdrawal from Representation**

The attorney client relationship is one of mutual trust and confidence. If you, for whatever reason, wish us to cease representing you, you may request that we do so. If we feel we no longer wish to represent you, we will request that the court (if an appearance has been filed) to permit us to terminate our representation of you. We will only do so in the following circumstances: (a) a lack

of cooperation by you in promptly submitting necessary requested information; (b) your knowingly providing us, your adversaries or the court with false information; (c) your disregard of advice about matters of critical importance to your case; (d) your failure to promptly pay legal fees; or (e) for any other reason provided advance notice is provided.

Upon such termination, however, you would remain liable for any unpaid fees and costs. We also shall be authorized to reveal this agreement and any other necessary documents to any court or agency if the same should prove necessary to effect withdrawal or collection of our fees.

It is the policy of this firm to make every effort to have our clients feel that they are treated on a fair basis. We welcome an honest discussion of our fees and our services and encourage our clients to inquire about any matter relating to our fee arrangement or monthly statements that are in anyway unclear or appear unsatisfactory. If you have any questions, please do not hesitate to call us.

6. **Future Services**

This agreement will also apply to services rendered for such future matters that we agree will be handled by the Firm. If, however, such services, are substantially different from those to which this agreement applies (for instance, an appearance on your behalf in court), either party may request that a new agreement be executed, or that this agreement be reacknowledged.

If this letter correctly sets forth your understanding of the scope of the services to be rendered to the company by the Firm, and if the terms of the engagement are satisfactory, please execute the enclosed copy of this letter and return it us. If the scope of the services described is incorrect or if the terms of the engagement set forth in this letter are not satisfactory to you, please let us know in writing so that we can discuss either aspect.

By executing this agreement, you acknowledge that there is uncertainty concerning the outcome of this matter and that the Firm and the undersigned attorneys have made no guarantees as to the disposition of any phase of this matter. All representations and expression relative to the outcome of this matter, are only expressions of the said attorney's opinions and do not constitute guarantees. We look forward to continuing to work with you and thank you once again for the opportunity to serve.

Very truly yours,

Eric L. Green

READ, AGREED AND CONSENTED TO:

_____   _____
Manager Joseph   Date

Form 2848
(Rev. February 2020)
Department of the Treasury
Internal Revenue Service

Power of Attorney and Declaration of Representative

▶ Go to *www.irs.gov/Form2848* for instructions and the latest information.

OMB No. 1545-0150

For IRS Use Only
Received by:
Name _____
Telephone _____
Function _____
Date __ / __ / __

Part I Power of Attorney

Caution: A separate Form 2848 must be completed for each taxpayer. Form 2848 will not be honored for any purpose other than representation before the IRS.

1 Taxpayer information. Taxpayer must sign and date this form on page 2, line 7.

Manager Joe
Street Address, City, State, Zip

Taxpayer identification number(s)
XXX-XX-XXXXX

Daytime telephone number
(203) 111-XXXX

Plan number (if applicable)

hereby appoints the following representative(s) as attorney(s)-in-fact:

2 Representative(s) must sign and date this form on page 2, Part II.

Name and address
Representative
Reps Address

CAF No. XXXX-XXXXXR
PTIN P00000000
Telephone No. (203) XXX-XXXX
Fax No. (203) XXX-XXXX

Check if to be sent copies of notices and communications ☐   Check if new: Address ☐   Telephone No. ☐   Fax No. ☐

Name and address

CAF No. _____
PTIN _____
Telephone No. _____
Fax No. _____

Check if to be sent copies of notices and communications ☐   Check if new: Address ☐   Telephone No. ☐   Fax No. ☐

Name and address

CAF No. _____
PTIN _____
Telephone No. _____
Fax No. _____

(**Note:** IRS sends notices and communications to only two representatives.)   Check if new: Address ☐   Telephone No. ☐   Fax No. ☐

Name and address

CAF No. _____
PTIN _____
Telephone No. _____
Fax No. _____

(**Note:** IRS sends notices and communications to only two representatives.)   Check if new: Address ☐   Telephone No. ☐   Fax No. ☐

to represent the taxpayer before the Internal Revenue Service and perform the following acts:

3 Acts authorized (you are required to complete this line 3). With the exception of the acts described in line 5b, I authorize my representative(s) to receive and inspect my confidential tax information and to perform acts that I can perform with respect to the tax matters described below. For example, my representative(s) shall have the authority to sign any agreements, consents, or similar documents (see instructions for line 5a for authorizing a representative to sign a return).

Description of Matter (Income, Employment, Payroll, Excise, Estate, Gift, Whistleblower, Practitioner Discipline, PLR, FOIA, Civil Penalty, Sec. 4980H Shared Responsibility Payment, etc.) (see instructions)	Tax Form Number (1040, 941, 720, etc.) (if applicable)	Year(s) or Period(s) (if applicable) (see instructions)
Income Tax	1040	12/31/2000 - 12/31/2021
Civil Penalties	IRC 6672	3/31/2000 - 12/31/2021

4 Specific use not recorded on Centralized Authorization File (CAF). If the power of attorney is for a specific use not recorded on CAF, check this box. See *Line 4. Specific Use Not Recorded on CAF* in the instructions . . . . ▶ ☐

5a Additional acts authorized. In addition to the acts listed on line 3 above, I authorize my representative(s) to perform the following acts (see instructions for line 5a for more information):   ☑ Access my IRS records via an Intermediate Service Provider;
☐ Authorize disclosure to third parties;   ☑ Substitute or add representative(s);   ☐ Sign a return; _____

☐ Other acts authorized: _____

For Privacy Act and Paperwork Reduction Act Notice, see the instructions.   Cat. No. 11980J   Form **2848** (Rev. 2-2020)

Form 2848 (Rev. 2-2020) Page **2**

- **b** **Specific acts not authorized.** My representative(s) is (are) not authorized to endorse or otherwise negotiate any check (including directing or accepting payment by any means, electronic or otherwise, into an account owned or controlled by the representative(s) or any firm or other entity with whom the representative(s) is (are) associated) issued by the government in respect of a federal tax liability.
List any other specific deletions to the acts otherwise authorized in this power of attorney (see instructions for line 5b): _____

6 **Retention/revocation of prior power(s) of attorney.** The filing of this power of attorney automatically revokes all earlier power(s) of attorney on file with the Internal Revenue Service for the same matters and years or periods covered by this document. If you **do not** want to revoke a prior power of attorney, check here . . . . ▶ ☐

YOU MUST ATTACH A COPY OF ANY POWER OF ATTORNEY YOU WANT TO REMAIN IN EFFECT.

7 **Signature of taxpayer.** If a tax matter concerns a year in which a joint return was filed, each spouse must file a separate power of attorney even if they are appointing the same representative(s). If signed by a corporate officer, partner, guardian, tax matters partner, partnership representative (or designated individual, if applicable), executor, receiver, administrator, or trustee on behalf of the taxpayer, I certify that I have the legal authority to execute this form on behalf of the taxpayer.

▶ **IF NOT COMPLETED, SIGNED, AND DATED, THE IRS WILL RETURN THIS POWER OF ATTORNEY TO THE TAXPAYER.**

_____ _____ _____
Signature   Date   Title (if applicable)

Taxpayer's Name

_____   _____
Print name   Print name of taxpayer from line 1 if other than individual

Part II Declaration of Representative

Under penalties of perjury, by my signature below I declare that:
- I am not currently suspended or disbarred from practice, or ineligible for practice, before the Internal Revenue Service;
- I am subject to regulations contained in Circular 230 (31 CFR, Subtitle A, Part 10), as amended, governing practice before the Internal Revenue Service;
- I am authorized to represent the taxpayer identified in Part I for the matter(s) specified there; and
- I am one of the following:

  a Attorney—a member in good standing of the bar of the highest court of the jurisdiction shown below.
  b Certified Public Accountant—a holder of an active license to practice as a certified public accountant in the jurisdiction shown below.
  c Enrolled Agent—enrolled as an agent by the IRS per the requirements of Circular 230.
  d Officer—a bona fide officer of the taxpayer organization.
  e Full-Time Employee—a full-time employee of the taxpayer.
  f Family Member—a member of the taxpayer's immediate family (spouse, parent, child, grandparent, grandchild, step-parent, step-child, brother, or sister).
  g Enrolled Actuary—enrolled as an actuary by the Joint Board for the Enrollment of Actuaries under 29 U.S.C. 1242 (the authority to practice before the IRS is limited by section 10.3(d) of Circular 230).
  h Unenrolled Return Preparer—Authority to practice before the IRS is limited. An unenrolled return preparer may represent, provided the preparer (1) prepared and signed the return or claim for refund (or prepared if there is no signature space on the form); (2) was eligible to sign the return or claim for refund; (3) has a valid PTIN; and (4) possesses the required Annual Filing Season Program Record of Completion(s). **See Special Rules and Requirements for Unenrolled Return Preparers** in the instructions for additional information.
  k Qualifying Student—receives permission to represent taxpayers before the IRS by virtue of his/her status as a law, business, or accounting student working in an LITC or STCP. See instructions for Part II for additional information and requirements.
  r Enrolled Retirement Plan Agent—enrolled as a retirement plan agent under the requirements of Circular 230 (the authority to practice before the Internal Revenue Service is limited by section 10.3(e)).

▶ **IF THIS DECLARATION OF REPRESENTATIVE IS NOT COMPLETED, SIGNED, AND DATED, THE IRS WILL RETURN THE POWER OF ATTORNEY. REPRESENTATIVES MUST SIGN IN THE ORDER LISTED IN PART I, LINE 2.**

Note: For designations d–f, enter your title, position, or relationship to the taxpayer in the "Licensing jurisdiction" column.

Designation— Insert above letter **(a–r).**	Licensing jurisdiction (State) or other licensing authority (if applicable)	Bar, license, certification, registration, or enrollment number (if applicable)	Signature	Date

Form **2848** (Rev. 2-2020)

Internal Revenue Service　　　　　　　　　　**Department of the Treasury**

Date:　　March 12, 2020	**Number of this Letter:**　　1153
	Person to Contact:　　Revenue Officer Name
	Employee Number:　　10000789
	IRS Contact Address:　　150 Court Street, New Haven, CT
	IRS Telephone Number:　　203-XXX-XXXX
	Employer Identification Number:　　06-XXXXXXX
	Business Name and Address:　　Global Construction, Inc.

Dear　Manager Joseph

Our efforts to collect the federal employment or excise taxes due from the business named above have not resulted in full payment of the liability. We therefore propose to assess a penalty against you as a person required to collect, account for, and pay over withhold taxes for the above business.

Under the provisions of Internal Revenue Code section 6672, individuals who were required to collect, account for, and pay over these taxes for the business may be personally liable for a penalty if the business doesn't pay the taxes. These taxes, described in the enclosed Form 2751, consist of employment taxes you withheld (or should have withheld) from the employees' wages (and didn't pay) or excise taxes you collected (or should have collected) from patrons (and didn't pay), and are commonly referred to as "trust fund taxes."

The penalty we propose to assess against you is a personal liability called the Trust Fund Recovery Penalty. It is equal to the unpaid trust fund taxes which the business still owes the government. If you agree with this penalty for each tax period shown, please sign Part 1 of the enclosed Form 2751 and return it to us in the enclosed envelope.

If you don't agree, have additional information to support your case, and wish to try to resolve the matter informally, contact the person named at the top of this letter within ten days from the date of this letter.

You also have the right to appeal or protest this action. To preserve your appeal rights you need to mail us your written appeal within 60 days from the date of this letter (75 days if this letter is addressed to you outside the United States). The instructions below explain how to make the request.

Letter 1153 (DO) (Rev. 3-2002)
Catalog Number: 40545C

APPEALS

You may appeal your case to the local Appeals Office. Send your written appeal to the attention of the Person to Contact at the address shown at the top of this letter. The dollar amount of the proposed liability for each specific tax period you are protesting affects the form your appeal should take.

For each period you are protesting, if the proposed penalty amount is:	You should:
$25,000 or less	Send a letter listing the issues you disagree with and explain why you disagree. (Small Case Request).
More than $25,000	Submit a formal Written Protest.

One protest will suffice for all the periods listed on the enclosed Form 2751, however if any one of those periods is more than $25,000, a formal protest must be filed. Include any additional information that you want the Settlement Officer/Appeals Officer to consider. You may still appeal without additional information, but including it at this stage will help us to process your request promptly.

A SMALL CASE REQUEST should include:

   1. A copy of this letter, or your name, address, social security number, and any information that will help us locate your file;

   2. A statement that you want an Appeal's conference;

   3. A list of the issues you disagree with and an explanation of why you disagree. Usually, penalty cases like this one involve issues of responsibility and willfulness. Willfulness means that an action was intentional, deliberate or voluntary and not an accident or mistake. Therefore, your statement should include a clear explanation of your duties and responsibilities; and specifically, your duty and authority to collect, account for, and pay the trust fund taxes. Should you disagree with how we calculated the penalty, your statement should identify the dates and amounts of payments that you believe we didn't consider and or/ any computation errors that you believe we made.

Please submit two copies of your Small Case Request.

A formal **WRITTEN PROTEST should** include the items below. Pay particular attention to item 6 and the note that follows it.

Letter 1153 (DO) (Rev. 3-2002)
Catalog Number: 40545C

1. Your name, address, and social security number;

2. A statement that you want a conference;

3. A copy of this letter, or the date and number of this letter;

4. The tax periods involved (see Form 2751);

5. A list of the findings you disagree with;

6. A statement of fact, signed under penalties of perjury, that explains why you disagree and why you believe you shouldn't be charged with the penalty. Include specific dates, names, amounts, and locations which support your position. Usually, penalty cases like this one involve issues of responsibility and willfulness. Willfulness means that an action was intentional, deliberate or voluntary and not an accident or mistake. Therefore, your statement should include a clear explanation of your duties and responsibilities; and specifically, your duty and authority to collect, account for, and pay the trust fund taxes. Should you disagree with how we calculated the penalty, your statement should identify the dates and amounts of payments that you believe we didn't consider and/or any computation errors you believe we made;

   NOTE:

   To declare that the statement in item 6 is true under penalties of perjury, you must add the following to your statement and sign it:

   "Under penalties of perjury, I declare that I have examined the facts presented in this statement and any accompanying information, and, to the best of my knowledge and belief, they are true, correct, and complete."

7. If you rely on a law or other authority to support your arguments, explain what it is and how it applies.

REPRESENTATION

You may represent yourself at your conference or have someone who is qualified to practice before the Internal Revenue Service represent you. This may be your attorney, a certified public accountant, or another individual enrolled to practice before the IRS. If your representative attends a conference without you, he or she must file a power of attorney or tax information authorization before receiving or inspecting confidential tax information. Form 2848, Power of Attorney and Declaration of Representative, or Form 8821, Tax Information Authorization, may be used for this purpose. Both forms are available from any IRS office. A properly written power of attorney or authorization is acceptable.

If your representative prepares and signs the protest for you, he or she must substitute a declaration stating:

1. That he or she submitted the protest and accompanying documents, and

2. Whether he or she knows personally that the facts stated in the protest and accompanying documents are true and correct.

CLAIMS FOR REFUND AND CONSIDERATION BY THE COURTS

CONSIDERATION BY THE COURTS

If you and the IRS still disagree after your conference, we will send you a bill. However, by following the procedures outlined below, you may take your case to the United States Court of Federal Claims or to your United States District Court. These courts have no connection with the IRS.

Before you can file a claim with these courts, you must pay a portion of the tax liability and file a claim for refund with the IRS, as described below.

SPECIAL BOND TO DELAY IRS COLLECTION ACTIONS FOR ANY PERIOD AS SOON AS A CLAIM FOR REFUND IS FILED

To request a delay in collection of the penalty by the IRS for any period as soon as you file a claim for refund for that period, you must do the following within 30 days of the date of the official notice of assessment and demand (the first bill) for that period:

1. Pay the tax for one employee for each period (quarter) of liability that you wish to contest, if we've based the amount of the penalty on unpaid employment taxes; or pay the tax for one transaction for each period that you wish to contest, if we've based the amount of the penalty on unpaid excise tax.

2. File a claim for a refund of the amount(s) you paid using Form(s) 843, Claim for Refund and Request for Abatement.

3. Post a bond with the IRS for one and one half times the amount of the penalty that is left after you have made the payment in Item 1.

If the IRS denies your claim when you have posted this bond, you then have 30 days to file suit in your United States District Court or the United States Court of Federal Claims before the IRS may apply the bond to your trust fund recovery penalty and the interest accruing on this debt.

Letter 1153 (DO) (Rev. 3-2002)
Catalog Number: 40545C

Form 2751 (Rev. 7-2002)

Department of the Treasury-Internal Revenue Service

Proposed Assessment of Trust Fund Recovery Penalty

(Sec. 6672, Internal Revenue Code, or corresponding provisions of prior internal revenue laws)

Report of Business Taxpayer's Unpaid Tax Liability

Name and address of business: Global Construction, Inc.
STREET ADDRESS CITY,
STATE, ZIP

Tax Return Form Number	Tax Period Ended	Date Return Filed	Date Tax Assessed	Identifying Number	Amount Outstanding	Penalty
941	12/31/2018	11/20/2019	11/20/2019	06-xxxxxxxx	$71,928.62	$45,939.84
941	03/31/2019	11/20/2019	11/20/2019	06-xxxxxxxx	$86,143.81	$54,929.60
941	06/30/2019	11/20/2019	11/20/2019	06-xxxxxxxx	$72,568.00	$44,929.60
941	09/31/2019	11/20/2019	11/20/2019	06-xxxxxxxx	$86,680.57	$54,880.90
Totals:					**$317,321**	**$200,68**

Agreement to Assessment and Collection of Trust Fund Recovery Penalty

Name, address, and social security number of person responsible:
Manager Joseph
xxx-xx-1111
Street Adress
City, State Zip

I consent to the assessment and collection of the penalty shown for each period, which is equal either to the amount of federal employment taxes withheld from employees' wages or to the amount of federal excise taxes collected from patrons or members, and which was not paid over to the Government by the business named above. I waive the 60 day restriction on notice and demand set forth in Internal Revenue Code Section 6672(b).

Signature of person responsible _____ **Date** _____

Part 1— Please sign and return this copy to Internal Revenue Service   Catalog No. 21955U   www.irs.gov   Form **2751** (Rev. 7-200

CLAIM FOR REFUND WITH NO SPECIAL BOND

If you do not file a special bond with a prompt claim for refund, as described above, you may still file a claim for refund following above action items 1 and 2, except these action items do not have to be taken in the first 30 days after the date of the official notice of assessment and demand for the period.

If IRS has not acted on your claim within 6 months from the date you filed it, you can file a suit for refund. You can also file a suit for refund within 2 years after IRS has disallowed your claim.

You should be aware that if IRS finds that the collection of this penalty is in jeopardy, we may take immediate action to collect it without regard to the 60-day period for submitting a protest mentioned above.

For further information about filing a suit you may contact the Clerk of your District Court or the Clerk of the United States Court of Federal Claims, 717 Madison Place, NW, Washington, D.C. 20005.

If we do not hear from you within 60 days from the date of this letter (or 75 days if this letter is addressed to you outside the United States), we will assess the penalty and begin collection action.

Sincerely yours,

Revenue Officer

Enclosures:
Form 2751
Publication 1
Envelope

Letter 1153 (DO) (Rev. 3-2002)
Catalog Number: 40545C

March ___, 2020

Internal Revenue Service
ATTN: _____
Street Address
City, State Zip

RE: Manager Joseph
      Street Address
      City, State Zip
      SSN: _____

Dear _____:

My power of attorney (Form 2848) to represent the taxpayer in this matter is included.

Reference is made to the March 12, 2020 letter that proposed an assessment for unpaid trust funds in regard to the above named taxpayer for Global Construction Inc., a copy of which is attached. This is to protest the proposed assessment and to request a conference with the Appeals Division. The following information is submitted in support of this appeal.

I. **CONFERENCE**

The taxpayer wants to appeal the determination of the Internal Revenue Service, and requests a hearing before the Regional Office of Appeals in the East Hartford, Connecticut Appeals office.

II. **NAME AND ADDRESS**

Manager Joseph
Street Address
City, State Zip
SSN: _____

III. **DATE AND SYMBOLS FROM LETTER**

March 12, 2020
Letter 1153 (DO)(Rev. 3-2002)

IV. TAX PERIODS

12/31/2018
03/31/2019
06/30/2019
09/30/2019

V. ITEMIZED SCHEDULE OF APPEAL ITEMS

The determination that the taxpayer is a responsible person as defined in IRC § 6672 for the unpaid trust funds for the tax periods listed above in the amount of $200,680.

VI. STATEMENT OF FACTS

The taxpayer worked as job site manager for Global Construction, Inc., ("GLOBAL"). GLOBAL was in the construction business, and the taxpayer was responsible for managing the job site operations and overseeing the actual construction activities. The taxpayer's specific duties included supervising of all job personnel, reviewing of job budgets, scheduling, attending job meetings, and consulting with the Company's agents and employees as required.

The President of GLOBAL, Mr. Smith, was responsible for the finances. Mr. Smith ran operations in the office, and only he signed payroll checks and other documents as the sole shareholder. The taxpayer had no financial responsibilities in the Companies. The taxpayer had no signature authority, never signed a single check, legal document, or tax document. Ms. Carol D, who was in charge of payroll function for the years of 2012 to 2019, affirms that the taxpayer had nothing to do with nor signed a single check. A copy of her affidavit is attached.

VII. LAW AND AUTHORITIES

The issue is whether the taxpayer meets the definition of a "responsible person" who willfully failed to have the payroll taxes paid over to the government IRC § 6672.

IRC § 6672 states the following:

Any person *required to collect, truthfully account for, and pay over* any tax imposed by this title who *willfully* fails to collect such tax, or truthfully account for and pay over such tax, or willfully attempts in any manner to evade or defeat any such tax or the payment thereof, shall, in addition to other penalties provided by law, be liable to a penalty equal to the total amount of the tax evaded, or not collected, or not accounted for and paid over.

In other words, pursuant to IRC § 6672 and Regulation § 301.6672-1, the Trust Fund Recovery penalty is only imposed on individuals who:
1. Were required to collect, account for and pay over the taxes, and
2. Willfully failed to do so.

Based upon the foregoing, the taxpayer, though a manager, lacked the functional responsibility for the payroll taxes of GLOBAL. He was never involved with the payroll function and in 10 years never signed a check or return for the Companies. It was not until the IRS sent him a letter that he learned that GLOBAL owed payroll taxes. Prior to that he had no knowledge nor access to the financial information of the company, and was never made aware by anyone that the company had failed to pay its payroll taxes or even had a money issue. Given that the taxpayer was never involved in GLOBAL's taxes and did not have knowledge of the payroll tax problem, he therefore lacked the requisite willfulness required under IRC § 6672. The taxpayer therefore should not be held responsible for GLOBAL's unpaid payroll taxes.

This protest was prepared by the undersigned based upon direct involvement of TAXPAYER. To the best of my knowledge and understanding all of the statements of facts contained in the protest are true and correct.

Very truly yours,

REPRESENTATIVE'S NAME

Enclosures
C. Manager Joseph

February 28, 2020

VIA FAX: 877-807-9215
IRS FOIA Request
HQ FOIA
Stop 211
PO Box 621506
Atlanta, GA 30362-3006

      Re: **Taxpayer: Manager Joseph**
                Current Address: _____
                SSN: _____

Dear Sir or Madam:

This is a request under the Freedom of Information Act.

1.   **Name and Address**

        Requestor:
        Representative's Name
        Reps Street Address
        Rep City, State and Zip

        Client:
        Manager Joseph
        Taxpayer's Street Address
        Taxpayer's City, State and Zip

2.   **Description of the Requested Records**

        The undersigned represents Manager Joseph (the "Requestor"). We respectfully request copies of the taxpayers' administrative file regarding his civil penalties under IRC § 6672 for the quarters 12/31/2018 through and including 12/31/2019.

3.   **Proof of Identity**

        As proof of identity, I am including a photocopy of my driver's license and a copy of my Power of Attorney and Declaration of Representative (Form 2848).

4.   **Commitment to Pay Any Fees Which May Apply**

{00050475.1 }

The undersigned is willing to pay for fees associated with this request. If the request shall exceed $100, the undersigned requests to be notified.

5.   Compelling Need for Speedy Response

We are in the middle of an Appeal of these civil penalties and require the information to properly present our case.

I declare that the above stated information is true and accurate to the best of my knowledge under the penalty of perjury.

Please call me with any questions.

Very truly yours,

Your Name

State of Connecticut)
) ss. Town of **Orange**
County of New Haven)

AFFIDAVIT

I, Carol D., of Orange, Connecticut hereby aver as follows:

1. That I am over eighteen years of age and believe in the obligations of an oath;

2. I was an employee of Global Construction, Inc. ("Company") during the period of 2012 through its dissolution in 2019.

3. My role was Supervisor in-charge of payroll for the Company.

4. During Mr. Manager Joseph's time as a work site manager at the Company he never signed a payroll check.

5. Manager Joseph never signed any tax returns or payroll-related documents

6. Manager Joseph was not involved in the payroll process at all.

7. The only person who signed payroll checks and determined which vendors to pay and not pay during my time with the company was the owner, Mr. Smith.

8. I am aware this affidavit is being submitted to the Internal Revenue Service for their consideration of a material tax matter.

Subscribed and sworn to, under penalty of perjury, this 23rd day of March, 2020.

_____
WITNESSES NAME

Dated at Orange, Connecticut, this 23rd day of March, 2020.

_____
Notary Public

Case Study 2

This is the same situation as Case Study #1, except that Joe now comes to us 6 months after the proposed assessment. He now has received an IRS Letter 11, Final Notice of Intent to Levy, from the IRS Collection Division. All the other facts in case Study #1 are the same. Now we need to challenge an existing assessment, so the protest is no longer available.

Joe now has two options for challenging the assessment: he can pay for one employee for each quarter and then seek a refund, or he can file a Doubt-as-to-Liability Offer. In speaking with Joe about both options, he tells us he cannot afford to litigate the refund claim if it is denied. Given that Joe does not have the means to litigate, and he has not yet been levied, we advise Joe to do a Doubt-as-to-Liability Offer ("DATL"). The reason is it is much more economical and, because there is no refund he will want from a levy, the DATL makes sense. We explain to Joe that a DATL is an offer to settle the existing debt, so any funds that had already been levied and taken could not be recovered with a DATL.

As examples, we have included here the following:

1. The retainer agreement
2. The Power of Attorney
3. Our Freedom of Information Act ("FOIA") request for the administrative file
4. The 656-L for the DATL and the explanation and the affidavit we drafted and Carol D. signed (both the explanation and affidavit would be attached to the 656-L when it is submitted)

March 14, 2020

Manager Joseph
Street
City, State, Zip

    Re: **Client Retention Agreement**

Dear Mr. Joseph:

We are pleased you have requested that Green & Sklarz LLC ("G&S" or "Firm") provide you with representation as set forth below. We would appreciate receiving written acknowledgement of this agreement for our files. The Bar recommends that there be a written fee agreement between attorneys and their clients. Additionally, we feel that it is in the best interest of our clients that they be fully informed of our billing practices. The purpose of this letter, therefore, is to set forth the scope of our engagement as legal counsel to you, to set forth the financial arrangements regarding our engagement and to verify our agreement of the foregoing:

1.   **Scope of Engagement**

Subject to the terms and conditions herein, including without limitation advance payment of the retainer and a signed copy of this agreement G&S will perform those legal services which you requested and, more specifically, to represent you before the Internal Revenue Service in regards to the trust fund assessment it has made against you (the "Engagement").

2.   **Fee for Representation**

Our billing practice is to charge for our services based on the hourly rate of the attorney involved. We bill in increments of no less than 1/10 of one hour. Please note, we bill for all services our office provides, including but not limited to: correspondence, telephone calls, document preparation, legal research, electronic legal research, inter-office conference, depositions, trials, meetings, etc. We use the amount of time devoted to a matter by a particular attorney at that attorney's hourly rate. These hourly rates are based upon experience, expertise and standing. In addition, we try to use associate, paralegal, legal assistant and/or secretarial support on projects whenever possible. All hourly rates are reviewed from time to time and may be adjusted and/or increased without notice. It is likely that all of these hourly rates will be increased annually usually commencing at the beginning of each calendar year and you hereby consent to such increase. My hourly rate is $475/hour. Our firm's rates for staff range from $75 - $275/hour, and for partners from $350 - $550/hour.

The detail and the monthly statement will inform you not only of the fees and disbursements incurred but also of the nature and progress of the work performed. These statements are due and payable upon receipt, but in any event, no later than thirty days thereafter.

We reserve the right to charge interest at an appropriate rate (currently 1% per month) calculated monthly starting forty-five days after issuance of the statement and continuing until fully paid. You will be sent monthly billing statements as to work performed. We generally bill clients on either the 1st or 15th of the month. If you have a preference as to when you receive a bill, please let me know.

We do our best to see that our clients are satisfied not only with our services but also with the reasonableness of the fees and disbursements charged for these services. Therefore, if you have any questions about or objection to a statement or the basis for our fees to you, you should raise it promptly and not more than thirty (30) days after you receive a bill for discussion. If you object only to a portion of the statement, we ask you pay the remainder, which will not constitute a waiver of your objections.

3. **Disbursements**

The performance of legal services involves costs and expenses, some of which must be paid to third parties. These expenses include, but are not limited to, filing fees, court reporters, deposition fees, travel costs, copying costs, telecopier costs, messenger services, long distance telephone charges, computerized research expenses and expenses of experts whom we deem appropriate to assist in our representation of you. We do not charge for internal copying costs, but if a production job is large and must be sent out we will charge you the actual expense. We expect that you will either pay directly or reimburse us for such costs. If such costs may be calculated beforehand and appear to be substantial, we may ask you to advance us those sums before we expend them or to reimburse the vendor directly.

4. **Retainer**

We will require a payment of $5,000.00 prior to commencement of work on Your behalf, the amount to be determined at that time depending upon the scope of the work you require. Should the Engagement require work beyond the anticipated scope, we may require an additional retainer be paid. If the retainer is exhausted and you receive a bill, please pay the amount due. At the conclusion of the Firm's representation of You, any remaining positive retainer balance will be returned to You. You also agree that the retainer payment may be deposited in the Firm's general operating account and comingled with other funds.

Please note, we have tried to keep the retainer amount as low as possible, however, given the nature and complexity of the Engagement, it is possible that the retainer amount may be exceeded.

5. **Withdrawal from Representation**

The attorney client relationship is one of mutual trust and confidence. If you, for whatever reason, wish us to cease representing you, you may request that we do so. If we feel we no longer wish to represent you, we will request that the court (if an appearance has been filed) to permit us to terminate our representation of you. We will only do so in the following circumstances: (a) a lack

of cooperation by you in promptly submitting necessary requested information; (b) your knowingly providing us, your adversaries or the court with false information; (c) your disregard of advice about matters of critical importance to your case; (d) your failure to promptly pay legal fees; or (e) for any other reason provided advance notice is provided.

Upon such termination, however, you would remain liable for any unpaid fees and costs. We also shall be authorized to reveal this agreement and any other necessary documents to any court or agency if the same should prove necessary to effect withdrawal or collection of our fees.

It is the policy of this firm to make every effort to have our clients feel that they are treated on a fair basis. We welcome an honest discussion of our fees and our services and encourage our clients to inquire about any matter relating to our fee arrangement or monthly statements that are in anyway unclear or appear unsatisfactory. If you have any questions, please do not hesitate to call us.

6.   Future Services

This agreement will also apply to services rendered for such future matters that we agree will be handled by the Firm. If, however, such services, are substantially different from those to which this agreement applies (for instance, an appearance on your behalf in court), either party may request that a new agreement be executed, or that this agreement be reacknowledged.

If this letter correctly sets forth your understanding of the scope of the services to be rendered to the company by the Firm, and if the terms of the engagement are satisfactory, please execute the enclosed copy of this letter and return it us. If the scope of the services described is incorrect or if the terms of the engagement set forth in this letter are not satisfactory to you, please let us know in writing so that we can discuss either aspect.

By executing this agreement, you acknowledge that there is uncertainty concerning the outcome of this matter and that the Firm and the undersigned attorneys have made no guarantees as to the disposition of any phase of this matter. All representations and expression relative to the outcome of this matter, are only expressions of the said attorney's opinions and do not constitute guarantees. We look forward to continuing to work with you and thank you once again for the opportunity to serve.

Very truly yours,

Eric L. Green

READ, AGREED AND CONSENTED TO:

_____   _____
Manager Joseph   Date

Form 2848
(Rev. February 2020)
Department of the Treasury
Internal Revenue Service

Power of Attorney and Declaration of Representative

▶ Go to *www.irs.gov/Form2848* for instructions and the latest information.

OMB No. 1545-0150

For IRS Use Only
Received by:
Name _____
Telephone _____
Function _____
Date / /

Part I Power of Attorney

Caution: A separate Form 2848 must be completed for each taxpayer. Form 2848 will not be honored for any purpose other than representation before the IRS.

1 Taxpayer information. Taxpayer must sign and date this form on page 2, line 7.

Manager Joe
Street Address, City, State, Zip

Taxpayer identification number(s)
XXX-XX-XXXXX

Daytime telephone number	Plan number (if applicable)
(203) 111-XXXX	

hereby appoints the following representative(s) as attorney(s)-in-fact:

2 Representative(s) must sign and date this form on page 2, Part II.

Name and address
Representative
Reps Address

CAF No. _____ XXXX-XXXXXR
PTIN _____ P00000000
Telephone No. _____ (203) XXX-XXXX
Fax No. _____ (203) XXX-XXXX

Check if to be sent copies of notices and communications ☐
Check if new: Address ☐ Telephone No. ☐ Fax No. ☐

Name and address

CAF No. _____
PTIN _____
Telephone No. _____
Fax No. _____

Check if to be sent copies of notices and communications ☐
Check if new: Address ☐ Telephone No. ☐ Fax No. ☐

Name and address

CAF No. _____
PTIN _____
Telephone No. _____
Fax No. _____

(**Note:** IRS sends notices and communications to only two representatives.)
Check if new: Address ☐ Telephone No. ☐ Fax No. ☐

Name and address

CAF No. _____
PTIN _____
Telephone No. _____
Fax No. _____

(**Note:** IRS sends notices and communications to only two representatives.)
Check if new: Address ☐ Telephone No. ☐ Fax No. ☐

to represent the taxpayer before the Internal Revenue Service and perform the following acts:

3 Acts authorized (you are required to complete this line 3). With the exception of the acts described in line 5b, I authorize my representative(s) to receive and inspect my confidential tax information and to perform acts that I can perform with respect to the tax matters described below. For example, my representative(s) shall have the authority to sign any agreements, consents, or similar documents (see instructions for line 5a for authorizing a representative to sign a return).

Description of Matter (Income, Employment, Payroll, Excise, Estate, Gift, Whistleblower, Practitioner Discipline, PLR, FOIA, Civil Penalty, Sec. 4980H Shared Responsibility Payment, etc.) (see instructions)	Tax Form Number (1040, 941, 720, etc.) (if applicable)	Year(s) or Period(s) (if applicable) (see instructions)
Income Tax	1040	12/31/2000 - 12/31/2021
Civil Penalties	IRC 6672	3/31/2000 - 12/31/2021

4 Specific use not recorded on Centralized Authorization File (CAF). If the power of attorney is for a specific use not recorded on CAF, check this box. See *Line 4. Specific Use Not Recorded on CAF* in the instructions . . . . ▶ ☐

5a Additional acts authorized. In addition to the acts listed on line 3 above, I authorize my representative(s) to perform the following acts (see instructions for line 5a for more information): ☑ Access my IRS records via an Intermediate Service Provider;
☐ Authorize disclosure to third parties;   ☑ Substitute or add representative(s);   ☐ Sign a return; _____

☐ Other acts authorized: _____

For Privacy Act and Paperwork Reduction Act Notice, see the instructions.   Cat. No. 11980J   Form **2848** (Rev. 2-2020)

b Specific acts not authorized. My representative(s) is (are) not authorized to endorse or otherwise negotiate any check (including directing or accepting payment by any means, electronic or otherwise, into an account owned or controlled by the representative(s) or any firm or other entity with whom the representative(s) is (are) associated) issued by the government in respect of a federal tax liability.
List any other specific deletions to the acts otherwise authorized in this power of attorney (see instructions for line 5b): _____

6 Retention/revocation of prior power(s) of attorney. The filing of this power of attorney automatically revokes all earlier power(s) of attorney on file with the Internal Revenue Service for the same matters and years or periods covered by this document. If you **do not** want to revoke a prior power of attorney, check here . . . . ▶ ☐
YOU MUST ATTACH A COPY OF ANY POWER OF ATTORNEY YOU WANT TO REMAIN IN EFFECT.

7 Signature of taxpayer. If a tax matter concerns a year in which a joint return was filed, each spouse must file a separate power of attorney even if they are appointing the same representative(s). If signed by a corporate officer, partner, guardian, tax matters partner, partnership representative (or designated individual, if applicable), executor, receiver, administrator, or trustee on behalf of the taxpayer, I certify that I have the legal authority to execute this form on behalf of the taxpayer.

▶ **IF NOT COMPLETED, SIGNED, AND DATED, THE IRS WILL RETURN THIS POWER OF ATTORNEY TO THE TAXPAYER.**

Signature	Date	Title (if applicable)

Taxpayer's Name

Print name	Print name of taxpayer from line 1 if other than individual

Part II Declaration of Representative

Under penalties of perjury, by my signature below I declare that:
- I am not currently suspended or disbarred from practice, or ineligible for practice, before the Internal Revenue Service;
- I am subject to regulations contained in Circular 230 (31 CFR, Subtitle A, Part 10), as amended, governing practice before the Internal Revenue Service;
- I am authorized to represent the taxpayer identified in Part I for the matter(s) specified there; and
- I am one of the following:
  - **a** Attorney—a member in good standing of the bar of the highest court of the jurisdiction shown below.
  - **b** Certified Public Accountant—a holder of an active license to practice as a certified public accountant in the jurisdiction shown below.
  - **c** Enrolled Agent—enrolled as an agent by the IRS per the requirements of Circular 230.
  - **d** Officer—a bona fide officer of the taxpayer organization.
  - **e** Full-Time Employee—a full-time employee of the taxpayer.
  - **f** Family Member—a member of the taxpayer's immediate family (spouse, parent, child, grandparent, grandchild, step-parent, step-child, brother, or sister).
  - **g** Enrolled Actuary—enrolled as an actuary by the Joint Board for the Enrollment of Actuaries under 29 U.S.C. 1242 (the authority to practice before the IRS is limited by section 10.3(d) of Circular 230).
  - **h** Unenrolled Return Preparer—Authority to practice before the IRS is limited. An unenrolled return preparer may represent, provided the preparer (1) prepared and signed the return or claim for refund (or prepared if there is no signature space on the form); (2) was eligible to sign the return or claim for refund; (3) has a valid PTIN; and (4) possesses the required Annual Filing Season Program Record of Completion(s). **See Special Rules and Requirements for Unenrolled Return Preparers** *in the instructions for additional information.*
  - **k** Qualifying Student—receives permission to represent taxpayers before the IRS by virtue of his/her status as a law, business, or accounting student working in an LITC or STCP. See instructions for Part II for additional information and requirements.
  - **r** Enrolled Retirement Plan Agent—enrolled as a retirement plan agent under the requirements of Circular 230 (the authority to practice before the Internal Revenue Service is limited by section 10.3(e)).

▶ **IF THIS DECLARATION OF REPRESENTATIVE IS NOT COMPLETED, SIGNED, AND DATED, THE IRS WILL RETURN THE POWER OF ATTORNEY. REPRESENTATIVES MUST SIGN IN THE ORDER LISTED IN PART I, LINE 2.**

Note: For designations d–f, enter your title, position, or relationship to the taxpayer in the "Licensing jurisdiction" column.

Designation— Insert above letter **(a–r).**	Licensing jurisdiction (State) or other licensing authority (if applicable)	Bar, license, certification, registration, or enrollment number (if applicable)	Signature	Date

February 28, 2020

VIA FAX: 877-807-9215
IRS FOIA Request
HQ FOIA
Stop 211
PO Box 621506
Atlanta, GA 30362-3006

    Re: **Taxpayer: Manager Joseph**
            Current Address: _____
            SSN: _____

Dear Sir or Madam:

This is a request under the Freedom of Information Act.

1. **Name and Address**

    Requestor:
    Representative's Name
    Reps Street Address
    Rep City, State and Zip

    Client:
    Manager Joseph
    Taxpayer's Street Address
    Taxpayer's City, State and Zip

2. **Description of the Requested Records**

    The undersigned represents Manager Joseph (the "Requestor"). We respectfully request copies of the taxpayers' administrative file regarding his civil penalties under IRC § 6672 for the quarters 12/31/2018 through and including 12/31/2019.

3. **Proof of Identity**

    As proof of identity, I am including a photocopy of my driver's license and a copy of my Power of Attorney and Declaration of Representative (Form 2848).

4. **Commitment to Pay Any Fees Which May Apply**

The undersigned is willing to pay for fees associated with this request. If the request shall exceed $100, the undersigned requests to be notified.

5. Compelling Need for Speedy Response

We are in the middle of an Appeal of these civil penalties and require the information to properly present our case.

I declare that the above stated information is true and accurate to the best of my knowledge under the penalty of perjury.

Please call me with any questions.

Very truly yours,

Your Name

Page 5

Form 656-L (January 2018)

Department of the Treasury - Internal Revenue Service

Offer in Compromise *(Doubt as to Liability)*

OMB Number 1545-1686

IRS Received Date

▶ **To: Commissioner of Internal Revenue Service**
In the following agreement, the pronoun "we" may be assumed in place of "I" when there are joint liabilities and both parties are signing this agreement.
I submit this offer to compromise the tax liabilities plus any interest, penalties, additions to tax, and additional amounts required by law for the tax type and period(s) marked below:

Section 1 — Individual Information (Form 1040 filers)

Your First Name, Middle Initial, Last Name
Manager Joseph

Social Security Number (SSN)
XXX - XX - XXXX

If a Joint Offer: Spouse's First Name, Middle Initial, Last Name

Social Security Number (SSN)
 - -

Your Physical Home Address *(Street, City, State, ZIP Code)*
Street, City, State, Zip

Your Mailing Address *(if different from your Physical Home Address or Post Office Box Number)*

Is this a new address?
☐ Yes ☒ No

If yes, would you like us to update our records to this address?
☐ Yes ☒ No

Employer Identification Number *(For self-employed individuals only)*
-

Individual Tax Periods

☐ **1040** U.S. Individual Income Tax Return [List all year(s); for example 2009, 2010, etc.]

☐ **941** Employer's Quarterly Federal Tax Return [List all quarterly period(s); for example 03/31/2010, 06/30/2010, 09/30/2010, etc.]

☐ **940** Employer's Annual Federal Unemployment (FUTA) Tax Return [List all year(s); for example 2010, 2011, etc.]

☐ **Trust Fund Recovery Penalty** as a responsible person of *(enter business name)* Global Construction, Inc. ,
for failure to pay withholding and Federal Insurance Contributions Act taxes (Social Security taxes), for period(s) ending [List all quarterly period(s); for example 03/31/2009, 06/30/2009, etc.]
12/31/18, 3/31/19, 6/30/19, 9/30/19

☐ **Other Federal Tax(es)** [specify type(s) and period(s)]

Section 2 — Business Information (Form 1120, 1065, etc., filers)

Business Name

Business Physical Address *(Street, City, State, ZIP Code)*

Business Mailing Address *(Street, City, State, ZIP Code)*

Employer Identification Number *(EIN)*
-

Name and Title of Primary Contact

Telephone Number
( ) -

Business Tax Periods

☐ **1120** U.S. Corporate Income Tax Return [List all year(s); for example 1120 2010, 1120 2013, etc.]

☐ **941** Employer's Quarterly Federal Tax Return [List all quarterly period(s); for example 03/31/2010, 06/30/2010, 09/30/2010, etc.]

☐ **940** Employer's Annual Federal Unemployment (FUTA) Tax Return [List all year(s); for example 2010, 2011, etc.]

☐ **Other Federal Tax(es)** [specify type(s) and period(s)]

Note: If you need more space, use a separate sheet of paper and title it "Attachment to Form 656-L Dated _____." Sign and date the attachment following the listing of the tax periods.

Catalog Number 47516R   www.irs.gov   Form **656-L** (Rev. 1-2018)

Page 6

Section 3 — Amount of the Offer

I offer to pay $ __10__

Must be $1 or more and payable within 90 days of the notification of acceptance, unless an alternative payment term is approved at the time the offer is accepted. **Do not send any payment with this form.** If you do not offer at least $1, your offer will be returned without consideration.

Section 4 — Terms

By submitting this offer, I have read, understand and agree to the following terms and conditions:

Terms, Conditions, and Legal Agreement

a) The IRS will apply payments made under the terms of this offer in the best interest of the government.

IRS will keep my payments and fees

b) I voluntarily submit all payments made on this offer.

c) The IRS will keep all payments and credits made, received, or applied to the total original tax debt before I send in the offer or while it is under consideration, including any refunds from tax returns and/or credits from tax years prior to the year in which the offer was accepted.

d) The IRS may levy under section 6331(a) up to the time that the IRS official signs and acknowledges my offer as pending, which is accepted for processing, and the IRS may keep any proceeds arising from such a levy.

e) If the Doubt as to Liability offer determines that I do not owe the taxes, or the IRS ultimately over-collected the compromised tax liability, the IRS will return the over-collected amount to me, unless such refund is legally prohibited by statute.

f) If the IRS served a continuous levy on wages, salary, or certain federal payments under sections 6331(e) or (h), then the IRS could choose to either retain or release the levy. No levy may be made during the time an offer in compromise is pending.

I agree to the time extensions allowed by law

g) To have my offer considered, I agree to the extension of time limit provided by law to assess my tax debt (statutory period of assessment). I agree that the date by which the IRS must assess my tax debt will now be the date by which my debt must currently be assessed plus the period of time my offer is pending plus one additional year if the IRS rejects, returns, or terminates my offer, or I withdraw it. [Paragraph (l) of this section defines pending and withdrawal]. I understand I have the right not to waive the statutory period of assessment or to limit the waiver to a certain length or certain periods or issues. I understand, however, the IRS may not consider my offer if I decline to waive the statutory period of assessment or if I provide only a limited waiver. I also understand the statutory period for collecting my tax debt will be suspended during the time my offer is pending with the IRS, for 30 days after any rejection of my offer by the IRS, and during the time any rejection of my offer is being considered by the Appeals Office.

I understand I remain responsible for the full amount of the tax liability

h) The IRS cannot collect more than the full amount of the tax debt under this offer.

i) I understand I remain responsible for the full amount of the tax debt, unless and until the IRS partially or fully abates the tax, or accepts the offer in writing and I have met all the terms and conditions of the offer. The IRS will not remove the original amount of the tax debt from its records until I have met all the terms of the offer.

j) I understand the tax I offer to compromise is and will remain a tax debt until I meet all the terms and conditions of this offer. If I file bankruptcy before the terms and conditions of this offer are completed, any claim the IRS files in bankruptcy proceedings will be a tax claim.

k) Once the IRS accepts the offer in writing, I have no right to contest, in court or otherwise, the amount of the tax debt.

Pending status of an offer and right to appeal

l) The offer is pending starting with the date an authorized IRS official signs this form. The offer remains pending until an authorized IRS official accepts, rejects, returns, or acknowledges withdrawal of the offer in writing. If I appeal an IRS rejection decision on the offer, the IRS will continue to treat the offer as pending until the Appeals Office accepts or rejects the offer in writing. If an offer is rejected, no levy may be made during the 30 days of rejection. If I do not file a protest within 30 days of the date the IRS notifies me of the right to protest the decision, I waive the right to a hearing before the Appeals Office about the offer.

I understand if IRS fails to make a decision in 24-months my offer will be accepted

m) I understand under Internal Revenue Code (IRC) § 7122(f), my offer will be accepted, by law, unless IRS notifies me otherwise, in writing, within 24 months of the date my offer was initially received.

I understand what will happen if I fail to meet the terms of my offer (e.g. default)

n) If I fail to meet any of the terms of this offer, the IRS may levy or sue me to collect any amount ranging from the unpaid balance of the offer to the original amount of the tax debt (less payments made) plus penalties and interest that have accrued from the time the underlying tax liability arose. The IRS will continue to add interest, as required by Section § 6601 of the Internal Revenue Code, on the amount of the IRS determines is due after default.

I understand the IRS may file a Notice of Federal Tax Lien on my/our property

o) The IRS may file a Notice of Federal Tax Lien to protect the Government's interest during the offer investigation. The tax lien will be released 30 days after the payment terms have been satisfied and the payment has been verified. If the offer is accepted, the tax lien will be released within 30 days of when the payment terms have been satisfied and the payment has been verified. The time it takes to verify the payment varies based on the form of payment.

Page 7

Section 4 — Terms (continued)

I authorize the IRS to contact relevant third parties in order to process my/our offer

p) I understand that IRS employees may contact third parties in order to respond to this request, and I authorize the IRS to make such contacts. Further, in connection with this request, by authorizing the IRS to contact third parties, I understand that I will not receive notice of third parties contacted as is otherwise required by IRC § 7602(c).

Section 5 — Explanation of Circumstances

THIS SECTION MUST BE COMPLETED.

Explain why you believe the tax is incorrect. Reminder: if your explanation indicates you cannot afford to pay, do not file a Form 656-L. Refer to page 4 "What if I agree with the tax debt but cannot afford to pay in full?", for additional information. **Note: You may attach additional sheets if necessary. Please include your name and SSN and/or EIN on all additional sheets or supporting documentation.**

See attached Letter

Section 6 — Signature(s)

Taxpayer Attestation: If I submit this offer on a substitute form, I affirm this form is a verbatim duplicate of the official Form 656-L, and I agree to be bound by all the terms and conditions set forth in the official Form 656-L. Under penalties of perjury, I declare that I have examined this offer, including accompanying schedules and statements, and to the best of my knowledge and belief, it is true, correct and complete.

▶ Signature of Taxpayer/Corporation Name | Daytime Telephone Number ( ) - | Today's date (mm/dd/yyyy)

☐ The IRS may contact you by telephone about this offer. By checking this box, you authorize the IRS to leave detailed messages concerning your offer on your voice mail or answering machine.

▶ Signature of Spouse/Authorized Corporate Officer | Today's date (mm/dd/yyyy)

☐ The IRS may contact you by telephone about this offer. By checking this box, you authorize the IRS to leave detailed messages concerning your offer on your voice mail or answering machine.

Section 7 — Application Prepared by Someone Other than the Taxpayer

If this application was prepared by someone other than you (the taxpayer), please fill in that person's name and address below.

Name

Address (Street, City, State, ZIP Code) | Daytime Telephone Number ( ) -

Section 8 — Paid Preparer Use Only

Signature of Preparer

☐ The IRS may contact you by telephone about this offer. By checking this box, you authorize the IRS to leave detailed messages concerning your offer on your voice mail or answering machine.

Name of Preparer | Today's date (mm/dd/yyyy) | Preparer's CAF no. or PTIN

Firm's Name, Address, and ZIP Code | Daytime Telephone Number ( ) -

If you would like to have someone represent you during the offer investigation, include a valid, signed Form 2848 or 8821 with this application, or a copy of a previously filed form.

Catalog Number 47516R www.irs.gov Form **656-L** (Rev. 1-2018)

Page 8

IRS Use Only		
I accept the waiver of the statutory period of limitations on assessment for the Internal Revenue Service, as described in Section 4(g).		
Signature of Authorized IRS Official	Title	Today's date *(mm/dd/yyyy)*

Privacy Act Statement

We ask for the information on this form to carry out the internal revenue laws of the United States. Our authority to request this information is contained in Section 7801 of the Internal Revenue Code.

Our purpose for requesting the information is to determine if it is in the best interests of the IRS to accept an offer. You are not required to make an offer; however, if you choose to do so, you must provide all of the information requested. Failure to provide all of the information may prevent us from processing your request.

If you are a paid preparer and you prepared the Form 656-L for the taxpayer submitting an offer, we request that you complete and sign Section 8 on the Form 656-L, and provide identifying information. Providing this information is voluntary. This information will be used to administer and enforce the internal revenue laws of the United States and may be used to regulate practice before the Internal Revenue Service for those persons subject to Treasury Department Circular No. 230, Regulations Governing the Practice of Attorneys, Certified Public Accountants, Enrolled Agents, Enrolled Actuaries, and Appraisers before the Internal Revenue Service. Information on this form may be disclosed to the Department of Justice for civil and criminal litigation.

We may also disclose this information to cities, states and the District of Columbia for use in administering their tax laws and to combat terrorism. Providing false or fraudulent information on this form may subject you to criminal prosecution and penalties.

APPLICATION CHECKLIST

☐ Did you include supporting documentation and an explanation as to why you doubt you owe the tax?

☐ Did you complete all fields on the Form 656-L?

☐ Did you make an offer amount that is $1 or more?

Note: The amount of your offer should be based on what you believe the correct amount of the tax debt should be. However, you must offer at least $1. If you do not want to offer $1 or more, you should pursue the alternative solutions provided under "What alternatives do I have to sending in an Offer in Compromise (Doubt as to Liability)?" found on page 3.

☐ If someone other than you completed the Form 656-L, did that person sign it?

☐ Did you sign and include the Form 656-L?

☐ If you want a third party to represent you during the offer process, did you include a Form 2848 or Form 8821 unless one is already on file?

Note: There is no application fee or deposit required for a Doubt as to Liability offer. Do not send any payments with this offer.

Mail your package to:

Brookhaven Internal Revenue Service
COIC Unit
P.O. Box 9008
Stop 681-D
Holtsville, NY 11742-9008

IRS Form 656-L, Section 5, Explanation of Circumstances

Manager Joseph (the "Taxpayer") worked as job site manager for Global Construction, Inc., ("GLOBAL"). GLOBAL was in the construction business, and the taxpayer was responsible for managing the job site operations and overseeing the actual construction activities. The Taxpayer's specific duties included supervising of all job personnel, reviewing of job budgets, scheduling, attending job meetings, and consulting with the Company's agents and employees as required.

The President of GLOBAL, Mr. Smith, was responsible for the finances. Mr. Smith ran operations in the office, and only he signed payroll checks and other documents as the sole shareholder. The Taxpayer had no financial responsibilities in the Companies. The Taxpayer had no signature authority, never signed a single check, legal document, or tax document. Ms. Carol D, who was in charge of payroll function for the years of 2012 to 2019, affirms that the Taxpayer had nothing to do with nor signed a single check. A copy of her affidavit is attached.

The issue is whether the Taxpayer meets the definition of a "responsible person" who willfully failed to have the payroll taxes paid over to the government IRC § 6672.

IRC § 6672 states the following:

Any person *required to collect, truthfully account for, and pay over* any tax imposed by this title who *willfully* fails to collect such tax, or truthfully account for and pay over such tax, or willfully attempts in any manner to evade or defeat any such tax or the payment thereof, shall, in addition to other penalties provided by law, be liable to a penalty equal to the total amount of the tax evaded, or not collected, or not accounted for and paid over.

In other words, pursuant to IRC § 6672 and Regulation § 301.6672-1, the Trust Fund Recovery penalty is only imposed on individuals who:
1. Were required to collect, account for and pay over the taxes, and
2. Willfully failed to do so.

Based upon the foregoing, the Taxpayer, though a manager, lacked the functional responsibility for the payroll taxes of GLOBAL. He was never involved with the payroll function and in 10 years never signed a check or return for the Companies. It was not until the IRS sent him a letter that he learned that GLOBAL owed payroll taxes. Prior to that he had no knowledge nor access to the financial information of the company and was never made aware by anyone that the company had failed to pay its payroll taxes or even had a money issue. Given that the Taxpayer was never involved in GLOBAL's taxes and did not have knowledge of the payroll tax problem, he therefore lacked the requisite willfulness required under IRC § 6672. The Taxpayer therefore should not be held responsible for GLOBAL's unpaid payroll taxes.

State of Connecticut   )
)   ss. Town of Orange
County of New Haven)

AFFIDAVIT

I, Carol D., of Orange, Connecticut hereby aver as follows:

1. That I am over eighteen years of age and believe in the obligations of an oath;

2. I was an employee of Global Construction, Inc. ("Company") during the period of 2012 through its dissolution in 2019.

3. My role was Supervisor in-charge of payroll for the Company.

4. During Mr. Manager Joseph's time as a work site manager at the Company he never signed a payroll check.

5. Manager Joseph never signed any tax returns or payroll-related documents

6. Manager Joseph was not involved in the payroll process at all.

7. The only person who signed payroll checks and determined which vendors to pay and not pay during my time with the company was the owner, Mr. Smith.

8. I am aware this affidavit is being submitted to the Internal Revenue Service for their consideration of a material tax matter.

Subscribed and sworn to, under penalty of perjury, this 23rd day of March, 2020.

_____
WITNESSES NAME

Dated at Orange, Connecticut, this 23rd day of March, 2020.

_____
Notary Public

Case Study 3

Michael comes to see us. His company is behind in payroll taxes and he has not filed his personal 1040 tax returns since 2016. He has concluded that the company is not viable and wants to shut it down. His friend who owns his own company has offered Michael a job. Michael would like to take his tools and pickup truck and go work for his friend. The truck is worth $8,500 according to Kelly Blue Book and his hand tools about $500.

The 1153 arrives and with it the IRS Form 2751 waiver. It shows that Michael is responsible for unpaid trust fund taxes of around $200,000. Michael was the sole owner and signature on the accounts. He has no defense to the issue of his being a responsible person for purposes of the Trust Fund assessment.

We would dissolve the legal entity, have Michael close the bank accounts and send whatever little money is left to the IRS. We would also complete and file a Final 433-B with the IRS showing the company is dissolved, along with the final bank statement or printout showing the final balance and a copy of the check that it was sent to the IRS. We would also complete a Form 14135 to request the hand tools and pick-up truck be discharged from the IRS lien. The assets are worth $9,000 ($8,500 for the truck and $500 for the tools), and so we would offer $7,200, which is the "Quick Sale Value" of the assets.[57]

The IRS Revenue Officer will review the information and send it on to the IRS Technical Services Group that handles tax liens. Assuming they agree, the Taxpayer should receive a letter stating they will receive the lien release and can take the assets and have good title upon the payment of the $7,200 in either "certified funds" or by a "cashier's check". Personal checks will not suffice and will delay the release by 30 days.

Once this is done, Michael will have to resolve his personal tax case, including getting into compliance and filing his missing 1040 returns and resolving the outstanding balance of any income tax and the trust fund tax balance.

---

[57] The IRS, for collection, assumes if it seized and sold an asset it would only receive 80% of fair-market-value. This 80% rule is called the assets "Quick Sale Value". Given that is all the IRS would normally expect it is usually all we offer.

As examples, we have included here the following:

1. The retainer agreement
2. The Power of Attorney
3. The IRS Letter 1153
4. The IRS Form 2751
5. The Final 433-B
6. The Form 14135

March 14, 2020

Owner Michael
Street
City, State, Zip

    Re: **Client Retention Agreement**

Dear Mr. Michael:

We are pleased you have requested that Green & Sklarz LLC ("G&S" or "Firm") provide you with representation as set forth below. We would appreciate receiving written acknowledgement of this agreement for our files. The Bar recommends that there be a written fee agreement between attorneys and their clients. Additionally, we feel that it is in the best interest of our clients that they be fully informed of our billing practices. The purpose of this letter, therefore, is to set forth the scope of our engagement as legal counsel to you, to set forth the financial arrangements regarding our engagement and to verify our agreement of the foregoing:

1.   **Scope of Engagement**

Subject to the terms and conditions herein, including without limitation advance payment of the retainer and a signed copy of this agreement G&S will perform those legal services which you requested and, more specifically, to represent you before the Internal Revenue Service in regards to the payroll tax issue with your company (the "Engagement").

2.   **Fee for Representation**

Our billing practice is to charge for our services based on the hourly rate of the attorney involved. We bill in increments of no less than 1/10 of one hour. Please note, we bill for all services our office provides, including but not limited to: correspondence, telephone calls, document preparation, legal research, electronic legal research, inter-office conference, depositions, trials, meetings, etc. We use the amount of time devoted to a matter by a particular attorney at that attorney's hourly rate. These hourly rates are based upon experience, expertise and standing. In addition, we try to use associate, paralegal, legal assistant and/or secretarial support on projects whenever possible. All hourly rates are reviewed from time to time and may be adjusted and/or increased without notice. It is likely that all of these hourly rates will be increased annually usually commencing at the beginning of each calendar year and you hereby consent to such increase. My hourly rate is $475/hour. Our firm's rates for staff range from $75 - $275/hour, and for partners from $350 - $550/hour.

The detail and the monthly statement will inform you not only of the fees and disbursements incurred but also of the nature and progress of the work performed. These statements are due and payable upon receipt, but in any event, no later than thirty days thereafter.

{00160416.1 }

We reserve the right to charge interest at an appropriate rate (currently 1% per month) calculated monthly starting forty-five days after issuance of the statement and continuing until fully paid. You will be sent monthly billing statements as to work performed. We generally bill clients on either the 1st or 15th of the month. If you have a preference as to when you receive a bill, please let me know.

We do our best to see that our clients are satisfied not only with our services but also with the reasonableness of the fees and disbursements charged for these services. Therefore, if you have any questions about or objection to a statement or the basis for our fees to you, you should raise it promptly and not more than thirty (30) days after you receive a bill for discussion. If you object only to a portion of the statement, we ask you pay the remainder, which will not constitute a waiver of your objections.

3. **Disbursements**

The performance of legal services involves costs and expenses, some of which must be paid to third parties. These expenses include, but are not limited to, filing fees, court reporters, deposition fees, travel costs, copying costs, telecopier costs, messenger services, long distance telephone charges, computerized research expenses and expenses of experts whom we deem appropriate to assist in our representation of you. We do not charge for internal copying costs, but if a production job is large and must be sent out we will charge you the actual expense. We expect that you will either pay directly or reimburse us for such costs. If such costs may be calculated beforehand and appear to be substantial, we may ask you to advance us those sums before we expend them or to reimburse the vendor directly.

4. **Retainer**

We will require an initial retainer of $5,000.00 prior to commencement of work on Your behalf, the amount to be determined at that time depending upon the scope of the work you require. Should the Engagement require work beyond the anticipated scope, we may require an additional retainer be paid. If the retainer is exhausted and you receive a bill, please pay the amount due. At the conclusion of the Firm's representation of You, any remaining positive retainer balance will be returned to You. You also agree that the retainer payment may be deposited in the Firm's general operating account and comingled with other funds.

Please note, we have tried to keep the retainer amount as low as possible, however, given the nature and complexity of the Engagement, it is possible that the retainer amount may be exceeded.

5. **Withdrawal from Representation**

The attorney client relationship is one of mutual trust and confidence. If you, for whatever reason, wish us to cease representing you, you may request that we do so. If we feel we no longer wish to represent you, we will request that the court (if an appearance has been filed) to permit us to terminate our representation of you. We will only do so in the following circumstances: (a) a lack

of cooperation by you in promptly submitting necessary requested information; (b) your knowingly providing us, your adversaries or the court with false information; (c) your disregard of advice about matters of critical importance to your case; (d) your failure to promptly pay legal fees; or (e) for any other reason provided advance notice is provided.

Upon such termination, however, you would remain liable for any unpaid fees and costs. We also shall be authorized to reveal this agreement and any other necessary documents to any court or agency if the same should prove necessary to effect withdrawal or collection of our fees.

It is the policy of this firm to make every effort to have our clients feel that they are treated on a fair basis. We welcome an honest discussion of our fees and our services and encourage our clients to inquire about any matter relating to our fee arrangement or monthly statements that are in anyway unclear or appear unsatisfactory. If you have any questions, please do not hesitate to call us.

6. **Future Services**

This agreement will also apply to services rendered for such future matters that we agree will be handled by the Firm. If, however, such services, are substantially different from those to which this agreement applies (for instance, an appearance on your behalf in court), either party may request that a new agreement be executed, or that this agreement be reacknowledged.

If this letter correctly sets forth your understanding of the scope of the services to be rendered to the company by the Firm, and if the terms of the engagement are satisfactory, please execute the enclosed copy of this letter and return it us. If the scope of the services described is incorrect or if the terms of the engagement set forth in this letter are not satisfactory to you, please let us know in writing so that we can discuss either aspect.

By executing this agreement, you acknowledge that there is uncertainty concerning the outcome of this matter and that the Firm and the undersigned attorneys have made no guarantees as to the disposition of any phase of this matter. All representations and expression relative to the outcome of this matter, are only expressions of the said attorney's opinions and do not constitute guarantees. We look forward to continuing to work with you and thank you once again for the opportunity to serve.

Very truly yours,

Eric L. Green

READ, AGREED AND CONSENTED TO:

_____   _____
Owner Michael   Date

Form 2848
(Rev. February 2020)
Department of the Treasury
Internal Revenue Service

Power of Attorney
and Declaration of Representative

▶ Go to www.irs.gov/Form2848 for instructions and the latest information.

OMB No. 1545-0150

For IRS Use Only
Received by:
Name _____
Telephone _____
Function _____
Date ___/___/___

Part I Power of Attorney

Caution: A separate Form 2848 must be completed for each taxpayer. Form 2848 will not be honored for any purpose other than representation before the IRS.

1 Taxpayer information. Taxpayer must sign and date this form on page 2, line 7.

Owner Michael
Street Address, City, State, Zip

Taxpayer identification number(s)
XXX-XX-XXXXX

Daytime telephone number
(203) 111-XXXX

Plan number (if applicable)

hereby appoints the following representative(s) as attorney(s)-in-fact:

2 Representative(s) must sign and date this form on page 2, Part II.

Name and address
Representative
Reps Address

CAF No. XXXX-XXXXXR
PTIN P00000000
Telephone No. (203) XXX-XXXX
Fax No. (203) XXX-XXXX

Check if to be sent copies of notices and communications ☐   Check if new: Address ☐   Telephone No. ☐   Fax No. ☐

Name and address

CAF No. _____
PTIN _____
Telephone No. _____
Fax No. _____

Check if to be sent copies of notices and communications ☐   Check if new: Address ☐   Telephone No. ☐   Fax No. ☐

Name and address

CAF No. _____
PTIN _____
Telephone No. _____
Fax No. _____

(**Note:** IRS sends notices and communications to only two representatives.)   Check if new: Address ☐   Telephone No. ☐   Fax No. ☐

Name and address

CAF No. _____
PTIN _____
Telephone No. _____
Fax No. _____

(**Note:** IRS sends notices and communications to only two representatives.)   Check if new: Address ☐   Telephone No. ☐   Fax No. ☐

to represent the taxpayer before the Internal Revenue Service and perform the following acts:

3 Acts authorized (you are required to complete this line 3). With the exception of the acts described in line 5b, I authorize my representative(s) to receive and inspect my confidential tax information and to perform acts that I can perform with respect to the tax matters described below. For example, my representative(s) shall have the authority to sign any agreements, consents, or similar documents (see instructions for line 5a for authorizing a representative to sign a return).

Description of Matter (Income, Employment, Payroll, Excise, Estate, Gift, Whistleblower, Practitioner Discipline, PLR, FOIA, Civil Penalty, Sec. 4980H Shared Responsibility Payment, etc.) (see instructions)	Tax Form Number (1040, 941, 720, etc.) (if applicable)	Year(s) or Period(s) (if applicable) (see instructions)
Income Tax	1040	12/31/2000 - 12/31/2021
Civil Penalties	IRC 6672	3/31/2000 - 12/31/2021

4 Specific use not recorded on Centralized Authorization File (CAF). If the power of attorney is for a specific use not recorded on CAF, check this box. See *Line 4. Specific Use Not Recorded on CAF* in the instructions . . . . ▶ ☐

5a Additional acts authorized. In addition to the acts listed on line 3 above, I authorize my representative(s) to perform the following acts (see instructions for line 5a for more information):   ☑ Access my IRS records via an Intermediate Service Provider;
☐ Authorize disclosure to third parties;   ☑ Substitute or add representative(s);   ☐ Sign a return; _____

☐ Other acts authorized: _____

For Privacy Act and Paperwork Reduction Act Notice, see the instructions.   Cat. No. 11980J   Form **2848** (Rev. 2-2020)

Form 2848 (Rev. 2-2020) Page **2**

b **Specific acts not authorized.** My representative(s) is (are) not authorized to endorse or otherwise negotiate any check (including directing or accepting payment by any means, electronic or otherwise, into an account owned or controlled by the representative(s) or any firm or other entity with whom the representative(s) is (are) associated) issued by the government in respect of a federal tax liability.

List any other specific deletions to the acts otherwise authorized in this power of attorney (see instructions for line 5b): _____

6 **Retention/revocation of prior power(s) of attorney.** The filing of this power of attorney automatically revokes all earlier power(s) of attorney on file with the Internal Revenue Service for the same matters and years or periods covered by this document. If you **do not** want to revoke a prior power of attorney, check here . . . . ▶ ☐

YOU MUST ATTACH A COPY OF ANY POWER OF ATTORNEY YOU WANT TO REMAIN IN EFFECT.

7 **Signature of taxpayer.** If a tax matter concerns a year in which a joint return was filed, each spouse must file a separate power of attorney even if they are appointing the same representative(s). If signed by a corporate officer, partner, guardian, tax matters partner, partnership representative (or designated individual, if applicable), executor, receiver, administrator, or trustee on behalf of the taxpayer, I certify that I have the legal authority to execute this form on behalf of the taxpayer.

▶ **IF NOT COMPLETED, SIGNED, AND DATED, THE IRS WILL RETURN THIS POWER OF ATTORNEY TO THE TAXPAYER.**

Signature	Date	Title (if applicable)

Taxpayer's Name

Print name	Print name of taxpayer from line 1 if other than individual

Part II Declaration of Representative

Under penalties of perjury, by my signature below I declare that:
- I am not currently suspended or disbarred from practice, or ineligible for practice, before the Internal Revenue Service;
- I am subject to regulations contained in Circular 230 (31 CFR, Subtitle A, Part 10), as amended, governing practice before the Internal Revenue Service;
- I am authorized to represent the taxpayer identified in Part I for the matter(s) specified there; and
- I am one of the following:

  a Attorney—a member in good standing of the bar of the highest court of the jurisdiction shown below.

  b Certified Public Accountant—a holder of an active license to practice as a certified public accountant in the jurisdiction shown below.

  c Enrolled Agent—enrolled as an agent by the IRS per the requirements of Circular 230.

  d Officer—a bona fide officer of the taxpayer organization.

  e Full-Time Employee—a full-time employee of the taxpayer.

  f Family Member—a member of the taxpayer's immediate family (spouse, parent, child, grandparent, grandchild, step-parent, step-child, brother, or sister).

  g Enrolled Actuary—enrolled as an actuary by the Joint Board for the Enrollment of Actuaries under 29 U.S.C. 1242 (the authority to practice before the IRS is limited by section 10.3(d) of Circular 230).

  h Unenrolled Return Preparer—Authority to practice before the IRS is limited. An unenrolled return preparer may represent, provided the preparer (1) prepared and signed the return or claim for refund (or prepared if there is no signature space on the form); (2) was eligible to sign the return or claim for refund; (3) has a valid PTIN; and (4) possesses the required Annual Filing Season Program Record of Completion(s). **See Special Rules and Requirements for Unenrolled Return Preparers** *in the instructions for additional information.*

  k Qualifying Student—receives permission to represent taxpayers before the IRS by virtue of his/her status as a law, business, or accounting student working in an LITC or STCP. See instructions for Part II for additional information and requirements.

  r Enrolled Retirement Plan Agent—enrolled as a retirement plan agent under the requirements of Circular 230 (the authority to practice before the Internal Revenue Service is limited by section 10.3(e)).

▶ **IF THIS DECLARATION OF REPRESENTATIVE IS NOT COMPLETED, SIGNED, AND DATED, THE IRS WILL RETURN THE POWER OF ATTORNEY. REPRESENTATIVES MUST SIGN IN THE ORDER LISTED IN PART I, LINE 2.**

Note: For designations d–f, enter your title, position, or relationship to the taxpayer in the "Licensing jurisdiction" column.

Designation— Insert above letter **(a–r)**.	Licensing jurisdiction (State) or other licensing authority (if applicable)	Bar, license, certification, registration, or enrollment number (if applicable)	Signature	Date

Form **2848** (Rev. 2-2020)

Form 2848
(Rev. February 2020)
Department of the Treasury
Internal Revenue Service

Power of Attorney
and Declaration of Representative

▶ Go to www.irs.gov/Form2848 for instructions and the latest information.

OMB No. 1545-0150
For IRS Use Only
Received by:
Name _____
Telephone _____
Function _____
Date   /   /

Part I Power of Attorney

Caution: A separate Form 2848 must be completed for each taxpayer. Form 2848 will not be honored for any purpose other than representation before the IRS.

1 Taxpayer information. Taxpayer must sign and date this form on page 2, line 7.

Owner Michael's Company
Street Address, City, State, Zip

Taxpayer identification number(s)
XX-XXXXXXX

Daytime telephone number
(203) 111-XXXX

Plan number (if applicable)

hereby appoints the following representative(s) as attorney(s)-in-fact:

2 Representative(s) must sign and date this form on page 2, Part II.

Name and address
Representative
Reps Address

CAF No. _____ XXXX-XXXXXR
PTIN _____ P00000000
Telephone No. _____ (203) XXX-XXXX
Fax No. _____ (203) XXX-XXXX

Check if to be sent copies of notices and communications ☐   Check if new: Address ☐   Telephone No. ☐   Fax No. ☐

Name and address

CAF No. _____
PTIN _____
Telephone No. _____
Fax No. _____

Check if to be sent copies of notices and communications ☐   Check if new: Address ☐   Telephone No. ☐   Fax No. ☐

Name and address

CAF No. _____
PTIN _____
Telephone No. _____
Fax No. _____

(**Note:** IRS sends notices and communications to only two representatives.)   Check if new: Address ☐   Telephone No. ☐   Fax No. ☐

Name and address

CAF No. _____
PTIN _____
Telephone No. _____
Fax No. _____

(**Note:** IRS sends notices and communications to only two representatives.)   Check if new: Address ☐   Telephone No. ☐   Fax No. ☐

to represent the taxpayer before the Internal Revenue Service and perform the following acts:

3 Acts authorized (you are required to complete this line 3). With the exception of the acts described in line 5b, I authorize my representative(s) to receive and inspect my confidential tax information and to perform acts that I can perform with respect to the tax matters described below. For example, my representative(s) shall have the authority to sign any agreements, consents, or similar documents (see instructions for line 5a for authorizing a representative to sign a return).

Description of Matter (Income, Employment, Payroll, Excise, Estate, Gift, Whistleblower, Practitioner Discipline, PLR, FOIA, Civil Penalty, Sec. 4980H Shared Responsibility Payment, etc.) (see instructions)	Tax Form Number (1040, 941, 720, etc.) (if applicable)	Year(s) or Period(s) (if applicable) (see instructions)
Income Tax	1040	12/31/2000 - 12/31/2021
Employment Tax	941	3/31/2000 - 12/31/2021
Employment Tax	940	12/31/2000 - 12/31/2021

4 Specific use not recorded on Centralized Authorization File (CAF). If the power of attorney is for a specific use not recorded on CAF, check this box. See *Line 4. Specific Use Not Recorded on CAF* in the instructions . . . . ▶ ☐

5a Additional acts authorized. In addition to the acts listed on line 3 above, I authorize my representative(s) to perform the following acts (see instructions for line 5a for more information): ☑ Access my IRS records via an Intermediate Service Provider;
☐ Authorize disclosure to third parties;   ☑ Substitute or add representative(s);   ☐ Sign a return; _____

☐ Other acts authorized: _____

For Privacy Act and Paperwork Reduction Act Notice, see the instructions.   Cat. No. 11980J   Form **2848** (Rev. 2-2020)

Form 2848 (Rev. 2-2020) Page **2**

- b **Specific acts not authorized.** My representative(s) is (are) not authorized to endorse or otherwise negotiate any check (including directing or accepting payment by any means, electronic or otherwise, into an account owned or controlled by the representative(s) or any firm or other entity with whom the representative(s) is (are) associated) issued by the government in respect of a federal tax liability.
List any other specific deletions to the acts otherwise authorized in this power of attorney (see instructions for line 5b): _____

6 **Retention/revocation of prior power(s) of attorney.** The filing of this power of attorney automatically revokes all earlier power(s) of attorney on file with the Internal Revenue Service for the same matters and years or periods covered by this document. If you **do not** want to revoke a prior power of attorney, check here . . . . ▶ ☐
YOU MUST ATTACH A COPY OF ANY POWER OF ATTORNEY YOU WANT TO REMAIN IN EFFECT.

7 **Signature of taxpayer.** If a tax matter concerns a year in which a joint return was filed, each spouse must file a separate power of attorney even if they are appointing the same representative(s). If signed by a corporate officer, partner, guardian, tax matters partner, partnership representative (or designated individual, if applicable), executor, receiver, administrator, or trustee on behalf of the taxpayer, I certify that I have the legal authority to execute this form on behalf of the taxpayer.

▶ **IF NOT COMPLETED, SIGNED, AND DATED, THE IRS WILL RETURN THIS POWER OF ATTORNEY TO THE TAXPAYER.**

Owner

| Signature | Date | Title (if applicable) |

Taxpayer's Name

| Print name | Print name of taxpayer from line 1 if other than individual |

Part II   Declaration of Representative

Under penalties of perjury, by my signature below I declare that:
- I am not currently suspended or disbarred from practice, or ineligible for practice, before the Internal Revenue Service;
- I am subject to regulations contained in Circular 230 (31 CFR, Subtitle A, Part 10), as amended, governing practice before the Internal Revenue Service;
- I am authorized to represent the taxpayer identified in Part I for the matter(s) specified there; and
- I am one of the following:

  a Attorney—a member in good standing of the bar of the highest court of the jurisdiction shown below.
  b Certified Public Accountant—a holder of an active license to practice as a certified public accountant in the jurisdiction shown below.
  c Enrolled Agent—enrolled as an agent by the IRS per the requirements of Circular 230.
  d Officer—a bona fide officer of the taxpayer organization.
  e Full-Time Employee—a full-time employee of the taxpayer.
  f Family Member—a member of the taxpayer's immediate family (spouse, parent, child, grandparent, grandchild, step-parent, step-child, brother, or sister).
  g Enrolled Actuary—enrolled as an actuary by the Joint Board for the Enrollment of Actuaries under 29 U.S.C. 1242 (the authority to practice before the IRS is limited by section 10.3(d) of Circular 230).
  h Unenrolled Return Preparer—Authority to practice before the IRS is limited. An unenrolled return preparer may represent, provided the preparer (1) prepared and signed the return or claim for refund (or prepared if there is no signature space on the form); (2) was eligible to sign the return or claim for refund; (3) has a valid PTIN; and (4) possesses the required Annual Filing Season Program Record of Completion(s). **See Special Rules and Requirements for Unenrolled Return Preparers *in the instructions for additional information.***
  k Qualifying Student—receives permission to represent taxpayers before the IRS by virtue of his/her status as a law, business, or accounting student working in an LITC or STCP. See instructions for Part II for additional information and requirements.
  r Enrolled Retirement Plan Agent—enrolled as a retirement plan agent under the requirements of Circular 230 (the authority to practice before the Internal Revenue Service is limited by section 10.3(e)).

▶ **IF THIS DECLARATION OF REPRESENTATIVE IS NOT COMPLETED, SIGNED, AND DATED, THE IRS WILL RETURN THE POWER OF ATTORNEY. REPRESENTATIVES MUST SIGN IN THE ORDER LISTED IN PART I, LINE 2.**

Note: For designations d–f, enter your title, position, or relationship to the taxpayer in the "Licensing jurisdiction" column.

Designation— Insert above letter **(a–r)**.	Licensing jurisdiction (State) or other licensing authority (if applicable)	Bar, license, certification, registration, or enrollment number (if applicable)	Signature	Date

Form **2848** (Rev. 2-2020)

Internal Revenue Service   **Department of the Treasury**

Date: March 12, 2020

Number of this Letter:	1153
Person to Contact:	Revenue Officer Name
Employee Number:	10000789
IRS Contact Address:	150 Court Street, New Haven, CT
IRS Telephone Number:	203-XXX-XXXX
Employer Identification Number:	06-XXXXXXX
Business Name and Address:	Michael's Company

Dear   Owner Michael

Our efforts to collect the federal employment or excise taxes due from the business named above have not resulted in full payment of the liability. We therefore propose to assess a penalty against you as a person required to collect, account for, and pay over withhold taxes for the above business.

Under the provisions of Internal Revenue Code section 6672, individuals who were required to collect, account for, and pay over these taxes for the business may be personally liable for a penalty if the business doesn't pay the taxes. These taxes, described in the enclosed Form 2751, consist of employment taxes you withheld (or should have withheld) from the employees' wages (and didn't pay) or excise taxes you collected (or should have collected) from patrons (and didn't pay), and are commonly referred to as "trust fund taxes."

The penalty we propose to assess against you is a personal liability called the Trust Fund Recovery Penalty. It is equal to the unpaid trust fund taxes which the business still owes the government. If you agree with this penalty for each tax period shown, please sign Part 1 of the enclosed Form 2751 and return it to us in the enclosed envelope.

If you don't agree, have additional information to support your case, and wish to try to resolve the matter informally, contact the person named at the top of this letter within ten days from the date of this letter.

You also have the right to appeal or protest this action. To preserve your appeal rights you need to mail us your written appeal within 60 days from the date of this letter (75 days if this letter is addressed to you outside the United States). The instructions below explain how to make the request.

Letter 1153 (DO) (Rev. 3-2002)
Catalog Number: 40545C

APPEALS

You may appeal your case to the local Appeals Office. Send your written appeal to the attention of the Person to Contact at the address shown at the top of this letter. The dollar amount of the proposed liability for each specific tax period you are protesting affects the form your appeal should take.

For each period you are protesting, if the proposed penalty amount is:	You should:
$25,000 or less	Send a letter listing the issues you disagree with and explain why you disagree. (Small Case Request).
More than $25,000	Submit a formal Written Protest.

One protest will suffice for all the periods listed on the enclosed Form 2751, however if any one of those periods is more than $25,000, a formal protest must be filed. Include any additional information that you want the Settlement Officer/Appeals Officer to consider. You may still appeal without additional information, but including it at this stage will help us to process your request promptly.

A SMALL CASE REQUEST should include:

1. A copy of this letter, or your name, address, social security number, and any information that will help us locate your file;

2. A statement that you want an Appeal's conference;

3. A list of the issues you disagree with and an explanation of why you disagree. Usually, penalty cases like this one involve issues of responsibility and willfulness. Willfulness means that an action was intentional, deliberate or voluntary and not an accident or mistake. Therefore, your statement should include a clear explanation of your duties and responsibilities; and specifically, your duty and authority to collect, account for, and pay the trust fund taxes. Should you disagree with how we calculated the penalty, your statement should identify the dates and amounts of payments that you believe we didn't consider and or/ any computation errors that you believe we made.

Please submit two copies of your Small Case Request.

A formal **WRITTEN PROTEST should** include the items below. Pay particular attention to item 6 and the note that follows it.

Letter 1153 (DO) (Rev. 3-2002)
Catalog Number: 40545C

1. Your name, address, and social security number;

2. A statement that you want a conference;

3. A copy of this letter, or the date and number of this letter;

4. The tax periods involved (see Form 2751);

5. A list of the findings you disagree with;

6. A statement of fact, signed under penalties of perjury, that explains why you disagree and why you believe you shouldn't be charged with the penalty. Include specific dates, names, amounts, and locations which support your position. Usually, penalty cases like this one involve issues of responsibility and willfulness. Willfulness means that an action was intentional, deliberate or voluntary and not an accident or mistake. Therefore, your statement should include a clear explanation of your duties and responsibilities; and specifically, your duty and authority to collect, account for, and pay the trust fund taxes. Should you disagree with how we calculated the penalty, your statement should identify the dates and amounts of payments that you believe we didn't consider and/or any computation errors you believe we made;

NOTE:

To declare that the statement in item 6 is true under penalties of perjury, you must add the following to your statement and sign it:

"Under penalties of perjury, I declare that I have examined the facts presented in this statement and any accompanying information, and, to the best of my knowledge and belief, they are true, correct, and complete."

7. If you rely on a law or other authority to support your arguments, explain what it is and how it applies.

REPRESENTATION

You may represent yourself at your conference or have someone who is qualified to practice before the Internal Revenue Service represent you. This may be your attorney, a certified public accountant, or another individual enrolled to practice before the IRS. If your representative attends a conference without you, he or she must file a power of attorney or tax information authorization before receiving or inspecting confidential tax information. Form 2848, Power of Attorney and Declaration of Representative, or Form 8821, Tax Information Authorization, may be used for this purpose. Both forms are available from any IRS office. A properly written power of attorney or authorization is acceptable.

If your representative prepares and signs the protest for you, he or she must substitute a declaration stating:

1. That he or she submitted the protest and accompanying documents, and

2. Whether he or she knows personally that the facts stated in the protest and accompanying documents are true and correct.

CLAIMS FOR REFUND AND CONSIDERATION BY THE COURTS

CONSIDERATION BY THE COURTS

If you and the IRS still disagree after your conference, we will send you a bill. However, by following the procedures outlined below, you may take your case to the United States Court of Federal Claims or to your United States District Court. These courts have no connection with the IRS.

Before you can file a claim with these courts, you must pay a portion of the tax liability and file a claim for refund with the IRS, as described below.

SPECIAL BOND TO DELAY IRS COLLECTION ACTIONS FOR ANY PERIOD AS SOON AS A CLAIM FOR REFUND IS FILED

To request a delay in collection of the penalty by the IRS for any period as soon as you file a claim for refund for that period, you must do the following within 30 days of the date of the official notice of assessment and demand (the first bill) for that period:

1. Pay the tax for one employee for each period (quarter) of liability that you wish to contest, if we've based the amount of the penalty on unpaid employment taxes; or pay the tax for one transaction for each period that you wish to contest, if we've based the amount of the penalty on unpaid excise tax.

2. File a claim for a refund of the amount(s) you paid using Form(s) 843, Claim for Refund and Request for Abatement.

3. Post a bond with the IRS for one and one half times the amount of the penalty that is left after you have made the payment in Item 1.

If the IRS denies your claim when you have posted this bond, you then have 30 days to file suit in your United States District Court or the United States Court of Federal Claims before the IRS may apply the bond to your trust fund recovery penalty and the interest accruing on this debt.

Letter 1153 (DO) (Rev. 3-2002)
Catalog Number: 40545C

CLAIM FOR REFUND WITH NO SPECIAL BOND

If you do not file a special bond with a prompt claim for refund, as described above, you may still file a claim for refund following above action items 1 and 2, except these action items do not have to be taken in the first 30 days after the date of the official notice of assessment and demand for the period.

If IRS has not acted on your claim within 6 months from the date you filed it, you can file a suit for refund. You can also file a suit for refund within 2 years after IRS has disallowed your claim.

You should be aware that if IRS finds that the collection of this penalty is in jeopardy, we may take immediate action to collect it without regard to the 60-day period for submitting a protest mentioned above.

For further information about filing a suit you may contact the Clerk of your District Court or the Clerk of the United States Court of Federal Claims, 717 Madison Place, NW, Washington, D.C. 20005.

If we do not hear from you within 60 days from the date of this letter (or 75 days if this letter is addressed to you outside the United States), we will assess the penalty and begin collection action.

Sincerely yours,

Revenue Officer

Enclosures:
Form 2751
Publication 1
Envelope

Form 2751 (Rev. 7-2002)

Department of the Treasury-Internal Revenue Service

Proposed Assessment of Trust Fund Recovery Penalty

(Sec. 6672, Internal Revenue Code, or corresponding provisions of prior internal revenue laws)

Report of Business Taxpayer's Unpaid Tax Liability

Name and address of business: MICHAEL'S COMPANY
STREET ADDRESS CITY,
STATE, ZIP

Tax Return Form Number	Tax Period Ended	Date Return Filed	Date Tax Assessed	Identifying Number	Amount Outstanding	Penalty
941	12/31/2018	11/20/2019	11/20/2019	06-xxxxxxxx	$71,928.62	$45,939.84
941	03/31/2019	11/20/2019	11/20/2019	06-xxxxxxxx	$86,143.81	$54,929.60
941	06/30/2019	11/20/2019	11/20/2019	06-xxxxxxxx	$72,568.00	$44,929.60
941	09/31/2019	11/20/2019	11/20/2019	06-xxxxxxxx	$86,680.57	$54,880.96
Totals:					$317,321	$200,68

Agreement to Assessment and Collection of Trust Fund Recovery Penalty

Name, address, and social security number of person responsible:
Owner Michael
xxx-xx-1111
Street Adress
City, State Zip

I consent to the assessment and collection of the penalty shown for each period, which is equal either to the amount of federal employment taxes withheld employees' wages or to the amount of federal excise taxes collected from patrons or members, and which was not paid over to the Government by the busir named above. I waive the 60 day restriction on notice and demand set forth in Internal Revenue Code Section 6672(b).

Signature of person responsible | Date

Part 1— Please sign and return this copy to Internal Revenue Service   Catalog No. 21955U   www.irs.gov

Form 433-B (February 2019)
Department of the Treasury
Internal Revenue Service

BUSINESS CLOSED AS OF 10/1/2019

Collection Information Statement for Businesses

Note: *Complete all entry spaces with the current data available or "N/A" (not applicable). Failure to complete all entry spaces may result in rejection of your request or significant delay in account resolution.* **Include attachments if additional space is needed to respond completely to any question.**

Section 1: Business Information

1a	Business Name: **Michael's Company**	2a	Employer Identification No. (EIN) **xx-xxxxxxx**
1b	Business Street Address: **Street, City, State and Zip** Mailing Address: **Same** City ____ State ____ ZIP ____	2b	Type of entity *(Check appropriate box below)* ☐ Partnership ☐ Corporation ☐ Other ____ ☐ Limited Liability Company (LLC) classified as a corporation ☑ Other LLC - Include number of members **1**
1c	County **List the County**	2c	Date Incorporated/Established **1/1/2008** *mmddyyyy*
1d	Business Telephone (**203**) xxx-xxxx	3a	Number of Employees **0**
1e	Type of Business: **Construction**	3b	Monthly Gross Payroll **0**
		3c	Frequency of Tax Deposits **0**
1f	Business Website (web address): **n/a**	3d	Is the business enrolled in Electronic Federal Tax Payment System (EFTPS) ☑ Yes ☐ No
4	Does the business engage in e-Commerce *(Internet sales)* If yes, complete 5a and 5b.		☐ Yes ☐ No

PAYMENT PROCESSOR *(e.g., PayPal, Authorize.net, Google Checkout, etc.)* Include virtual currency wallet, exchange or digital currency exchange.

	Name and Address *(Street, City, State, ZIP code)*	Payment Processor Account Number
5a	**Was Merchant Services but closed 9/30/2019**	**Was XXXXXXXXXXX**
5b		

CREDIT CARDS ACCEPTED BY THE BUSINESS

Type of Credit Card *(e.g., Visa, Mastercard, etc.)*	Merchant Account Number	Issuing Bank Name and Address *(Street, City, State, ZIP code)*
n/a		
6a		Phone
6b		Phone
6c		Phone

Section 2: Business Personnel and Contacts

PARTNERS, OFFICERS, LLC MEMBERS, MAJOR SHAREHOLDERS (Foreign and Domestic), ETC.

7a	Full Name **Owner Michael** Title **Member** Home Address **Street** City **City** State **State** ZIP **Zip** Responsible for Depositing Payroll Taxes ☐ Yes ☐ No	Taxpayer Identification Number **xxx-xx-xxxx** Home Telephone (**203**) xxx-xxxx Work/Cell Phone (**203**) xxx-xxxx Ownership Percentage & Shares or Interest **100** Annual Salary/Draw **$60,000**
7b	Full Name ____ Title ____ Home Address ____ City ____ State ____ ZIP ____ Responsible for Depositing Payroll Taxes ☐ Yes ☐ No	Taxpayer Identification Number ____ Home Telephone ( ) Work/Cell Phone ( ) Ownership Percentage & Shares or Interest ____ Annual Salary/Draw ____
7c	Full Name ____ Title ____ Home Address ____ City ____ State ____ ZIP ____ Responsible for Depositing Payroll Taxes ☐ Yes ☐ No	Taxpayer Identification Number ____ Home Telephone ( ) Work/Cell Phone ( ) Ownership Percentage & Shares or Interest ____ Annual Salary/Draw ____
7d	Full Name ____ Title ____ Home Address ____ City ____ State ____ ZIP ____ Responsible for Depositing Payroll Taxes ☐ Yes ☐ No	Taxpayer Identification Number ____ Home Telephone ( ) Work/Cell Phone ( ) Ownership Percentage & Shares or Interest ____ Annual Salary/Draw ____

Form 433-B (Rev. 2-2019) Page **2**

Section 3: Other Financial Information *(Attach copies of all applicable documents)*

8 Does the business use a Payroll Service Provider or Reporting Agent *(If yes, answer the following)* ☐ Yes ☑ No

Name and Address *(Street, City, State, ZIP code)* closed 9/30/19	Effective dates *(mmddyyyy)*

9 Is the business a party to a lawsuit *(If yes, answer the following)* ☐ Yes ☑ No

☐ Plaintiff ☐ Defendant	Location of Filing	Represented by	Docket/Case No.
Amount of Suit $	Possible Completion Date *(mmddyyyy)*	Subject of Suit	

10 Has the business ever filed bankruptcy *(If yes, answer the following)* ☐ Yes ☑ No

Date Filed *(mmddyyyy)*	Date Dismissed *(mmddyyyy)*	Date Discharged *(mmddyyyy)*	Petition No.	District of Filing

11 Do any related parties *(e.g., officers, partners, employees)* have outstanding amounts owed to the business *(If yes, answer the following)* ☐ Yes ☑ No

Name and Address *(Street, City, State, ZIP code)*	Date of Loan	Current Balance As of *mmddyyyy* $	Payment Date	Payment Amount $

12 Have any assets been transferred, in the last 10 years, from this business for less than full value *(If yes, answer the following)* ☐ Yes ☑ No

List Asset	Value at Time of Transfer $	Date Transferred *(mmddyyyy)*	To Whom or Where Transferred

13 Does this business have other business affiliations *(e.g., subsidiary or parent companies)* *(If yes, answer the following)* ☐ Yes ☑ No

Related Business Name and Address *(Street, City, State, ZIP code)*	Related Business EIN:

14 Any increase/decrease in income anticipated *(If yes, answer the following)* ☑ Yes ☐ No

Explain *(Use attachment if needed)* Operations ceased 9/30/19 - no longer aby income	How much will it increase/decrease $	When will it increase/decrease Totally 10/1/19

15 Is the business a Federal Government Contractor *(Include Federal Government contracts in #18, Accounts/Notes Receivable)* ☐ Yes ☑ No

Section 4: Business Asset and Liability Information (Foreign and Domestic)

16a **CASH ON HAND** *Include cash that is not in the bank* Total Cash on Hand $ 0

16b Is there a safe on the business premises ☐ Yes ☑ No Contents

BUSINESS BANK ACOUNTS Include online and mobile accounts *(e.g., PayPal)*, money market accounts, savings accounts, checking accounts and stored value cards *(e.g., payroll cards, government benefit cards, etc.)*
List safe deposit boxes including location, box number and value of contents. Attach list of contents.

	Type of Account	Full Name and Address *(Street, City, State, ZIP code)* of Bank, Savings & Loan, Credit Union or Financial Institution	Account Number	Account Balance As of _____ *mmddyyyy*
17a	Checking	Closed 10/1/19 - see attached statement		$ 0
17b				$
17c				$
17d	Total Cash in Banks *(Add lines 17a through 17c and amounts from any attachments)*			$ 0

Form 433-B (Rev. 2-2019) Page 3

ACCOUNTS/NOTES RECEIVABLE Include e-payment accounts receivable and factoring companies, and any bartering or online auction accounts. *(List all contracts separately including contracts awarded, but not started).* **Include Federal, state and local government grants and contracts.**

Name & Address *(Street, City, State, ZIP code)*	Status *(e.g., age, factored, other)*	Date Due *(mmddyyy)*	Invoice Number or Government Grant or Contract Number	Amount Due
18a None Contact Name Phone				$
18b Contact Name Phone				$
18c Contact Name Phone				$
18d Contact Name Phone				$
18e Contact Name Phone				$
18f Outstanding Balance *(Add lines 18a through 18e and amounts from any attachments)*				$ 0

INVESTMENTS List all investment assets below. Include stocks, bonds, mutual funds, stock options, certificates of deposit, commodities (e.g., gold, silver, copper, etc.) and virtual currency (e.g., Bitcoin, Ripple and Litecoin).

Name of Company & Address *(Street, City, State, ZIP code)*	Used as collateral on loan	Current Value	Loan Balance	**Equity** Value Minus Loan
19a None Phone	☐ Yes ☐ No	$	$	$
19b Phone	☐ Yes ☐ No	$	$	$
19c Total Investments *(Add lines 19a, 19b, and amounts from any attachments)*				$ 0

AVAILABLE CREDIT Include all lines of credit and credit cards.

Full Name & Address *(Street, City, State, ZIP code)*	Credit Limit	Amount Owed As of _____ *mmddyyyy*	**Available Credit** As of _____ *mmddyyyy*
20a None Account No.	$	$	$
20b Account No.	$	$	$
20c Total Credit Available *(Add lines 20a, 20b, and amounts from any attachments)*			$ 0

Catalog Number 16649P www.irs.gov Form **433-B** (Rev. 2-2019)

Form 433-B (Rev. 2-2019) — Page 4

REAL PROPERTY Include all real property and land contracts the business owns/leases/rents.

	Purchase/Lease Date (mmddyyyy)	Current Fair Market Value (FMV)	Current Loan Balance	Amount of Monthly Payment	Date of Final Payment (mmddyyyy)	Equity FMV Minus Loan
21a Property Description **None**		$	$	$		$ 0
Location (Street, City, State, ZIP code) and County		Lender/Lessor/Landlord Name, Address, (Street, City, State, ZIP code) and Phone Phone				
21b Property Description		$	$	$		$
Location (Street, City, State, ZIP code) and County		Lender/Lessor/Landlord Name, Address, (Street, City, State, ZIP code) and Phone Phone				
21c Property Description		$	$	$		$
Location (Street, City, State, ZIP code) and County		Lender/Lessor/Landlord Name, Address, (Street, City, State, ZIP code) and Phone Phone				
21d Property Description		$	$	$		$
Location (Street, City, State, ZIP code) and County		Lender/Lessor/Landlord Name, Address, (Street, City, State, ZIP code) and Phone Phone				

21e Total Equity (Add lines 21a through 21d and amounts from any attachments) $ 0

VEHICLES, LEASED AND PURCHASED Include boats, RVs, motorcycles, all-terrain and off-road vehicles, trailers, mobile homes, etc.

		Purchase/Lease Date (mmddyyyy)	Current Fair Market Value (FMV)	Current Loan Balance	Amount of Monthly Payment	Date of Final Payment (mmddyyyy)	Equity FMV Minus Loan
22a Year 2010	Make/Model F150	2/2011	$ 8,500	$ 0	$ 0	0	$ 8,500
Mileage 187,600	License/Tag Number xxxxxx	Lender/Lessor Name, Address, (Street, City, State, ZIP code) and Phone					
Vehicle Identification Number (VIN) x1x1x1x1x1xx1x1						Phone	
22b Year	Make/Model		$	$	$		$
Mileage	License/Tag Number	Lender/Lessor Name, Address, (Street, City, State, ZIP code) and Phone					
Vehicle Identification Number (VIN)						Phone	
22c Year	Make/Model		$	$	$		$
Mileage	License/Tag Number	Lender/Lessor Name, Address, (Street, City, State, ZIP code) and Phone					
Vehicle Identification Number (VIN)						Phone	
22d Year	Make/Model		$	$	$		$
Mileage	License/Tag Number	Lender/Lessor Name, Address, (Street, City, State, ZIP code) and Phone					
Vehicle Identification Number (VIN)						Phone	

22e Total Equity (Add lines 22a through 22d and amounts from any attachments) $ 8,500

Form 433-B (Rev. 2-2019) — Page 5

BUSINESS EQUIPMENT AND INTANGIBLE ASSETS Include all machinery, equipment, merchandise inventory, and other assets in 23a through 23d. List intangible assets in 23e through 23g *(licenses, patents, logos, domain names, trademarks, copyrights, software, mining claims, goodwill and trade secrets.)*

	Purchase/ Lease Date *(mmddyyyy)*	Current Fair Market Value (FMV)	Current Loan Balance	Amount of Monthly Payment	Date of Final Payment *(mmddyyyy)*	**Equity** FMV Minus Loan
23a Asset Description **Hand Tools**		$ 500	$ 0	$ 0	n/a	$ 500
Location of asset *(Street, City, State, ZIP code)* and County **Owner's address**		Lender/Lessor Name, Address, *(Street, City, State, ZIP code)* and Phone n/a Phone				
23b Asset Description		$	$	$		$
Location of asset *(Street, City, State, ZIP code)* and County		Lender/Lessor Name, Address, *(Street, City, State, ZIP code)* and Phone Phone				
23c Asset Description		$	$	$		$
Location of asset *(Street, City, State, ZIP code)* and County		Lender/Lessor Name, Address, *(Street, City, State, ZIP code)* and Phone Phone				
23d Asset Description		$	$	$		$
Location of asset *(Street, City, State, ZIP code)* and County		Lender/Lessor Name, Address, *(Street, City, State, ZIP code)* and Phone Phone				
23e Intangible Asset Description						$
23f Intangible Asset Description						$
23g Intangible Asset Description						$
23h Total Equity *(Add lines 23a through 23g and amounts from any attachments)*						$ 500.00

BUSINESS LIABILITIES Include notes and judgements not listed previously on this form.

Business Liabilities	Secured/ Unsecured	Date Pledged *(mmddyyyy)*	Balance Owed	Date of Final Payment *(mmddyyyy)*	Payment Amount
24a Description: **IRS**	☑ Secured ☐ Unsecured		$ 317,321		$ 0
Name Street Address City/State/ZIP code			Phone		
24b Description: **Capital One Bank**	☐ Secured ☑ Unsecured		$ 15,000		$789
Name Street Address City/State/ZIP code			Phone		
24c Total Payments *(Add lines 24a and 24b and amounts from any attachments)*				$	$789

Catalog Number 16649P — www.irs.gov — Form **433-B** (Rev. 2-2019)

Form 433-B (Rev. 2-2019) Page **6**

Section 5: Monthly Income/Expenses Statement for Business

Accounting Method Used: ☑ Cash ☐ Accrual
Use the prior 3, 6, 9 or 12 month period to determine your typical business income and expenses.

Income and Expenses during the period (mmddyyyy) _____ to (mmddyyyy) _____

Provide a breakdown below of your average monthly income and expenses, based on the period of time used above.

Total Monthly Business Income			Total Monthly Business Expenses		
	Income Source	Gross Monthly		Expense items	Actual Monthly
25	Gross Receipts from Sales/Services	$	36	Materials Purchased [1]	$
26	Gross Rental Income	$	37	Inventory Purchased [2]	$
27	Interest Income	$	38	Gross Wages & Salaries	$
28	Dividends	$	39	Rent	$
29	Cash Receipts (Not included in lines 25-28)	$	40	Supplies [3]	$
	Other Income (Specify below)		41	Utilities/Telephone [4]	$
30		$	42	Vehicle Gasoline/Oil	$
31		$	43	Repairs & Maintenance	$
32		$	44	Insurance	$
33		$	45	Current Taxes [5]	$
34		$	46	Other Expenses (Specify)	$ 0
35	**Total Income** (Add lines 25 through 34)	$ 0	47	IRS Use Only-Allowable Installment Payments	$
			48	**Total Expenses** (Add lines 36 through 47)	$
			49	**Net Income** (Line 35 minus Line 48)	$ 0

1. **Materials Purchased:** Materials are items directly related to the production of a product or service.
2. **Inventory Purchased:** Goods bought for resale.
3. **Supplies:** Supplies are items used to conduct business and are consumed or used up within one year. This could be the cost of books, office supplies, professional equipment, etc.
4. **Utilities/Telephone:** Utilities include gas, electricity, water, oil, other fuels, trash collection, telephone, cell phone and business internet.
5. **Current Taxes:** Real estate, state, and local income tax, excise, franchise, occupational, personal property, sales and the employer's portion of employment taxes.

Certification: *Under penalties of perjury, I declare that to the best of my knowledge and belief this statement of assets, liabilities, and other information is true, correct, and complete.*

Signature	Title	Date
	Owner	3/20/2020

Print Name of Officer, Partner or LLC Member

Owner Michael

After we review the completed Form 433-B, you may be asked to provide verification for the assets, encumbrances, income and expenses reported. Documentation may include previously filed income tax returns, profit and loss statements, bank and investment statements, loan statements, financing statements, bills or statements for recurring expenses, etc.

IRS USE ONLY (Notes)

Privacy Act: The information requested on this Form is covered under Privacy Acts and Paperwork Reduction Notices which have already been provided to the taxpayer.

Catalog Number 16649P www.irs.gov Form **433-B** (Rev. 2-2019)

Form 14135
(June 2010)

Department of the Treasury — Internal Revenue Service

Application for Certificate of Discharge of Property from Federal Tax Lien

OMB No. 1545-2174

Complete the entire application. Enter NA *(not applicable)*, when appropriate. Attachments and exhibits should be included as necessary. Additional information may be requested of you or a third party to clarify the details of the transaction(s).

1. Taxpayer Information *(Individual or Business named on the notice of lien)*:

Name *(Individual First, Middle Initial, Last)* or *(Business)* as it appears on lien		Primary Social Security Number *(last 4 digits only)*
Michaels Company		
Name Continuation *(Individual First, Middle Initial, Last)* or *(Business d/b/a)*		Secondary Social Security Number *(last 4 digits only)*
Address *(Number, Street, P.O. Box)*		Employer Identification Number
Street		XX-XXXXXXX
City	State	ZIP Code
City	State	Zip
Telephone Number *(with area code)*	Fax Number *(with area code)*	
203-xxx-xxxx	(203) xxx-xxxx	

2. Applicant Information: ☐ Check if also the Taxpayer *(If not the taxpayer, attach copy of lien. See Sec.10)*

Name *(First, Middle Initial, Last)*		Relationship to taxpayer
Owner Michael		Owner
Address *(Number, Street, P.O. Box)*		
Street		
City	State	ZIP Code
City	State	Zip
Telephone Number *(with area code)*	Fax Number *(with area code)*	
203-xxx-xxxx	n/a	

3. Purchase/Transferee/New Owner   ☒ Check if also the Applicant

	Relationship to taxpayer

4. Attorney/Representative Information   Attached: Form 8821 or Power of Attorney Form 2848   ☒ Yes   ☐ No

Name *(First, Middle Initial, Last)*		Interest Represented *(e.g. taxpayer, lender, etc.)*
Your Name		No
Address *(Number, Street, P.O. Box)*		
Your address		
City	State	ZIP Code
Your city	Your state	Your zip
Telephone Number *(with area code)*	Fax Number *(with area code)*	
Your #	Your #	

5. Lender/Finance Company Information - or *(Settlement/Escrow Company for applications under Section 6325(b)(3) only)*

Company Name	Contact Name	Contact Phone Number

Catalog Number 54727S   www.irs.gov   Form **14135** (Rev. 06-2010)

6. Monetary Information

Proposed sales price	$7,200
Expected proceeds to be paid to the United States in exchange for the certificate of discharge *(Enter NA if no proceeds are anticipated)*	$7,200

7. Basis for Discharge:
Check the box below that best addresses what you would like the United States to consider in your application for discharge. *(Publication 783 has additional descriptions of the Internal Revenue Code sections listed below.)*

- [ ] **6325(b)(1)** — Value of property remaining attached by the lien(s) is at least double the liability of the federal tax lien(s) plus other encumbrances senior to the lien(s)

- [x] **6325(b)(2)(A)** — The United States receives an amount not less than the value of the United States' interest.
    (Note: If you are applying under 6325(b)(2)(A) and are the property owner but not the taxpayer, see also section 16.)

- [ ] **6325(b)(2)(B)** — Interest of the United States in the property to be discharged has no value.

- [ ] **6325(b)(3)** — Proceeds from property sale held in escrow subject to the liens and claims of the United States.

- [ ] **6325(b)(4)** — Deposit made or bond furnished in an amount equal to the value of the United States' interest.
    (Note: This selection provides a remedy under 7426(a)(4) for return of deposit but is exclusively for a property owner not named as the taxpayer on the lien)

8. Description of property
(for example, 3 bedroom rental house; 2002 Cessna twin engine airplane, serial number AT919000000000X00; etc.):

2010 Ford F150 Truck, 187,000 miles, Vin 1x1x1x1x1x1x1
Miscellaneous used hand tools

Address of real property *(If this is personal property, list the address where the property is located)*:

Address *(Number, Street, P.O. Box)*
n/a

City	State	ZIP Code

FOR REAL ESTATE: a legible copy of the deed or title showing the legal description is required	☐ Attached	☒ NA
FOR Discharge Requests under Section 6325(b)(1): copy of deed(s) or title(s) for property remaining subject to the Federal Tax Lien is required	☐ Attached	☒ NA

9. Appraisal and Valuations

REQUIRED APPRAISAL Professional appraisal completed by a disinterested third party	☐ Attached
PLUS ONE OF THE FOLLOWING ADDITIONAL VALUATIONS:	
County valuation of property *(real property)*	☐ Attached
Informal valuation of property by disinterested third party	☒ Attached
Proposed selling price *(for property being sold at auction)*	☒ Attached
Other: _____	☐ Attached

AND for applications under Section 6325(b)(1), valuation information (of the type described above in this section) must also be provided for property remaining subject to the lien.

10. Copy of Federal Tax Lien(s) *(Complete if applicant and taxpayer differ)* ☒ Attached ☐ No
OR list the lien number(s) found near the top right corner on the lien document(s) *(if known)*

Lien #			

11. Copy of the sales contract/purchase agreement *(if available)* ☒ Attached ☐ No
OR
Describe how and when the taxpayer will be divested of his/her interest in the property:
Owner wishes to pay the quick-sale value of the used equipment so he can accept another job as a W-2 employee

12. Copy of a current title report ☒ Attached ☐ No
OR
List encumbrances senior to the Federal Tax Lien. Include name and address of holder; description of encumbrance, e.g., mortgage, state lien, etc.; date of agreement; original loan amount and interest rate; amount due at time of application; and family relationship, if applicable *(Attach additional sheets as needed)*:
Copy of the title of the truck is attached

13. Copy of proposed closing statement *(aka HUD-1)* ☐ Attached ☒ No
OR
Itemize all proposed costs, commissions, and expenses of any transfer or sale associated with property *(Attach additional sheets as needed)*:
None

14. Additional information that may have a bearing on this request, such as pending litigation, explanations of unusual situations, etc., is attached for consideration ☐ Attached ☒ No

15. Escrow Agreement *(For applications under IRC 6325(b)(3))* ☐ Attached ☒ No
Escrow agreement must specify type of account, name and depositary for account, conditions under which payment will be made, cost of escrow, name and address of any party identified as part of escrow agreement, and signatures of all parties involved including Advisory Group Manager. Terms for agreement must be reached before discharge approved.

16. WAIVER *(For applications made by third parties under IRC 6325(b)(2))*
If you are applying as an owner of the property and you are not the taxpayer, to have this application considered under section 6325(b)(2), you must waive the rights that would be available if the application were made under section 6325(b)(4). If you choose not to waive these rights, the application will be treated as one made under 6325(b)(4) and any payment will be treated like a deposit under that section. Please check the appropriate box.

I understand that an application and payment made under section 6325(b)(2) does not provide the judicial remedy available under section 7426(a)(4). In making such an application / payment, I waive the option to have the payment treated as a deposit under section 6325(b)(4) and the right to request a return of funds and to bring an action under section 7426(a)(4). ☒ Waive ☐ No

17. Declaration
Under penalties of perjury, I declare that I have examined this application, including any accompanying schedules, exhibits, affidavits, and statements and to the best of my knowledge and belief it is true, correct and complete.

Signature/Title   Date

Signature/Title   Date

DEPARTMENT OF THE TREASURY
INTERNAL REVENUE SERVICE
Washington, D.C. 20224

SMALL BUSINESS/SELF-EMPLOYED DIVISION

Rep Name

Rep Street Address

City, State Zip

Re: Owner Michael

Dear REP NAME:

This letter is to transmit to you the Certificate of Discharge of Property From Federal Tax Lien pursuant to Internal Revenue Code Section 6325(b)(2)(A), relating to the business Michael's Company LLC.

The Certificate of Discharge is enclosed. This is the original document. You may wish to record this certificate with the office where the Federal Tax Lien is filed.

If we can be of further assistance or if you have any questions concerning this matter, please write to Internal Revenue Service, Advisory Group, 380 Westminster Street, Providence, RI 02903 or you may contact me by phone at (401) 528-1854 or by fax at (401) 528-1860.

Sincerely yours,

Advisor
Badge# XX-XXXXX

Enclosure

Form 669-B	Department of the Treasury – Internal Revenue Service
(Rev. September 2008)	**Certificate of Discharge of Property From Federal Tax Lien**
	(Section 6325(b)(2)(A) of the Internal Revenue Code)

Owner Michael of ____ Main Street Town, State Zip is indebted to the United States for unpaid internal revenue tax as evidenced by:

Notice of Federal Tax Lien Serial Number (a)	Recording Information (b)	Date Recorded (c)	Taxpayer Identification Number (d)	Amount Shown on Lien (e)
xxxxxxxx	Book: xxx Page: 141	02/16/2019	XXX-XX-XXXX	$71,928.62
xxxxxxxx	Book: xxx Page: 297	05/14/2019	XXX-XX-XXXX	$86,143.81
xxxxxxxx	Book: xxxx Page: 490	01/09/2020	XXX-XX-XXXX	$159,248.57

A lien attaching to all the property of the taxpayer was filed to secure the amount owed. The notice of lien was filed with the Farmington Town Clerk, Hartford County, State of Connecticut, in accordance with the applicable provisions of law.

The lien listed above is attached to certain property described as:

Ford F150, Vin 1x1x1x1x1x1xx1, Miscellaneous hand tools

The Internal Revenue Service acknowledges receipt of $7,200.00, the Internal Revenue Service discharges the above described property from the lien. However, the lien remains in effect for all other property, or rights to property, to which the lien is attached.

Signature	Title	

(Note: Certificate of officer authorized by law to take acknowledgements is not essential to the validity of Discharge of Federal Tax Lien. Rev. Rul. 71-466, 1971-2, C.B. 409.)

Catalog No. 16752N

Form 669-B (Rev. 9-2008)

Case Study 4

Michael comes to see us just like in Case Study #3. In this case, however, he tells us that the company is a good company. He has let half his employees go and the company now is on the upswing. He would like to work out a payment arrangement with the IRS. Again, he is the only signature on the company bank account and was the sole owner and manager, so he has no defense to not paying the payroll taxes, other than he was too busy and struggling with too little cash flow to manage his finances properly. The Revenue Officer he met with insists she needs to see the company either pay the liability or shut down. He hands us the Letter 1153 and Form 2751 she dropped off at his office that morning. She also included Final Notices of Intent to Levy for all four quarters at issue.

We would start the process by being retained and obtaining Power of Attorney for both the Company and for Michael himself. Once retained and we had Power of Attorney we would contact the Revenue Officer and discuss a game plan. We also file Form 12153 Request for Collection Due Process on the final notices to protect the taxpayer's appeal rights.

The revenue officer requests both Form 433-B for the company and Form 433-A for Michael. She also wants proof of current federal tax deposits faxed to her and a copy of the last filed Form 941, as it has not yet been processed and she needs to confirm Michael is in current tax compliance. It is critical Michael maintain current tax compliance while the revenue officer is working the case (and thereafter), as he must prove to her that the business is in fact viable. We advise Michael if he does not maintain current tax compliance, the IRS could file an injunction against the business for failure to make payroll deposits, essentially forcing him out of business.

We work with Michael to prepare a Form 433-B for the business as well as a Form 433-A for him personally. We discuss ways Michael may be able to free up funds to pay down the IRS debt, and Michael determines he is able to cut advertising expenses and in June, when his lease is up, he can move to a new space with much lower rent.

We present the Form 433-A and Form 433-B to the IRS, as well as proof of the new lease to show the IRS he is working with them to trim expenses and succeed in saving his business. The Form 433-A indicates he has $30,000 in a personal investment account for which he plans to cash out to make a self-directed payment towards the trust fund liability. The Form 433-A shows he has no excess funds available after taking his salary and paying his IRS allowable expenses. The Form 433-B shows that after paying Michael's salary and all necessary business expenses (including the reduced rent and current tax deposits), the business can pay $1500/month towards its payroll liability. We also send her the signed Forms 2751s, as Michael is responsible for the unpaid taxes and eagerly wants to get into a resolution and the IRS out of his life.

The revenue officer responds that she is pleased with the progress in the case, indicates she will continue to monitor payroll deposits for the rest of the quarter and then contact us to set up the installment agreement. We file a Form 12256 withdrawing the request for a collection due process hearing, as we have reached a satisfactory result with the revenue officer.

As examples, we have included here the following:

1. The retainer agreement
2. The Power of Attorney
3. The Form 433-A and Form 433-B
4. The letter designating payment of the trust funds

March 14, 2020

Owner Michael
Street
City, State, Zip

    Re: **Client Retention Agreement**

Dear Mr. Michael:

We are pleased you have requested that Green & Sklarz LLC ("G&S" or "Firm") provide you with representation as set forth below. We would appreciate receiving written acknowledgement of this agreement for our files. The Bar recommends that there be a written fee agreement between attorneys and their clients. Additionally, we feel that it is in the best interest of our clients that they be fully informed of our billing practices. The purpose of this letter, therefore, is to set forth the scope of our engagement as legal counsel to you, to set forth the financial arrangements regarding our engagement and to verify our agreement of the foregoing:

1.   **Scope of Engagement**

Subject to the terms and conditions herein, including without limitation advance payment of the retainer and a signed copy of this agreement G&S will perform those legal services which you requested and, more specifically, to represent you and your company, Michael's Company, before the Internal Revenue Service in regards to the payroll tax issue with your company (the "Engagement").

2.   **Fee for Representation**

Our billing practice is to charge for our services based on the hourly rate of the attorney involved. We bill in increments of no less than 1/10 of one hour. Please note, we bill for all services our office provides, including but not limited to: correspondence, telephone calls, document preparation, legal research, electronic legal research, inter-office conference, depositions, trials, meetings, etc. We use the amount of time devoted to a matter by a particular attorney at that attorney's hourly rate. These hourly rates are based upon experience, expertise and standing. In addition, we try to use associate, paralegal, legal assistant and/or secretarial support on projects whenever possible. All hourly rates are reviewed from time to time and may be adjusted and/or increased without notice. It is likely that all of these hourly rates will be increased annually usually commencing at the beginning of each calendar year and you hereby consent to such increase. My hourly rate is $475/hour. Our firm's rates for staff range from $75 - $275/hour, and for partners from $350 - $550/hour.

The detail and the monthly statement will inform you not only of the fees and disbursements incurred but also of the nature and progress of the work performed. These statements are due and payable upon receipt, but in any event, no later than thirty days thereafter. We reserve the right to charge interest at an appropriate rate (currently 1% per month) calculated monthly starting forty-five days after issuance of the statement and continuing until fully paid. You will be sent monthly billing statements as to work performed. We generally bill clients on either the 1st or 15th of the month. If you have a preference as to when you receive a bill, please let me know.

We do our best to see that our clients are satisfied not only with our services but also with the reasonableness of the fees and disbursements charged for these services. Therefore, if you have any questions about or objection to a statement or the basis for our fees to you, you should raise it promptly and not more than thirty (30) days after you receive a bill for discussion. If you object only to a portion of the statement, we ask you pay the remainder, which will not constitute a waiver of your objections.

3. **Disbursements**

The performance of legal services involves costs and expenses, some of which must be paid to third parties. These expenses include, but are not limited to, filing fees, court reporters, deposition fees, travel costs, copying costs, telecopier costs, messenger services, long distance telephone charges, computerized research expenses and expenses of experts whom we deem appropriate to assist in our representation of you. We do not charge for internal copying costs, but if a production job is large and must be sent out we will charge you the actual expense. We expect that you will either pay directly or reimburse us for such costs. If such costs may be calculated beforehand and appear to be substantial, we may ask you to advance us those sums before we expend them or to reimburse the vendor directly.

4. **Retainer**

We will require an initial retainer of $5,000.00 prior to commencement of work on Your behalf, the amount to be determined at that time depending upon the scope of the work you require. Should the Engagement require work beyond the anticipated scope, we may require an additional retainer be paid. If the retainer is exhausted and you receive a bill, please pay the amount due. At the conclusion of the Firm's representation of You, any remaining positive retainer balance will be returned to You. You also agree that the retainer payment may be deposited in the Firm's general operating account and comingled with other funds.

Please note, we have tried to keep the retainer amount as low as possible, however, given the nature and complexity of the Engagement, it is possible that the retainer amount may be exceeded.

5. **Withdrawal from Representation**

The attorney client relationship is one of mutual trust and confidence. If you, for whatever reason, wish us to cease representing you, you may request that we do so. If we feel we no longer wish to represent you, we will request that the court (if an appearance has been filed) to permit us to terminate our representation of you. We will only do so in the following circumstances: (a) a lack of cooperation by you in promptly submitting necessary requested information; (b) your knowingly providing us, your adversaries or the court with false information; (c) your disregard of advice about matters of critical importance to your case; (d) your failure to promptly pay legal fees; or (e) for any other reason provided advance notice is provided.

Upon such termination, however, you would remain liable for any unpaid fees and costs. We also shall be authorized to reveal this agreement and any other necessary documents to any court or agency if the same should prove necessary to effect withdrawal or collection of our fees.

It is the policy of this firm to make every effort to have our clients feel that they are treated on a fair basis. We welcome an honest discussion of our fees and our services and encourage our clients to inquire about any matter relating to our fee arrangement or monthly statements that are in anyway unclear or appear unsatisfactory. If you have any questions, please do not hesitate to call us.

6. **Future Services**

This agreement will also apply to services rendered for such future matters that we agree will be handled by the Firm. If, however, such services, are substantially different from those to which this agreement applies (for instance, an appearance on your behalf in court), either party may request that a new agreement be executed, or that this agreement be reacknowledged.

If this letter correctly sets forth your understanding of the scope of the services to be rendered to the company by the Firm, and if the terms of the engagement are satisfactory, please execute the enclosed copy of this letter and return it us. If the scope of the services described is incorrect or if the terms of the engagement set forth in this letter are not satisfactory to you, please let us know in writing so that we can discuss either aspect.

By executing this agreement, you acknowledge that there is uncertainty concerning the outcome of this matter and that the Firm and the undersigned attorneys have made no guarantees as to the disposition of any phase of this matter. All representations and expression relative to the outcome of this matter, are only expressions of the said attorney's opinions and do not constitute guarantees. We look forward to continuing to work with you and thank you once again for the opportunity to serve.

Very truly yours,

Eric L. Green

READ, AGREED AND CONSENTED TO:

_____   _____
Owner Michael   Date

_____   _____
Michael, Individually   Date

Form 2848
(Rev. February 2020)
Department of the Treasury
Internal Revenue Service

Power of Attorney and Declaration of Representative

▶ Go to www.irs.gov/Form2848 for instructions and the latest information.

OMB No. 1545-0150

For IRS Use Only
Received by:
Name _____
Telephone _____
Function _____
Date   /   /

Part I Power of Attorney

Caution: A separate Form 2848 must be completed for each taxpayer. Form 2848 will not be honored for any purpose other than representation before the IRS.

1 Taxpayer information. Taxpayer must sign and date this form on page 2, line 7.

Owner Michael
Street Address, City, State, Zip

Taxpayer identification number(s)
XXX-XX-XXXXX

Daytime telephone number
(203) 111-XXXX

Plan number (if applicable)

hereby appoints the following representative(s) as attorney(s)-in-fact:

2 Representative(s) must sign and date this form on page 2, Part II.

Name and address
Representative
Reps Address

CAF No. XXXX-XXXXXR
PTIN P00000000
Telephone No. (203) XXX-XXXX
Fax No. (203) XXX-XXXX

Check if to be sent copies of notices and communications ☐   Check if new: Address ☐   Telephone No. ☐   Fax No. ☐

Name and address

CAF No. _____
PTIN _____
Telephone No. _____
Fax No. _____

Check if to be sent copies of notices and communications ☐   Check if new: Address ☐   Telephone No. ☐   Fax No. ☐

Name and address

CAF No. _____
PTIN _____
Telephone No. _____
Fax No. _____

(**Note:** IRS sends notices and communications to only two representatives.) Check if new: Address ☐   Telephone No. ☐   Fax No. ☐

Name and address

CAF No. _____
PTIN _____
Telephone No. _____
Fax No. _____

(**Note:** IRS sends notices and communications to only two representatives.) Check if new: Address ☐   Telephone No. ☐   Fax No. ☐

to represent the taxpayer before the Internal Revenue Service and perform the following acts:

3 Acts authorized (you are required to complete this line 3). With the exception of the acts described in line 5b, I authorize my representative(s) to receive and inspect my confidential tax information and to perform acts that I can perform with respect to the tax matters described below. For example, my representative(s) shall have the authority to sign any agreements, consents, or similar documents (see instructions for line 5a for authorizing a representative to sign a return).

Description of Matter (Income, Employment, Payroll, Excise, Estate, Gift, Whistleblower, Practitioner Discipline, PLR, FOIA, Civil Penalty, Sec. 4980H Shared Responsibility Payment, etc.) (see instructions)	Tax Form Number (1040, 941, 720, etc.) (if applicable)	Year(s) or Period(s) (if applicable) (see instructions)
Income Tax	1040	12/31/2000 - 12/31/2021
Civil Penalties	IRC 6672	3/31/2000 - 12/31/2021

4 Specific use not recorded on Centralized Authorization File (CAF). If the power of attorney is for a specific use not recorded on CAF, check this box. See *Line 4. Specific Use Not Recorded on CAF* in the instructions . . . . ▶ ☐

5a Additional acts authorized. In addition to the acts listed on line 3 above, I authorize my representative(s) to perform the following acts (see instructions for line 5a for more information): ☑ Access my IRS records via an Intermediate Service Provider;
☐ Authorize disclosure to third parties;   ☑ Substitute or add representative(s);   ☐ Sign a return; _____

☐ Other acts authorized: _____

For Privacy Act and Paperwork Reduction Act Notice, see the instructions.   Cat. No. 11980J   Form **2848** (Rev. 2-2020)

Form 2848 (Rev. 2-2020) Page **2**

b **Specific acts not authorized.** My representative(s) is (are) not authorized to endorse or otherwise negotiate any check (including directing or accepting payment by any means, electronic or otherwise, into an account owned or controlled by the representative(s) or any firm or other entity with whom the representative(s) is (are) associated) issued by the government in respect of a federal tax liability.
List any other specific deletions to the acts otherwise authorized in this power of attorney (see instructions for line 5b): _____

6 **Retention/revocation of prior power(s) of attorney.** The filing of this power of attorney automatically revokes all earlier power(s) of attorney on file with the Internal Revenue Service for the same matters and years or periods covered by this document. If you **do not** want to revoke a prior power of attorney, check here . . . . ▶ ☐
YOU MUST ATTACH A COPY OF ANY POWER OF ATTORNEY YOU WANT TO REMAIN IN EFFECT.

7 **Signature of taxpayer.** If a tax matter concerns a year in which a joint return was filed, each spouse must file a separate power of attorney even if they are appointing the same representative(s). If signed by a corporate officer, partner, guardian, tax matters partner, partnership representative (or designated individual, if applicable), executor, receiver, administrator, or trustee on behalf of the taxpayer, I certify that I have the legal authority to execute this form on behalf of the taxpayer.
▶ **IF NOT COMPLETED, SIGNED, AND DATED, THE IRS WILL RETURN THIS POWER OF ATTORNEY TO THE TAXPAYER.**

Signature	Date	Title (if applicable)

Taxpayer's Name

Print name	Print name of taxpayer from line 1 if other than individual

Part II — Declaration of Representative

Under penalties of perjury, by my signature below I declare that:
- I am not currently suspended or disbarred from practice, or ineligible for practice, before the Internal Revenue Service;
- I am subject to regulations contained in Circular 230 (31 CFR, Subtitle A, Part 10), as amended, governing practice before the Internal Revenue Service;
- I am authorized to represent the taxpayer identified in Part I for the matter(s) specified there; and
- I am one of the following:

a Attorney—a member in good standing of the bar of the highest court of the jurisdiction shown below.
b Certified Public Accountant—a holder of an active license to practice as a certified public accountant in the jurisdiction shown below.
c Enrolled Agent—enrolled as an agent by the IRS per the requirements of Circular 230.
d Officer—a bona fide officer of the taxpayer organization.
e Full-Time Employee—a full-time employee of the taxpayer.
f Family Member—a member of the taxpayer's immediate family (spouse, parent, child, grandparent, grandchild, step-parent, step-child, brother, or sister).
g Enrolled Actuary—enrolled as an actuary by the Joint Board for the Enrollment of Actuaries under 29 U.S.C. 1242 (the authority to practice before the IRS is limited by section 10.3(d) of Circular 230).
h Unenrolled Return Preparer—Authority to practice before the IRS is limited. An unenrolled return preparer may represent, provided the preparer (1) prepared and signed the return or claim for refund (or prepared if there is no signature space on the form); (2) was eligible to sign the return or claim for refund; (3) has a valid PTIN; and (4) possesses the required Annual Filing Season Program Record of Completion(s). **See Special Rules and Requirements for Unenrolled Return Preparers** *in the instructions for additional information.*
k Qualifying Student—receives permission to represent taxpayers before the IRS by virtue of his/her status as a law, business, or accounting student working in an LITC or STCP. See instructions for Part II for additional information and requirements.
r Enrolled Retirement Plan Agent—enrolled as a retirement plan agent under the requirements of Circular 230 (the authority to practice before the Internal Revenue Service is limited by section 10.3(e)).

▶ **IF THIS DECLARATION OF REPRESENTATIVE IS NOT COMPLETED, SIGNED, AND DATED, THE IRS WILL RETURN THE POWER OF ATTORNEY. REPRESENTATIVES MUST SIGN IN THE ORDER LISTED IN PART I, LINE 2.**

Note: For designations d–f, enter your title, position, or relationship to the taxpayer in the "Licensing jurisdiction" column.

Designation— Insert above letter **(a–r)**.	Licensing jurisdiction (State) or other licensing authority (if applicable)	Bar, license, certification, registration, or enrollment number (if applicable)	Signature	Date

Form **2848** (Rev. 2-2020)

Form 2848
(Rev. February 2020)
Department of the Treasury
Internal Revenue Service

Power of Attorney and Declaration of Representative

▶ Go to *www.irs.gov/Form2848* for instructions and the latest information.

OMB No. 1545-0150

For IRS Use Only
Received by:
Name _____
Telephone _____
Function _____
Date / /

Part I Power of Attorney

Caution: A separate Form 2848 must be completed for each taxpayer. Form 2848 will not be honored for any purpose other than representation before the IRS.

1 Taxpayer information. Taxpayer must sign and date this form on page 2, line 7.

Owner Michael's Company
Street Address, City, State, Zip

Taxpayer identification number(s)
XX-XXXXXXX

Daytime telephone number
(203) 111-XXXX

Plan number (if applicable)

hereby appoints the following representative(s) as attorney(s)-in-fact:

2 Representative(s) must sign and date this form on page 2, Part II.

Name and address
Representative
Reps Address

CAF No. XXXX-XXXXXR
PTIN P00000000
Telephone No. (203) XXX-XXXX
Fax No. (203) XXX-XXXX

Check if to be sent copies of notices and communications ☐   Check if new: Address ☐   Telephone No. ☐   Fax No. ☐

Name and address

CAF No. _____
PTIN _____
Telephone No. _____
Fax No. _____

Check if to be sent copies of notices and communications ☐   Check if new: Address ☐   Telephone No. ☐   Fax No. ☐

Name and address

CAF No. _____
PTIN _____
Telephone No. _____
Fax No. _____

(**Note:** IRS sends notices and communications to only two representatives.)   Check if new: Address ☐   Telephone No. ☐   Fax No. ☐

Name and address

CAF No. _____
PTIN _____
Telephone No. _____
Fax No. _____

(**Note:** IRS sends notices and communications to only two representatives.)   Check if new: Address ☐   Telephone No. ☐   Fax No. ☐

to represent the taxpayer before the Internal Revenue Service and perform the following acts:

3 Acts authorized (you are required to complete this line 3). With the exception of the acts described in line 5b, I authorize my representative(s) to receive and inspect my confidential tax information and to perform acts that I can perform with respect to the tax matters described below. For example, my representative(s) shall have the authority to sign any agreements, consents, or similar documents (see instructions for line 5a for authorizing a representative to sign a return).

Description of Matter (Income, Employment, Payroll, Excise, Estate, Gift, Whistleblower, Practitioner Discipline, PLR, FOIA, Civil Penalty, Sec. 4980H Shared Responsibility Payment, etc.) (see instructions)	Tax Form Number (1040, 941, 720, etc.) (if applicable)	Year(s) or Period(s) (if applicable) (see instructions)
Income Tax	1040	12/31/2000 - 12/31/2021
Employment Tax	941	3/31/2000 - 12/31/2021
Employment Tax	940	12/31/2000 - 12/31/2021

4 Specific use not recorded on Centralized Authorization File (CAF). If the power of attorney is for a specific use not recorded on CAF, check this box. See *Line 4. Specific Use Not Recorded on CAF* in the instructions . . . . ▶ ☐

5a Additional acts authorized. In addition to the acts listed on line 3 above, I authorize my representative(s) to perform the following acts (see instructions for line 5a for more information): ☑ Access my IRS records via an Intermediate Service Provider;
☐ Authorize disclosure to third parties;   ☑ Substitute or add representative(s);   ☐ Sign a return; _____

☐ Other acts authorized: _____

For Privacy Act and Paperwork Reduction Act Notice, see the instructions.   Cat. No. 11980J   Form **2848** (Rev. 2-2020)

Form 2848 (Rev. 2-2020) Page **2**

b **Specific acts not authorized.** My representative(s) is (are) not authorized to endorse or otherwise negotiate any check (including directing or accepting payment by any means, electronic or otherwise, into an account owned or controlled by the representative(s) or any firm or other entity with whom the representative(s) is (are) associated) issued by the government in respect of a federal tax liability.
List any other specific deletions to the acts otherwise authorized in this power of attorney (see instructions for line 5b): _____

6 **Retention/revocation of prior power(s) of attorney.** The filing of this power of attorney automatically revokes all earlier power(s) of attorney on file with the Internal Revenue Service for the same matters and years or periods covered by this document. If you **do not** want to revoke a prior power of attorney, check here . . . . ▶ ☐
YOU MUST ATTACH A COPY OF ANY POWER OF ATTORNEY YOU WANT TO REMAIN IN EFFECT.

7 **Signature of taxpayer.** If a tax matter concerns a year in which a joint return was filed, each spouse must file a separate power of attorney even if they are appointing the same representative(s). If signed by a corporate officer, partner, guardian, tax matters partner, partnership representative (or designated individual, if applicable), executor, receiver, administrator, or trustee on behalf of the taxpayer, I certify that I have the legal authority to execute this form on behalf of the taxpayer.
▶ **IF NOT COMPLETED, SIGNED, AND DATED, THE IRS WILL RETURN THIS POWER OF ATTORNEY TO THE TAXPAYER.**

Owner

_____ _____ _____
Signature   Date   Title (if applicable)
Taxpayer's Name

_____   _____
Print name   Print name of taxpayer from line 1 if other than individual

Part II — Declaration of Representative

Under penalties of perjury, by my signature below I declare that:
- I am not currently suspended or disbarred from practice, or ineligible for practice, before the Internal Revenue Service;
- I am subject to regulations contained in Circular 230 (31 CFR, Subtitle A, Part 10), as amended, governing practice before the Internal Revenue Service;
- I am authorized to represent the taxpayer identified in Part I for the matter(s) specified there; and
- I am one of the following:

  a Attorney—a member in good standing of the bar of the highest court of the jurisdiction shown below.
  b Certified Public Accountant—a holder of an active license to practice as a certified public accountant in the jurisdiction shown below.
  c Enrolled Agent—enrolled as an agent by the IRS per the requirements of Circular 230.
  d Officer—a bona fide officer of the taxpayer organization.
  e Full-Time Employee—a full-time employee of the taxpayer.
  f Family Member—a member of the taxpayer's immediate family (spouse, parent, child, grandparent, grandchild, step-parent, step-child, brother, or sister).
  g Enrolled Actuary—enrolled as an actuary by the Joint Board for the Enrollment of Actuaries under 29 U.S.C. 1242 (the authority to practice before the IRS is limited by section 10.3(d) of Circular 230).
  h Unenrolled Return Preparer—Authority to practice before the IRS is limited. An unenrolled return preparer may represent, provided the preparer (1) prepared and signed the return or claim for refund (or prepared if there is no signature space on the form); (2) was eligible to sign the return or claim for refund; (3) has a valid PTIN; and (4) possesses the required Annual Filing Season Program Record of Completion(s). **See Special Rules and Requirements for Unenrolled Return Preparers** *in the instructions for additional information.*
  k Qualifying Student—receives permission to represent taxpayers before the IRS by virtue of his/her status as a law, business, or accounting student working in an LITC or STCP. See instructions for Part II for additional information and requirements.
  r Enrolled Retirement Plan Agent—enrolled as a retirement plan agent under the requirements of Circular 230 (the authority to practice before the Internal Revenue Service is limited by section 10.3(e)).

▶ **IF THIS DECLARATION OF REPRESENTATIVE IS NOT COMPLETED, SIGNED, AND DATED, THE IRS WILL RETURN THE POWER OF ATTORNEY. REPRESENTATIVES MUST SIGN IN THE ORDER LISTED IN PART I, LINE 2.**

Note: For designations d–f, enter your title, position, or relationship to the taxpayer in the "Licensing jurisdiction" column.

Designation— Insert above letter **(a–r)**.	Licensing jurisdiction (State) or other licensing authority (if applicable)	Bar, license, certification, registration, or enrollment number (if applicable)	Signature	Date

Form **2848** (Rev. 2-2020)

January 3, 2020

VIA FEDERAL EXPRESS
Department of Treasury
Internal Revenue Service
Attn: REVENUE OFFICER NAME
Street Address
City, State Zip

Re: **Owner Michael, SSN: xxx-xx-xxxx**
Directed Payment of Trust Fund Portion of Employment Taxes
Employer: Owner Michael's Company, Inc., EIN XX-XXXXXXX

Dear REVENUE OFFICER NAME:

This office represents TAXPAYERS NAME and COMPANY NAME, Inc. Enclosed please find a check in the amount of $30,000 (check # XXXX) payable to the U.S. Treasury. Pursuant to Rev. Proc. 2002-26, 2002-15 IRB 746, 2002-1 CB 746 and IRM 5.1.2.3 and 26 C.F.R. 301.7701-2(c)(2)(iv), this payment constitutes a voluntary payment and should be applied to reduce any trust fund recovery penalty and/or trust fund portions of employment taxes for which Owner Michael is personally liable.

If for any reason the Internal Revenue Service intends and/or expects to apply the enclosed payment *not* in accordance with this letter of direction, the U.S. Treasury is *not* authorized to deposit the enclosed check and it should be returned to me.

Please call me should you have any questions.

Very truly yours,

Eric L. Green

Form 433-A
(February 2019)
Department of the Treasury
Internal Revenue Service

Collection Information Statement for Wage Earners and Self-Employed Individuals

Wage Earners Complete Sections 1, 2, 3, 4, and 5 including the signature line on page 4. *Answer all questions or write N/A if the question is not applicable.*

Self-Employed Individuals Complete Sections 1, 3, 4, 5, 6 and 7 and the signature line on page 4. *Answer all questions or write N/A if the question is not applicable.*

For Additional Information, refer to Publication 1854, "How To Prepare a Collection Information Statement."

Include attachments if additional space is needed to respond completely to any question.

Name on Internal Revenue Service (IRS) Account	SSN or ITIN on IRS Account	Employer Identification Number EIN
Michael Smith	XXX-XX-XXXZ	XX-XXXXXXX

Section 1: Personal Information

1a Full Name of Taxpayer and Spouse *(if applicable)*
Michael Smith

1b Address *(Street, City, State, ZIP code) (County of Residence)*
ABC Street, City, Zip
New Haven County

1c Home Phone (203) xxx-xxxx
1d Cell Phone ( )
1e Business Phone ( )
1f Business Cell Phone ( )

2a Marital Status: ☐ Married ☑ Unmarried *(Single, Divorced, Widowed)*
2b Name, Age, and Relationship of dependent(s)
NA

	SSN or ITIN	Date of Birth *(mmddyyyy)*	Driver's License Number and State
3a Taxpayer	XXX-XX-XXXX	01011980	
3b Spouse			

Section 2: Employment Information for Wage Earners

If you or your spouse have self-employment income instead of, or in addition to wage income, complete Business Information in Sections 6 and 7.

Taxpayer	Spouse
4a Taxpayer's Employer Name Michael Company - See 433B	**5a** Spouse's Employer Name
4b Address *(Street, City, State, and ZIP code)*	**5b** Address *(Street, City, State, and ZIP code)*
4c Work Telephone Number ( ) / **4d** Does employer allow contact at work ☐ Yes ☐ No	**5c** Work Telephone Number ( ) / **5d** Does employer allow contact at work ☐ Yes ☐ No
4e How long with this employer (years) (months) / **4f** Occupation	**5e** How long with this employer (years) (months) / **5f** Occupation
4g Number of withholding allowances claimed on Form W-4 / **4h** Pay Period: ☐ Weekly ☐ Bi-weekly ☐ Monthly ☐ Other	**5g** Number of withholding allowances claimed on Form W-4 / **5h** Pay Period: ☐ Weekly ☐ Bi-weekly ☐ Monthly ☐ Other

Section 3: Other Financial Information *(Attach copies of applicable documentation)*

6 Are you a party to a lawsuit *(If yes, answer the following)* ☐ Yes ☑ No

☐ Plaintiff ☐ Defendant | Location of Filing | Represented by | Docket/Case No.

Amount of Suit $ | Possible Completion Date *(mmddyyyy)* | Subject of Suit

7 Have you ever filed bankruptcy *(If yes, answer the following)* ☐ Yes ☑ No

Date Filed *(mmddyyyy)* | Date Dismissed *(mmddyyyy)* | Date Discharged *(mmddyyyy)* | Petition No. | Location Filed

8 In the past 10 years, have you lived outside of the U.S for 6 months or longer *(If yes, answer the following)* ☐ Yes ☑ No

Dates lived abroad: from *(mmddyyyy)* | To *(mmddyyyy)*

9a Are you the beneficiary of a trust, estate, or life insurance policy *(If yes, answer the following)* ☐ Yes ☑ No

Place where recorded: | EIN:

Name of the trust, estate, or policy | Anticipated amount to be received $ | When will the amount be received

9b Are you a trustee, fiduciary, or contributor of a trust ☐ Yes ☑ No

Name of the trust: | EIN:

10 Do you have a safe deposit box (business or personal) *(If yes, answer the following)* ☐ Yes ☑ No

Location *(Name, address and box number(s))* | Contents | Value $

11 In the past 10 years, have you transferred any assets for less than their full value *(If yes, answer the following)* ☐ Yes ☑ No

List Asset(s) | Value at Time of Transfer $ | Date Transferred *(mmddyyyy)* | To Whom or Where was it Transferred

Form 433-A (Rev. 2-2019) Page 2

Section 4: Personal Asset Information for all Individuals (Foreign and Domestic)

12 CASH ON HAND Include cash that is not in a bank   **Total Cash on Hand** $ 50

PERSONAL BANK ACCOUNTS Include all checking, online and mobile (e.g., PayPal) accounts, money market accounts, savings accounts, and stored value cards (e.g., payroll cards, government benefit cards, etc.).

Type of Account	Full Name & Address (Street, City, State, ZIP code) of Bank, Savings & Loan, Credit Union, or Financial Institution	Account Number	Account Balance As of 03012020 mmddyyyy
13a Checking	ABC Bank, Street, Address	999999	$ 1,000
13b Money Market Acct	XYZ Bank	88888	$ 30,000
13c Total Cash (Add lines 13a, 13b, and amounts from any attachments)			$ 31,000

INVESTMENTS Include stocks, bonds, mutual funds, stock options, certificates of deposit, and retirement assets such as IRAs, Keogh, 401(k) plans and commodities (e.g., gold, silver, copper, etc.). Include all corporations, partnerships, limited liability companies, or other business entities in which you are an officer, director, owner, member, or otherwise have a financial interest. Include attachment(s) if additional space is needed to respond.

Type of Investment or Financial Interest	Full Name & Address (Street, City, State, ZIP code) of Company	Current Value	Loan Balance (if applicable) As of _____ mmddyyyy	Equity Value minus Loan
14a	Phone	$	$	$
14b	Phone	$	$	$

VIRTUAL CURRENCY (CRYPTOCURRENCY) List all virtual currency you own or in which you have a financial interest. (e.g., Bitcoin, Ethereum, Litecoin, Ripple, etc.) If applicable, attach a statement with each virtual currency's public key.

Type of Virtual Currency	Name of Virtual Currency Wallet, Exchange or Digital Currency Exchange (DCE)	Email Address Used to Set-up With the Virtual Currency Exchange or DCE	Location(s) of Virtual Currency (Mobile Wallet, Online, and/or External Hardware storage)	Virtual Currency Amount and Value in US dollars as of today (e.g., 10 Bitcoins $64,600.00 USD)
14c				$
14d				$
14e Total Equity (Add lines 14a through 14d and amounts from any attachments)				$

AVAILABLE CREDIT Include all lines of credit and bank issued credit cards.

Full Name & Address (Street, City, State, ZIP code) of Credit Institution	Credit Limit	Amount Owed As of _____ mmddyyyy	Available Credit As of _____ mmddyyyy
15a NA Acct. No	$	$	$
15b Acct. No	$	$	$
15c Total Available Credit (Add lines 15a, 15b and amounts from any attachments)			$

16a LIFE INSURANCE Do you own or have any interest in any life insurance policies with cash value (Term Life insurance does not have a cash value)
☐ Yes ☑ No   If yes, complete blocks 16b through 16f for each policy.

16b	Name and Address of Insurance Company(ies):				
16c	Policy Number(s)				
16d	Owner of Policy				
16e	Current Cash Value	$	$	$	
16f	Outstanding Loan Balance	$	$	$	
16g	Total Available Cash (Subtract amounts on line 16f from line 16e and include amounts from any attachments)				$

Catalog Number 20312N   www.irs.gov   Form **433-A** (Rev. 2-2019)

Form 433-A (Rev. 2-2019) Page **3**

REAL PROPERTY Include all real property owned or being purchased

		Purchase Date (mmddyyyy)	Current Fair Market Value (FMV)	Current Loan Balance	Amount of Monthly Payment	Date of Final Payment (mmddyyyy)	**Equity** FMV Minus Loan
17a	Property Description **NA**		$	$	$		$
	Location (Street, City, State, ZIP code) and County			Lender/Contract Holder Name, Address (Street, City, State, ZIP code), and Phone			
				Phone			
17b	Property Description		$	$	$		$
	Location (Street, City, State, ZIP code) and County			Lender/Contract Holder Name, Address (Street, City, State, ZIP code), and Phone			
				Phone			
17c	**Total Equity** (Add lines 17a, 17b and amounts from any attachments)						$

PERSONAL VEHICLES LEASED AND PURCHASED Include boats, RVs, motorcycles, all-terrain and off-road vehicles, trailers, etc.

Description (Year, Mileage, Make/Model, Tag Number, Vehicle Identification Number)		Purchase/ Lease Date (mmddyyyy)	Current Fair Market Value (FMV)	Current Loan Balance	Amount of Monthly Payment	Date of Final Payment (mmddyyyy)	**Equity** FMV Minus Loan
18a Year 2015	Make/Model **Honda Civic**	01012019	$ 10,000	$ 9,500	$ 500	08012022	$ 500
Mileage 60,000	License/Tag Number **XB87B**	Lender/Lessor Name, Address (Street, City, State, ZIP code), and Phone **ABC Bank**					
Vehicle Identification Number BBBBBBBBBB11111111					Phone		
18b Year	Make/Model		$	$	$		$
Mileage	License/Tag Number	Lender/Lessor Name, Address (Street, City, State, ZIP code), and Phone					
Vehicle Identification Number					Phone		
18c **Total Equity** (Add lines 18a, 18b and amounts from any attachments)							$ 500

PERSONAL ASSETS Include all furniture, personal effects, artwork, jewelry, collections (coins, guns, etc.), antiques or other assets. Include intangible assets such as licenses, domain names, patents, copyrights, mining claims, etc.

		Purchase/ Lease Date (mmddyyyy)	Current Fair Market Value (FMV)	Current Loan Balance	Amount of Monthly Payment	Date of Final Payment (mmddyyyy)	**Equity** FMV Minus Loan
19a	Property Description **Misc. Personal Effects**	Various	$ 2,500	$ NA	$ NA		$ 2,500
	Location (Street, City, State, ZIP code) and County			Lender/Lessor Name, Address (Street, City, State, ZIP code), and Phone			
				Phone			
19b	Property Description		$	$	$		$
	Location (Street, City, State, ZIP code) and County			Lender/Lessor Name, Address (Street, City, State, ZIP code), and Phone			
				Phone			
19c	**Total Equity** (Add lines 19a, 19b and amounts from any attachments)						$ 2,500

Form 433-A (Rev. 2-2019) Page 4

If you are self-employed, sections 6 and 7 must be completed before continuing.

Section 5: Monthly Income and Expenses

Monthly Income/Expense Statement *(For additional information, refer to Publication 1854.)*

Total Income			Total Living Expenses			IRS USE ONLY
	Source	Gross Monthly		Expense Items [6]	Actual Monthly	Allowable Expenses
20	Wages (Taxpayer) [1]	$	35 Food, Clothing and Misc. [7]		$ 715	
21	Wages (Spouse) [1]	$	36 Housing and Utilities [8]		$ 1,959	
22	Interest - Dividends	$	37 Vehicle Ownership Costs [9]		$ 500	
23	Net Business Income [2]	$	38 Vehicle Operating Costs [10]		$ 242	
24	Net Rental Income [3]	$	39 Public Transportation [11]		$	
25	Distributions (K-1, IRA, etc.) [4]	$ 10,000	40 Health Insurance		$ 2,000	
26	Pension (Taxpayer)	$	41 Out of Pocket Health Care Costs [12]		$ 56	
27	Pension (Spouse)	$	42 Court Ordered Payments		$ 1,200	
28	Social Security (Taxpayer)	$	43 Child/Dependent Care		$	
29	Social Security (Spouse)	$	44 Life Insurance		$ 400	
30	Child Support	$	45 Current year taxes (Income/FICA) [13]		$ 3,000	
31	Alimony	$	46 Secured Debts (Attach list)		$	
	Other Income (Specify below) [5]		47 Delinquent State or Local Taxes		$	
32		$	48 Other Expenses (Attach list)		$	
33		$	49 Total Living Expenses (add lines 35-48)		$ 10,072	
34	Total Income (add lines 20-33)	$ 10,000	50 Net difference (Line 34 minus 49)		$ 0	

1. **Wages, salaries, pensions, and social security**: Enter gross monthly wages and/or salaries. Do not deduct tax withholding or allotments taken out of pay, such as insurance payments, credit union deductions, car payments, etc. To calculate the gross monthly wages and/or salaries:

    If paid weekly - multiply weekly gross wages by 4.3. Example: $425.89 x 4.3 = $1,831.33

    If paid biweekly (every 2 weeks) - multiply biweekly gross wages by 2.17. Example: $972.45 x 2.17 = $2,110.22

    If paid semimonthly (twice each month) - multiply semimonthly gross wages by 2. Example: $856.23 x 2 = $1,712.46

2. **Net Income from Business**: Enter monthly net business income. This is the amount earned after ordinary and necessary monthly business expenses are paid. **This figure is the amount from page 6, line 89.** If the net business income is a loss, enter "0". Do not enter a negative number. If this amount is more or less than previous years, attach an explanation.

3. **Net Rental Income**: Enter monthly net rental income. This is the amount earned after ordinary and necessary monthly rental expenses are paid. Do not include deductions for depreciation or depletion. If the net rental income is a loss, enter "0." Do not enter a negative number.

4. **Distributions**: Enter the total distributions from partnerships and subchapter S corporations reported on Schedule K-1, and from limited liability companies reported on Form 1040, Schedule C, D or E. Enter total distributions from IRAs if not included under pension income.

5. **Other Income**: Include agricultural subsidies, unemployment compensation, gambling income, oil credits, rent subsidies, etc.

6. **Expenses not generally allowed**: We generally do not allow tuition for private schools, public or private college expenses, charitable contributions, voluntary retirement contributions or payments on unsecured debts. However, we may allow the expenses if proven that they are necessary for the health and welfare of the individual or family or the production of income. See Publication 1854 for exceptions.

7. **Food, Clothing and Miscellaneous**: Total of food, clothing, housekeeping supplies, and personal care products for one month. The miscellaneous allowance is for expenses incurred that are not included in any other allowable living expense items. Examples are credit card payments, bank fees and charges, reading material, and school supplies.

8. **Housing and Utilities**: For principal residence: Total of rent or mortgage payment. Add the average monthly expenses for the following: property taxes, homeowner's or renter's insurance, maintenance, dues, fees, and utilities. Utilities include gas, electricity, water, fuel, oil, other fuels, trash collection, telephone, cell phone, cable television and internet services.

9. **Vehicle Ownership Costs**: Total of monthly lease or purchase/loan payments.

10. **Vehicle Operating Costs**: Total of maintenance, repairs, insurance, fuel, registrations, licenses, inspections, parking, and tolls for one month.

11. **Public Transportation**: Total of monthly fares for mass transit *(e.g., bus, train, ferry, taxi, etc.)*

12. **Out of Pocket Health Care Costs**: Monthly total of medical services, prescription drugs and medical supplies *(e.g., eyeglasses, hearing aids, etc.)*

13. **Current Year Taxes**: Include state and Federal taxes withheld from salary or wages, or paid as estimated taxes.

Certification: *Under penalties of perjury, I declare that to the best of my knowledge and belief this statement of assets, liabilities, and other information is true, correct, and complete.*

Taxpayer's Signature	Spouse's signature	Date

After we review the completed Form 433-A, you may be asked to provide verification for the assets, encumbrances, income and expenses reported. Documentation may include previously filed income tax returns, pay statements, self-employment records, bank and investment statements, loan statements, bills or statements for recurring expenses, etc.

IRS USE ONLY *(Notes)*

Form 433-A (Rev. 2-2019) Page 5

Sections 6 and 7 must be completed only if you are SELF-EMPLOYED.

Section 6: Business Information

51 Is the business a sole proprietorship *(filing Schedule C)* ☐ **Yes**, Continue with Sections 6 and 7. ☑ **No**, Complete Form 433-B.
All other business entities, including limited liability companies, partnerships or corporations, must complete Form 433-B.

52 Business Name & Address *(if different than 1b)*

53 Employer Identification Number	54 Type of Business	55 Is the business a Federal Contractor ☐ Yes ☐ No
56 Business Website (web address)	57 Total Number of Employees	58 Average Gross Monthly Payroll
59 Frequency of Tax Deposits	60 Does the business engage in e-Commerce *(Internet sales)* If yes, complete *lines 61a and 61b*	☐ Yes ☐ No

PAYMENT PROCESSOR *(e.g., PayPal, Authorize.net, Google Checkout, etc.)* Include virtual currency wallet, exchange or digital currency exchange.

	Name & Address *(Street, City, State, ZIP code). Name & Address (Street, City, State, ZIP code)*	Payment Processor Account Number
61a		
61b		

CREDIT CARDS ACCEPTED BY THE BUSINESS

	Credit Card	Merchant Account Number	Issuing Bank Name & Address *(Street, City, State, ZIP code)*
62a			
62b			
62c			

63 **BUSINESS CASH ON HAND** Include cash that is not in a bank. **Total Cash on Hand** $

BUSINESS BANK ACCOUNTS Include checking accounts, online and mobile *(e.g., PayPal)* accounts, money market accounts, savings accounts, and stored value cards *(e.g., payroll cards, government benefit cards, etc.)*. Report Personal Accounts in Section 4.

	Type of Account	Full name & Address *(Street, City, State, ZIP code)* of Bank, Savings & Loan, Credit Union or Financial Institution.	Account Number	Account Balance As of _____ *mmddyyyy*
64a				$
64b				$
64c	Total Cash in Banks *(Add lines 64a, 64b and amounts from any attachments)*			$

ACCOUNTS/NOTES RECEIVABLE Include e-payment accounts receivable and factoring companies, and any bartering or online auction accounts. *(List all contracts separately, including contracts awarded, but not started.)* **Include Federal, state and local government grants and contracts.**

	Accounts/Notes Receivable & Address *(Street, City, State, ZIP code)*	Status *(e.g., age, factored, other)*	Date Due *(mmddyyyy)*	Invoice Number or Government Grant or Contract Number	Amount Due
65a					$
65b					$
65c					$
65d					$
65e					$
65f	Total Outstanding Balance *(Add lines 65a through 65e and amounts from any attachments)*				$

Catalog Number 20312N   www.irs.gov   Form **433-A** (Rev. 2-2019)

Form 433-A (Rev. 2-2019) Page **6**

BUSINESS ASSETS Include all tools, books, machinery, equipment, inventory or other assets used in trade or business. Include a list and show the value of all intangible assets such as licenses, patents, domain names, copyrights, trademarks, mining claims, etc.

		Purchase/ Lease Date (mmddyyyy)	Current Fair Market Value (FMV)	Current Loan Balance	Amount of Monthly Payment	Date of Final Payment (mmddyyyy)	Equity FMV Minus Loan
66a	Property Description		$	$	$		$
	Location (Street, City, State, ZIP code) and Country		Lender/Lessor/Landlord Name, Address (Street, City, State, ZIP code), and Phone Phone				
66b	Property Description		$	$	$		$
	Location (Street, City, State, ZIP code) and Country		Lender/Lessor/Landlord Name, Address (Street, City, State, ZIP code), and Phone Phone				
66c	Total Equity (Add lines 66a, 66b and amounts from any attachments)						$

Section 7 should be completed only if you are SELF-EMPLOYED

Section 7: Sole Proprietorship Information (lines 67 through 87 should reconcile with business Profit and Loss Statement)

Accounting Method Used: ☐ Cash ☐ Accrual
Use the prior 3, 6, 9 or 12 month period to determine your typical business income and expenses.

Income and Expenses during the period (mmddyyyy) _____ to (mmddyyyy) _____

Provide a breakdown below of your average monthly income and expenses, based on the period of time used above.

	Total Monthly Business Income			Total Monthly Business Expenses (Use attachments as needed)	
	Source	Gross Monthly		Expense Items	Actual Monthly
67	Gross Receipts	$	77	Materials Purchased [1]	$
68	Gross Rental Income	$	78	Inventory Purchased [2]	$
69	Interest	$	79	Gross Wages & Salaries	$
70	Dividends	$	80	Rent	$
71	Cash Receipts not included in lines 67-70	$	81	Supplies [3]	$
	Other Income (Specify below)		82	Utilities/Telephone [4]	$
72		$	83	Vehicle Gasoline/Oil	$
73		$	84	Repairs & Maintenance	$
74		$	85	Insurance	$
75		$	86	Current Taxes [5]	$
76	Total Income (Add lines 67 through 75)	$	87	Other Expenses, including installment payments (Specify)	$
			88	**Total Expenses (Add lines 77 through 87)**	$
			89	**Net Business Income (Line 76 minus 88)** [6]	$

Enter the monthly net income amount from line 89 on line 23, section 5. If line 89 is a loss, enter "0" on line 23, section 5.
Self-employed taxpayers must return to page 4 to sign the certification.

1. **Materials Purchased:** Materials are items directly related to the production of a product or service.
2. **Inventory Purchased:** Goods bought for resale.
3. **Supplies:** Supplies are items used in the business that are consumed or used up within one year. This could be the cost of books, office supplies, professional equipment, etc.
4. **Utilities/Telephone:** Utilities include gas, electricity, water, oil, other fuels, trash collection, telephone, cell phone and business internet.
5. **Current Taxes:** Real estate, excise, franchise, occupational, personal property, sales and employer's portion of employment taxes.
6. **Net Business Income:** Net profit from Form 1040, Schedule C may be used if duplicated deductions are eliminated (e.g., expenses for business use of home already included in housing and utility expenses on page 4). Deductions for depreciation and depletion on Schedule C are not cash expenses and must be added back to the net income figure. In addition, interest cannot be deducted if it is already included in any other installment payments allowed.

IRS USE ONLY (Notes)

Privacy Act: The information requested on this Form is covered under Privacy Acts and Paperwork Reduction Notices which have already been provided to the taxpayer.

Form 433-B (February 2019)

Department of the Treasury
Internal Revenue Service

Collection Information Statement for Businesses

Note: Complete all entry spaces with the current data available or "N/A" (not applicable). Failure to complete all entry spaces may result in rejection of your request or significant delay in account resolution. **Include attachments if additional space is needed to respond completely to any question.**

Section 1: Business Information

1a Business Name: **Michael's Company**
1b Business Street Address: **Street, City, State and Zip**
  Mailing Address: **Same**
  City _____ State _____ ZIP _____
1c County: **List the County**
1d Business Telephone: (**203**) **xxx-xxxx**
1e Type of Business: **Construction**
1f Business Website (web address): **n/a**

2a Employer Identification No. (EIN): **xx-xxxxxxx**
2b Type of entity (Check appropriate box below)
  ☐ Partnership ☐ Corporation ☐ Other _____
  ☐ Limited Liability Company (LLC) classified as a corporation
  ☑ Other LLC - Include number of members **1**
2c Date Incorporated/Established: **1/1/2008** mmddyyyy
3a Number of Employees: **5**
3b Monthly Gross Payroll: **30,000**
3c Frequency of Tax Deposits: **weekly**
3d Is the business enrolled in Electronic Federal Tax Payment System (EFTPS) ☑ Yes ☐ No

4 Does the business engage in e-Commerce (Internet sales) If yes, complete 5a and 5b. ☐ Yes ☑ No

PAYMENT PROCESSOR (e.g., PayPal, Authorize.net, Google Checkout, etc.) Include virtual currency wallet, exchange or digital currency exchange.

	Name and Address (Street, City, State, ZIP code)	Payment Processor Account Number
5a	Merchant Services	XXXXXXXXXX
5b		

CREDIT CARDS ACCEPTED BY THE BUSINESS

Type of Credit Card (e.g., Visa, Mastercard, etc.)	Merchant Account Number	Issuing Bank Name and Address (Street, City, State, ZIP code)
n/a		
6a		Phone
6b		Phone
6c		Phone

Section 2: Business Personnel and Contacts

PARTNERS, OFFICERS, LLC MEMBERS, MAJOR SHAREHOLDERS (Foreign and Domestic), ETC.

7a Full Name: **Owner Michael**
  Title: **Member**
  Home Address: **Street**
  City **City** State **State** ZIP **Zip**
  Responsible for Depositing Payroll Taxes ☐ Yes ☐ No
  Taxpayer Identification Number: **xxx-xx-xxxx**
  Home Telephone: (**203**) **xxx-xxxx**
  Work/Cell Phone: (**203**) **xxx-xxxx**
  Ownership Percentage & Shares or Interest: **100**
  Annual Salary/Draw: **$120,000**

7b Full Name: _____
  Title: _____
  Home Address: _____
  City _____ State _____ ZIP _____
  Responsible for Depositing Payroll Taxes ☐ Yes ☐ No
  Taxpayer Identification Number: _____
  Home Telephone: (_____)
  Work/Cell Phone: (_____)
  Ownership Percentage & Shares or Interest: _____
  Annual Salary/Draw: _____

7c Full Name: _____
  Title: _____
  Home Address: _____
  City _____ State _____ ZIP _____
  Responsible for Depositing Payroll Taxes ☐ Yes ☐ No
  Taxpayer Identification Number: _____
  Home Telephone: (_____)
  Work/Cell Phone: (_____)
  Ownership Percentage & Shares or Interest: _____
  Annual Salary/Draw: _____

7d Full Name: _____
  Title: _____
  Home Address: _____
  City _____ State _____ ZIP _____
  Responsible for Depositing Payroll Taxes ☐ Yes ☐ No
  Taxpayer Identification Number: _____
  Home Telephone: (_____)
  Work/Cell Phone: (_____)
  Ownership Percentage & Shares or Interest: _____
  Annual Salary/Draw: _____

Catalog Number 16649P   www.irs.gov   Form **433-B** (Rev. 2-2019)

Form 433-B (Rev. 2-2019) Page **2**

Section 3: Other Financial Information *(Attach copies of all applicable documents)*

8 Does the business use a Payroll Service Provider or Reporting Agent *(If yes, answer the following)* ☐ Yes ☑ No

Effective dates *(mmddyyyy)*

9 Is the business a party to a lawsuit *(If yes, answer the following)* ☐ Yes ☑ No

☐ Plaintiff ☐ Defendant	Location of Filing	Represented by	Docket/Case No.
Amount of Suit $	Possible Completion Date *(mmddyyyy)*	Subject of Suit	

10 Has the business ever filed bankruptcy *(If yes, answer the following)* ☐ Yes ☑ No

Date Filed *(mmddyyyy)*	Date Dismissed *(mmddyyyy)*	Date Discharged *(mmddyyyy)*	Petition No.	District of Filing

11 Do any related parties *(e.g., officers, partners, employees)* have outstanding amounts owed to the business *(If yes, answer the following)* ☐ Yes ☑ No

Name and Address *(Street, City, State, ZIP code)*	Date of Loan	Current Balance As of *mmddyyyy* $	Payment Date	Payment Amount $

12 Have any assets been transferred, in the last 10 years, from this business for less than full value *(If yes, answer the following)* ☐ Yes ☑ No

List Asset	Value at Time of Transfer $	Date Transferred *(mmddyyyy)*	To Whom or Where Transferred

13 Does this business have other business affiliations *(e.g., subsidiary or parent companies)* *(If yes, answer the following)* ☐ Yes ☑ No

Related Business Name and Address *(Street, City, State, ZIP code)*	Related Business EIN:

14 Any increase/decrease in income anticipated *(If yes, answer the following)* ☑ Yes ☐ No

Moving to new office space in June 2020, which will free up $1200/month and decreasing advertising budget	How much will it increase/decrease $ $1,400	June 2020

15 Is the business a Federal Government Contractor *(Include Federal Government contracts in #18, Accounts/Notes Receivable)* ☐ Yes ☑ No

Section 4: Business Asset and Liability Information (Foreign and Domestic)

16a **CASH ON HAND** *Include cash that is not in the bank*   **Total Cash on Hand** $ 0

16b Is there a safe on the business premises ☐ Yes ☑ No   Contents

BUSINESS BANK ACCOUNTS Include online and mobile accounts *(e.g., PayPal)*, money market accounts, savings accounts, checking accounts and stored value cards *(e.g., payroll cards, government benefit cards, etc.)*
List safe deposit boxes including location, box number and value of contents. Attach list of contents.

	Type of Account	Full Name and Address *(Street, City, State, ZIP code)* of Bank, Savings & Loan, Credit Union or Financial Institution	Account Number	Account Balance As of 04012020 *mmddyyyy*
17a	Checking	ABC Bank, Address	9999999	$ 1,000
17b				$
17c				$
17d	Total Cash in Banks *(Add lines 17a through 17c and amounts from any attachments)*			$ 1,000

Form 433-B (Rev. 2-2019) Page **3**

ACCOUNTS/NOTES RECEIVABLE Include e-payment accounts receivable and factoring companies, and any bartering or online auction accounts. *(List all contracts separately including contracts awarded, but not started).* **Include Federal, state and local government grants and contracts.**

Name & Address *(Street, City, State, ZIP code)*	Status *(e.g., age, factored, other)*	Date Due *(mmddyyy)*	Invoice Number or Government Grant or Contract Number	**Amount Due**
18a None Contact Name Phone				$
18b Contact Name Phone				$
18c Contact Name Phone				$
18d Contact Name Phone				$
18e Contact Name Phone				$
18f Outstanding Balance *(Add lines 18a through 18e and amounts from any attachments)*				$ 0

INVESTMENTS List all investment assets below. Include stocks, bonds, mutual funds, stock options, certificates of deposit, commodities (e.g., gold, silver, copper, etc.) and virtual currency (e.g., Bitcoin, Ripple and Litecoin).

Name of Company & Address *(Street, City, State, ZIP code)*	Used as collateral on loan	Current Value	Loan Balance	**Equity** Value Minus Loan
19a None Phone	☐ Yes ☐ No	$	$	$
19b Phone	☐ Yes ☐ No	$	$	$
19c Total Investments *(Add lines 19a, 19b, and amounts from any attachments)*				$ 0

AVAILABLE CREDIT Include all lines of credit and credit cards.

Full Name & Address *(Street, City, State, ZIP code)*	Credit Limit	Amount Owed As of _____ *mmddyyyy*	**Available Credit** As of _____ *mmddyyyy*
20a None Account No.	$	$	$
20b Account No.	$	$	$
20c Total Credit Available *(Add lines 20a, 20b, and amounts from any attachments)*			$ 0

Catalog Number 16649P www.irs.gov Form **433-B** (Rev. 2-2019)

Form 433-B (Rev. 2-2019) Page **4**

REAL PROPERTY Include all real property and land contracts the business owns/leases/rents.

	Purchase/Lease Date (mmddyyyy)	Current Fair Market Value (FMV)	Current Loan Balance	Amount of Monthly Payment	Date of Final Payment (mmddyyyy)	**Equity** FMV Minus Loan
21a Property Description Commercial office space	06012020	$ rents property	$	$ 2,000	06012022	$ 0
Location (Street, City, State, ZIP code) and County ABC Street, City, Zip, County (As of June 2020.)			Lender/Lessor/Landlord Name, Address, (Street, City, State, ZIP code) and Phone ABC Landlord Phone			
21b Property Description		$	$	$		$
Location (Street, City, State, ZIP code) and County			Lender/Lessor/Landlord Name, Address, (Street, City, State, ZIP code) and Phone Phone			
21c Property Description		$	$	$		$
Location (Street, City, State, ZIP code) and County			Lender/Lessor/Landlord Name, Address, (Street, City, State, ZIP code) and Phone Phone			
21d Property Description		$	$	$		$
Location (Street, City, State, ZIP code) and County			Lender/Lessor/Landlord Name, Address, (Street, City, State, ZIP code) and Phone Phone			

21e Total Equity (Add lines 21a through 21d and amounts from any attachments) $ 0

VEHICLES, LEASED AND PURCHASED Include boats, RVs, motorcycles, all-terrain and off-road vehicles, trailers, mobile homes, etc.

	Purchase/Lease Date (mmddyyyy)	Current Fair Market Value (FMV)	Current Loan Balance	Amount of Monthly Payment	Date of Final Payment (mmddyyyy)	**Equity** FMV Minus Loan
22a Year 2010 Make/Model F150	2/2011	$ 8,500	$ 0	$ 0	0	$ 8,500
Mileage 187,600 License/Tag Number xxxxxx Vehicle Identification Number (VIN) x1x1x1x1x1xx1x1			Lender/Lessor Name, Address, (Street, City, State, ZIP code) and Phone Phone			
22b Year Make/Model		$	$	$		$
Mileage License/Tag Number Vehicle Identification Number (VIN)			Lender/Lessor Name, Address, (Street, City, State, ZIP code) and Phone Phone			
22c Year Make/Model		$	$	$		$
Mileage License/Tag Number Vehicle Identification Number (VIN)			Lender/Lessor Name, Address, (Street, City, State, ZIP code) and Phone Phone			
22d Year Make/Model		$	$	$		$
Mileage License/Tag Number Vehicle Identification Number (VIN)			Lender/Lessor Name, Address, (Street, City, State, ZIP code) and Phone Phone			

22e Total Equity (Add lines 22a through 22d and amounts from any attachments) $ 8,500

Catalog Number 16649P

Form 433-B (Rev. 2-2019) Page **5**

BUSINESS EQUIPMENT AND INTANGIBLE ASSETS Include all machinery, equipment, merchandise inventory, and other assets in 23a through 23d. List intangible assets in 23e through 23g *(licenses, patents, logos, domain names, trademarks, copyrights, software, mining claims, goodwill and trade secrets.)*

	Purchase/ Lease Date *(mmddyyyy)*	Current Fair Market Value (FMV)	Current Loan Balance	Amount of Monthly Payment	Date of Final Payment *(mmddyyyy)*	**Equity** FMV Minus Loan
23a Asset Description **Hand Tools**		$ 500	$ 0	$ 0	n/a	$ 500
Location of asset *(Street, City, State, ZIP code)* and County **Owner's address**		Lender/Lessor Name, Address, *(Street, City, State, ZIP code)* and Phone n/a Phone				
23b Asset Description		$	$	$		$
Location of asset *(Street, City, State, ZIP code)* and County		Lender/Lessor Name, Address, *(Street, City, State, ZIP code)* and Phone Phone				
23c Asset Description		$	$	$		$
Location of asset *(Street, City, State, ZIP code)* and County		Lender/Lessor Name, Address, *(Street, City, State, ZIP code)* and Phone Phone				
23d Asset Description		$	$	$		$
Location of asset *(Street, City, State, ZIP code)* and County		Lender/Lessor Name, Address, *(Street, City, State, ZIP code)* and Phone Phone				
23e Intangible Asset Description						$
23f Intangible Asset Description						$
23g Intangible Asset Description						$
23h Total Equity *(Add lines 23a through 23g and amounts from any attachments)*						$ 500.00

BUSINESS LIABILITIES Include notes and judgements not listed previously on this form.

Business Liabilities	Secured/ Unsecured	Date Pledged *(mmddyyyy)*	Balance Owed	Date of Final Payment *(mmddyyyy)*	Payment Amount
24a Description: **IRS**	☑ Secured ☐ Unsecured		$ 317,321		$ 0
Name Street Address City/State/ZIP code			Phone		
24b Description: **Capital One Bank**	☐ Secured ☑ Unsecured		$ 15,000		$789
Name Street Address City/State/ZIP code			Phone		
24c Total Payments *(Add lines 24a and 24b and amounts from any attachments)*					$789

Form 433-B (Rev. 2-2019) Page 6

Section 5: Monthly Income/Expenses Statement for Business

Accounting Method Used: ☑ Cash ☐ Accrual

Use the prior 3, 6, 9 or 12 month period to determine your typical business income and expenses.

Income and Expenses during the period (mmddyyyy) _____ to (mmddyyyy) _____

Provide a breakdown below of your average monthly income and expenses, based on the period of time used above.

Total Monthly Business Income			Total Monthly Business Expenses		
Income Source	Gross Monthly		Expense items		Actual Monthly
25 Gross Receipts from Sales/Services	$ 60,000		36 Materials Purchased [1]	$	7,000
26 Gross Rental Income	$		37 Inventory Purchased [2]	$	
27 Interest Income	$		38 Gross Wages & Salaries	$	30,000
28 Dividends	$		39 Rent	$	3,200 (decreasing to $2k on 6/1/2020)
29 Cash Receipts (Not included in lines 25-28)	$		40 Supplies [3]	$	1,800
Other Income (Specify below)			41 Utilities/Telephone [4]	$	
30	$		42 Vehicle Gasoline/Oil	$	
31	$		43 Repairs & Maintenance	$	
32	$		44 Insurance	$	1,700
33	$		45 Current Taxes [5]	$	6,000
34	$		46 Other Expenses (Specify)	$	300 (advertising)
35 Total Income (Add lines 25 through 34)	$ 60,000	0	47 IRS Use Only-Allowable Installment Payments	$	
			48 **Total Expenses** (Add lines 36 through 47)	$	50,000
			49 **Net Income** (Line 35 minus Line 48)	$	10,000

1. **Materials Purchased:** Materials are items directly related to the production of a product or service.
2. **Inventory Purchased:** Goods bought for resale.
3. **Supplies:** Supplies are items used to conduct business and are consumed or used up within one year. This could be the cost of books, office supplies, professional equipment, etc.
4. **Utilities/Telephone:** Utilities include gas, electricity, water, oil, other fuels, trash collection, telephone, cell phone and business internet.
5. **Current Taxes:** Real estate, state, and local income tax, excise, franchise, occupational, personal property, sales and the employer's portion of employment taxes.

Certification: Under penalties of perjury, I declare that to the best of my knowledge and belief this statement of assets, liabilities, and other information is true, correct, and complete.

Signature	Title	Date
	Owner	3/20/2020

Print Name of Officer, Partner or LLC Member

Owner Michael

After we review the completed Form 433-B, you may be asked to provide verification for the assets, encumbrances, income and expenses reported. Documentation may include previously filed income tax returns, profit and loss statements, bank and investment statements, loan statements, financing statements, bills or statements for recurring expenses, etc.

IRS USE ONLY (Notes)

Privacy Act: The information requested on this Form is covered under Privacy Acts and Paperwork Reduction Notices which have already been provided to the taxpayer.

Checklist: Payroll Tax Case

1. **New Client**
   a. Who is our client? (Business / Owner / Both)
   b. Retainer agreement
   c. Retainer check
   d. Power of Attorney (Business / Owner / Both)

2. **Compliance**
   a. Have the payroll tax returns due been filed?
   b. Have current quarter's tax payments been made?
   c. Are all W-2s and W-3s filed?
   d. Were 1099s filed (if necessary)?

3. **Obtain Both Employer's and Owner's Financial Information**
   a. Profit and Loss
   b. Balance Sheet
   c. Breakdown of any business receivables
   d. Proof of business loans and financing agreements
   e. Bank Statements – last three months (business and personal)
   f. Retirement Accounts
      a. Recent statement of value
      b. Copy of the plan document (to see if the taxpayer can access the funds)
   g. Investment Accounts – recent statement of value
   h. Life Insurance – statement of current cash value
   i. Real Estate (business and personal)
      a. Statement of Value (Zillow, etc.)
      b. Recent Mortgage Statement showing loan balance and monthly payment
   j. Automobiles (business and personal)
      a. Statement of Value (Kelly Blue Book)
      b. Current lease or loan statement showing outstanding balance and monthly payment amount

k. Collectables, Artwork, etc. – statements of values on collectables that can be used to pay the tax debt
l. Proof of income
   a. Profit & Loss
   b. Paystubs
j. Utility Bills – last 3 months (get proof of payments or highlight in the bank statements)
k. Proof of health insurance premium (get proof of payments or highlight in the bank statements)
l. Proof of term life insurance and premium amount (get proof of payments or highlight in the bank statements)
m. Proof of disability insurance (get proof of payments or highlight in the bank statements)
n. Proof of out-of-pocket medical expenses (get proof of payments or highlight in the bank statements)
o. Proof of alimony (Divorce Agreement or Decree)
p. Proof of child support (Divorce Agreement or Decree)
q. Proof of dependent care expenses (get proof of payments or highlight in the bank statements)
r. Proof of judgments and payments to creditors
s. Proof of current taxes being paid/withheld
t. Written agreement with state department of revenue and proof of payments

4. **Prepare Collection Information Statement (IRS Form 433)**
   a. Individual – 433-A (OIC)
   b. Each Business Interest – 433-B

5. **Analyze taxpayer's assets for collection**
   a. Analyze taxpayer's income vs. IRS allowable expenses
      i. Are the assets necessary to produce income?
      ii. Are there assets that are not necessary?
      iii. Can the assets be used to secure a loan?
   b. Analyze taxpayer's income vs. IRS allowable expenses

c. Calculate Net Equity in Assets

   d. Calculate RCP

6. **Prepare package for IRS**

7. **File with the IRS with a proposed Collection Alternative**

   a. Form 433-A

   b. Form 433-B

   c. All supporting documents

Exhibits

Exhibit Number	Exhibit
1	IRS Form 2848 Power of Attorney - Business
2	IRS Form 2848 Power of Attorney - Owner
3	CP-501 - Billing Notice
4	CP-503 - Reminder Notice
5	CP-504 - Threat To Levy
6	IRS Form 12153 - Request for Collection Due Process or Equivalent Hearing
7	IRS Form 12153 - Request for Collection Due Process or Equivalent Hearing
8	Sample Account Transcript
9	IRS Form 433-B - Collection Information Statement for Businesses
10	IRS Form 433-A - Collection Information Statement for Individuals
11	CP-523 - Notice of Intent to Terminate Your Installment Agreement
12	IRS Form 9423 - Collection Appeal Request
13	Letter Deeming the Taxpayer Uncollectible
14	IRS Form 656-B - Offer-in-Compromise Booklet
15	IRS Letter 903 - IRS Demand Letter to deposit Employment Taxes
16	Sample Injunction and Court Order to Make Payroll deposits
17	IRS Form 4180 - Trust Fund Interview Form

18	IRS Letter 1153 - Notice of Proposed Trust Fund Assessment
19	IRS Form 2751 - Agreement to Assessment and Collection of Trust Fund Recovery Penalty
20	Sample Protest of the Proposed trust Fund Assessment
21	Sample Freedom of Information Act Request
22	Sample Affidavit
23	IRS Form 656-L - Doubt-as-to-Liability Offer
24	IRS Form 843 - Request for Abatement or Refund
25	Sample Refund Suit Filed in United States District Court
26	Revenue Procedure 2002-26
27	Sample Letter Designating Trust Fund Payments
28	IRS Form 14135 - Request for Discharge from federal Tax Lien
29	Sample Indictment for Payroll Taxes

Form 2848
(Rev. February 2020)
Department of the Treasury
Internal Revenue Service

Power of Attorney
and Declaration of Representative

▶ Go to www.irs.gov/Form2848 for instructions and the latest information.

OMB No. 1545-0150

For IRS Use Only
Received by:
Name _____
Telephone _____
Function _____
Date __/__/__

Part I Power of Attorney

Caution: A separate Form 2848 must be completed for each taxpayer. Form 2848 will not be honored for any purpose other than representation before the IRS.

1 Taxpayer information. Taxpayer must sign and date this form on page 2, line 7.

Taxpayer name and address	Taxpayer identification number(s)
ABC Corporation 1 Main Street New Haven, CT 06511	XX-XXXXXXXX
	Daytime telephone number: **(203) 111-XXXX** Plan number (if applicable)

hereby appoints the following representative(s) as attorney(s)-in-fact:

2 Representative(s) must sign and date this form on page 2, Part II.

Name and address
Representative
Reps Address

CAF No. _____ XXXX-XXXXXR _____
PTIN _____ P00000000 _____
Telephone No. _____ (203) XXX-XXXX _____
Fax No. _____ (203) XXX-XXXX _____

Check if to be sent copies of notices and communications ☐   Check if new: Address ☐   Telephone No. ☐   Fax No. ☐

Name and address

CAF No. _____
PTIN _____
Telephone No. _____
Fax No. _____

Check if to be sent copies of notices and communications ☐   Check if new: Address ☐   Telephone No. ☐   Fax No. ☐

Name and address

CAF No. _____
PTIN _____
Telephone No. _____
Fax No. _____

(**Note:** IRS sends notices and communications to only two representatives.)   Check if new: Address ☐   Telephone No. ☐   Fax No. ☐

Name and address

CAF No. _____
PTIN _____
Telephone No. _____
Fax No. _____

(**Note:** IRS sends notices and communications to only two representatives.)   Check if new: Address ☐   Telephone No. ☐   Fax No. ☐

to represent the taxpayer before the Internal Revenue Service and perform the following acts:

3 Acts authorized (you are required to complete this line 3). With the exception of the acts described in line 5b, I authorize my representative(s) to receive and inspect my confidential tax information and to perform acts that I can perform with respect to the tax matters described below. For example, my representative(s) shall have the authority to sign any agreements, consents, or similar documents (see instructions for line 5a for authorizing a representative to sign a return).

Description of Matter (Income, Employment, Payroll, Excise, Estate, Gift, Whistleblower, Practitioner Discipline, PLR, FOIA, Civil Penalty, Sec. 4980H Shared Responsibility Payment, etc.) (see instructions)	Tax Form Number (1040, 941, 720, etc.) (if applicable)	Year(s) or Period(s) (if applicable) (see instructions)
Income Tax	1120-S	12/31/2000 - 12/31/2021
Employment Tax	941	3/31/2000 - 12/31/2021
Employment Tax	940	12/31/2000 - 12/31/2021

4 Specific use not recorded on Centralized Authorization File (CAF). If the power of attorney is for a specific use not recorded on CAF, check this box. See *Line 4. Specific Use Not Recorded on CAF* in the instructions . . . . ▶ ☐

5a Additional acts authorized. In addition to the acts listed on line 3 above, I authorize my representative(s) to perform the following acts (see instructions for line 5a for more information): ☑ Access my IRS records via an Intermediate Service Provider;
☐ Authorize disclosure to third parties;   ☑ Substitute or add representative(s);   ☐ Sign a return; _____

☐ Other acts authorized: _____

For Privacy Act and Paperwork Reduction Act Notice, see the instructions.   Cat. No. 11980J   Form **2848** (Rev. 2-2020)

EXHIBIT 1

Form 2848 (Rev. 2-2020) Page **2**

b **Specific acts not authorized.** My representative(s) is (are) not authorized to endorse or otherwise negotiate any check (including directing or accepting payment by any means, electronic or otherwise, into an account owned or controlled by the representative(s) or any firm or other entity with whom the representative(s) is (are) associated) issued by the government in respect of a federal tax liability.
List any other specific deletions to the acts otherwise authorized in this power of attorney (see instructions for line 5b): _____

6 **Retention/revocation of prior power(s) of attorney.** The filing of this power of attorney automatically revokes all earlier power(s) of attorney on file with the Internal Revenue Service for the same matters and years or periods covered by this document. If you **do not** want to revoke a prior power of attorney, check here . . . . ▶ ☐
YOU MUST ATTACH A COPY OF ANY POWER OF ATTORNEY YOU WANT TO REMAIN IN EFFECT.

7 **Signature of taxpayer.** If a tax matter concerns a year in which a joint return was filed, each spouse must file a separate power of attorney even if they are appointing the same representative(s). If signed by a corporate officer, partner, guardian, tax matters partner, partnership representative (or designated individual, if applicable), executor, receiver, administrator, or trustee on behalf of the taxpayer, I certify that I have the legal authority to execute this form on behalf of the taxpayer.

▶ **IF NOT COMPLETED, SIGNED, AND DATED, THE IRS WILL RETURN THIS POWER OF ATTORNEY TO THE TAXPAYER.**

President

| Signature | Date | Title (if applicable) |

President's Name

| Print name | Print name of taxpayer from line 1 if other than individual |

| Part II | Declaration of Representative |

Under penalties of perjury, by my signature below I declare that:
- I am not currently suspended or disbarred from practice, or ineligible for practice, before the Internal Revenue Service;
- I am subject to regulations contained in Circular 230 (31 CFR, Subtitle A, Part 10), as amended, governing practice before the Internal Revenue Service;
- I am authorized to represent the taxpayer identified in Part I for the matter(s) specified there; and
- I am one of the following:

a Attorney—a member in good standing of the bar of the highest court of the jurisdiction shown below.
b Certified Public Accountant—a holder of an active license to practice as a certified public accountant in the jurisdiction shown below.
c Enrolled Agent—enrolled as an agent by the IRS per the requirements of Circular 230.
d Officer—a bona fide officer of the taxpayer organization.
e Full-Time Employee—a full-time employee of the taxpayer.
f Family Member—a member of the taxpayer's immediate family (spouse, parent, child, grandparent, grandchild, step-parent, step-child, brother, or sister).
g Enrolled Actuary—enrolled as an actuary by the Joint Board for the Enrollment of Actuaries under 29 U.S.C. 1242 (the authority to practice before the IRS is limited by section 10.3(d) of Circular 230).
h Unenrolled Return Preparer—Authority to practice before the IRS is limited. An unenrolled return preparer may represent, provided the preparer (1) prepared and signed the return or claim for refund (or prepared if there is no signature space on the form); (2) was eligible to sign the return or claim for refund; (3) has a valid PTIN; and (4) possesses the required Annual Filing Season Program Record of Completion(s). **See Special Rules and Requirements for Unenrolled Return Preparers** *in the instructions for additional information.*
k Qualifying Student—receives permission to represent taxpayers before the IRS by virtue of his/her status as a law, business, or accounting student working in an LITC or STCP. See instructions for Part II for additional information and requirements.
r Enrolled Retirement Plan Agent—enrolled as a retirement plan agent under the requirements of Circular 230 (the authority to practice before the Internal Revenue Service is limited by section 10.3(e)).

▶ **IF THIS DECLARATION OF REPRESENTATIVE IS NOT COMPLETED, SIGNED, AND DATED, THE IRS WILL RETURN THE POWER OF ATTORNEY. REPRESENTATIVES MUST SIGN IN THE ORDER LISTED IN PART I, LINE 2.**

Note: For designations d–f, enter your title, position, or relationship to the taxpayer in the "Licensing jurisdiction" column.

Designation— Insert above letter **(a–r)**.	Licensing jurisdiction (State) or other licensing authority (if applicable)	Bar, license, certification, registration, or enrollment number (if applicable)	Signature	Date

Form **2848** (Rev. 2-2020)

Form 2848
(Rev. February 2020)
Department of the Treasury
Internal Revenue Service

Power of Attorney and Declaration of Representative

▶ Go to www.irs.gov/Form2848 for instructions and the latest information.

OMB No. 1545-0150

For IRS Use Only
Received by:
Name _____
Telephone _____
Function _____
Date __/__/__

Part I Power of Attorney

Caution: A separate Form 2848 must be completed for each taxpayer. Form 2848 will not be honored for any purpose other than representation before the IRS.

1 Taxpayer information. Taxpayer must sign and date this form on page 2, line 7.

Taxpayer name and address	Taxpayer identification number(s)
Shareholder Joe His Street Address New Haven, CT 06511	XXX-XX-XXXXX
	Daytime telephone number	Plan number (if applicable)
	(203) 111-XXXX	

hereby appoints the following representative(s) as attorney(s)-in-fact:

2 Representative(s) must sign and date this form on page 2, Part II.

Name and address	
Representative Reps Address	CAF No. _____ XXXX-XXXXXR PTIN _____ P00000000 Telephone No. _____ (203) XXX-XXXX Fax No. _____ (203) XXX-XXXX
Check if to be sent copies of notices and communications ☐	Check if new: Address ☐ Telephone No. ☐ Fax No. ☐

Name and address	
	CAF No. _____ PTIN _____ Telephone No. _____ Fax No. _____
Check if to be sent copies of notices and communications ☐	Check if new: Address ☐ Telephone No. ☐ Fax No. ☐

Name and address	
	CAF No. _____ PTIN _____ Telephone No. _____ Fax No. _____
(Note: IRS sends notices and communications to only two representatives.)	Check if new: Address ☐ Telephone No. ☐ Fax No. ☐

Name and address	
	CAF No. _____ PTIN _____ Telephone No. _____ Fax No. _____
(Note: IRS sends notices and communications to only two representatives.)	Check if new: Address ☐ Telephone No. ☐ Fax No. ☐

to represent the taxpayer before the Internal Revenue Service and perform the following acts:

3 Acts authorized (you are required to complete this line 3). With the exception of the acts described in line 5b, I authorize my representative(s) to receive and inspect my confidential tax information and to perform acts that I can perform with respect to the tax matters described below. For example, my representative(s) shall have the authority to sign any agreements, consents, or similar documents (see instructions for line 5a for authorizing a representative to sign a return).

Description of Matter (Income, Employment, Payroll, Excise, Estate, Gift, Whistleblower, Practitioner Discipline, PLR, FOIA, Civil Penalty, Sec. 4980H Shared Responsibility Payment, etc.) (see instructions)	Tax Form Number (1040, 941, 720, etc.) (if applicable)	Year(s) or Period(s) (if applicable) (see instructions)
Income Tax	1040	12/31/2000 - 12/31/2021
Civil Penalties	IRC 6672	3/31/2000 - 12/31/2021

4 Specific use not recorded on Centralized Authorization File (CAF). If the power of attorney is for a specific use not recorded on CAF, check this box. See *Line 4. Specific Use Not Recorded on CAF* in the instructions . . . . ▶ ☐

5a Additional acts authorized. In addition to the acts listed on line 3 above, I authorize my representative(s) to perform the following acts (see instructions for line 5a for more information): ☑ Access my IRS records via an Intermediate Service Provider;
☐ Authorize disclosure to third parties;   ☑ Substitute or add representative(s);   ☐ Sign a return; _____

☐ Other acts authorized: _____

For Privacy Act and Paperwork Reduction Act Notice, see the instructions.   Cat. No. 11980J   Form **2848** (Rev. 2-2020)

EXHIBIT 2

Form 2848 (Rev. 2-2020) Page **2**

b Specific acts not authorized. My representative(s) is (are) not authorized to endorse or otherwise negotiate any check (including directing or accepting payment by any means, electronic or otherwise, into an account owned or controlled by the representative(s) or any firm or other entity with whom the representative(s) is (are) associated) issued by the government in respect of a federal tax liability.
List any other specific deletions to the acts otherwise authorized in this power of attorney (see instructions for line 5b): _____

6 Retention/revocation of prior power(s) of attorney. The filing of this power of attorney automatically revokes all earlier power(s) of attorney on file with the Internal Revenue Service for the same matters and years or periods covered by this document. If you **do not** want to revoke a prior power of attorney, check here . . . . ▶ ☐
YOU MUST ATTACH A COPY OF ANY POWER OF ATTORNEY YOU WANT TO REMAIN IN EFFECT.

7 Signature of taxpayer. If a tax matter concerns a year in which a joint return was filed, each spouse must file a separate power of attorney even if they are appointing the same representative(s). If signed by a corporate officer, partner, guardian, tax matters partner, partnership representative (or designated individual, if applicable), executor, receiver, administrator, or trustee on behalf of the taxpayer, I certify that I have the legal authority to execute this form on behalf of the taxpayer.

▶ **IF NOT COMPLETED, SIGNED, AND DATED, THE IRS WILL RETURN THIS POWER OF ATTORNEY TO THE TAXPAYER.**

Signature	Date	Title (if applicable)

Taxpayer's Name

Print name	Print name of taxpayer from line 1 if other than individual

Part II   Declaration of Representative

Under penalties of perjury, by my signature below I declare that:
- I am not currently suspended or disbarred from practice, or ineligible for practice, before the Internal Revenue Service;
- I am subject to regulations contained in Circular 230 (31 CFR, Subtitle A, Part 10), as amended, governing practice before the Internal Revenue Service;
- I am authorized to represent the taxpayer identified in Part I for the matter(s) specified there; and
- I am one of the following:

  a Attorney—a member in good standing of the bar of the highest court of the jurisdiction shown below.
  b Certified Public Accountant—a holder of an active license to practice as a certified public accountant in the jurisdiction shown below.
  c Enrolled Agent—enrolled as an agent by the IRS per the requirements of Circular 230.
  d Officer—a bona fide officer of the taxpayer organization.
  e Full-Time Employee—a full-time employee of the taxpayer.
  f Family Member—a member of the taxpayer's immediate family (spouse, parent, child, grandparent, grandchild, step-parent, step-child, brother, or sister).
  g Enrolled Actuary—enrolled as an actuary by the Joint Board for the Enrollment of Actuaries under 29 U.S.C. 1242 (the authority to practice before the IRS is limited by section 10.3(d) of Circular 230).
  h Unenrolled Return Preparer—Authority to practice before the IRS is limited. An unenrolled return preparer may represent, provided the preparer (1) prepared and signed the return or claim for refund (or prepared if there is no signature space on the form); (2) was eligible to sign the return or claim for refund; (3) has a valid PTIN; and (4) possesses the required Annual Filing Season Program Record of Completion(s). **See Special Rules and Requirements for Unenrolled Return Preparers *in the instructions for additional information.***
  k Qualifying Student—receives permission to represent taxpayers before the IRS by virtue of his/her status as a law, business, or accounting student working in an LITC or STCP. See instructions for Part II for additional information and requirements.
  r Enrolled Retirement Plan Agent—enrolled as a retirement plan agent under the requirements of Circular 230 (the authority to practice before the Internal Revenue Service is limited by section 10.3(e)).

▶ **IF THIS DECLARATION OF REPRESENTATIVE IS NOT COMPLETED, SIGNED, AND DATED, THE IRS WILL RETURN THE POWER OF ATTORNEY. REPRESENTATIVES MUST SIGN IN THE ORDER LISTED IN PART I, LINE 2.**

Note: For designations d–f, enter your title, position, or relationship to the taxpayer in the "Licensing jurisdiction" column.

Designation— Insert above letter **(a–r)**.	Licensing jurisdiction (State) or other licensing authority (if applicable)	Bar, license, certification, registration, or enrollment number (if applicable)	Signature	Date

Form **2848** (Rev. 2-2020)

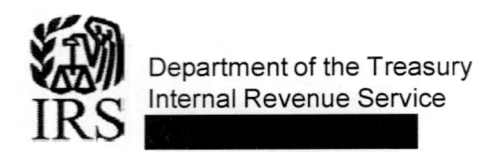

Notice	CP501
Tax Year	2014
Notice date	December 16, 2016
Social Security number	
To contact us	Phone
Your Caller ID	

Department of the Treasury
Internal Revenue Service

You have unpaid taxes for 2014

Amount due:

Our records show you have unpaid taxes for the tax year ending December 31, 2014 (Form 1040).

Billing Summary

Amount you owed
Failure-to-pay penalty
Interest charges
Amount due by January 26, 2015

What you need to do immediately

Pay immediately

- Pay the amount due of ▮ by January 26, 2015, to avoid additional penalty and interest charges. **You can pay online now at www.irs.gov/directpay.**

Continued on back...

Payment

Notice	CP501
Notice date	December 16, 2016
Social Security Number	

- Make your check or money order payable to the United States Treasury.
- Write your Social Security number ▮, the tax year (2014), and the form number (1040) on your payment and any correspondence.

Amount due by January 26, 2015

INTERNAL REVENUE SERVICE

EXHIBIT 3

Notice	CP501
Tax Year	2014
Notice date	December 16, 2016
Social Security number	

What you need to do immediately—continued

Pay immediately—**continued**

- If you can't pay the amount due, pay as much as you can now and make payment arrangements that allow you to pay off the rest over time. Visit www.irs.gov/payments for more information about:
  -- Credit and debit card payments
  -- Electronic payments
  -- Installment and payment plans:
    - Automatic deductions from your bank account
    - Payroll deductions

    - [Apply online or mail Form 9465, Installment Agreement Request.]

  -- Offer in Compromise- To see if you qualify for an offer, visit the Offer in Compromise Pre-Qualifier tool at www.irs.gov/Individuals/Offer-in-Compromise-1

Or, call us at 1-800-XXX-XXXX to discuss your options

If you need to pay your tax debt over time, we encourage you to apply for
a Direct Debit Installment Agreement. These agreements save you time
and money by having your monthly payment automatically withdrawn from your bank account. There are no checks to write and mail and these agreements have a reduced user fee.

[Apply for a payment plan using the Online Payment Agreement application at: www.irs.gov and search "online-payment.".]

Apply for a payment plan by completing Form 433-F prior to calling us at 1-800-XXX-XXXX. This will assist us in handling your call more efficiently.]

[By setting up an agreement online now, you may be able to avoid the filing of a Notice of Federal Tax Lien, if one hasn't already been filed. If a
Notice of Federal Tax Lien has been filed, certain taxpayers may request
the notice be withdrawn after establishing a Direct Debit Installment Agreement. For more information on liens, visit: www.irs.gov and search
"federal tax lien"].

If you already paid your balance in full within the past 14 days or made payment arrangements, please disregard this notice.

Notice	CP501
Tax Year	2014
Notice date	December 16, 2016
Social Security number	

If we don't hear from you

- If you don't pay ▮ by January 26, 2015, interest will increase and additional penalties may apply.
- If you don't pay the amount due or call us to make payment arrangements, we can file a Notice of Federal Tax Lien on your property at any time, if we haven't already done so.
- If the lien is in place, you may find it difficult to sell or borrow against your property. The tax lien would also appear on your credit report—which may harm your credit rating--and your creditors would also be publicly notified that the IRS has priority to seize your property.
- If you don't pay your tax debt, we have the right to seize ("levy") your property.

Penalties

We are required by law to charge any applicable penalties.

Failure-to-pay

Description	Amount
Total failure-to-pay	▮

When you pay your taxes after the due date, we charge a penalty of 0.5% of the unpaid amount due per month, up to 25% of the amount due. We count part of a month as a full month. (Internal Revenue Code Section 6651)

For a detailed calculation of your penalty charges, call 1-800-829-0922.

IRS

Notice	CP501
Notice date	December 16, 2016
Social Security Number	

Contact information

If your address has changed, please call 1-800-829-0922 or visit www.irs.gov.

☐ Please check here if you've included any correspondence. Write your Social Security number (▮), the tax year (2014), and the form number (1040) on any correspondence.

Primary phone	Best time to call	Secondary phone	Best time to call
	☐ a.m. ☐ p.m.		☐ a.m. ☐ p.m.

Notice	CP501
Tax Year	2014
Notice date	December 16, 2016
Social Security number	

Removal of penalties due to erroneous written advice from the IRS

If you were penalized based on written advice from the IRS, we will remove the penalty if you meet the following criteria:
- If you sent a written request to the IRS for written advice on a specific issue
- You gave us complete and accurate information
- You received written advice from us
- You reasonably relied on our written advice and were penalized based on that advice

To request removal of penalties based on erroneous written advice from us, submit a completed Claim for Refund and Request for Abatement (Form 843) to the IRS service center where you filed your tax return. For a copy of the form or to find your IRS service center, go to www.irs.gov or call 1-800-829-0922.

Removal or reduction of penalties

We understand that circumstances—such as serious illness or injury, a family member's death, or loss of financial records due to natural disaster—may make it difficult for you to meet your taxpayer responsibility in a timely manner.

If you would like us to consider removing or reducing any of your penalty charges, please do the following:
- Identify which penalty charges you would like us to remove or reduce (e.g., 2005 late filing penalty).
- For each penalty charge, explain why you believe removal or reduction is appropriate.
- Sign your statement, and mail it to us along with any supporting documents.

We will review your statement and let you know whether we accept your explanation as reasonable cause to reduce or remove the penalty charge(s).

Notice	CP501
Tax Year	2014
Notice date	December 16, 2016
Social Security number	

Interest charges

We are required by law to charge interest on unpaid tax from the date the tax return was due to the date the tax is paid in full. The interest is charged as long as there is an unpaid amount due, including penalties, if applicable. (Internal Revenue Code section 6601)

Description	Amount
Total interest	

The table below shows the rates used to calculate the interest on your unpaid amount due. For a detailed calculation of your interest, call 1-800-829-0922.

Period	Interest rate
July 1, 2013–December 31, 2013	8%
January 1, 2014–March 31, 2014	7%
April 1, 2014–June 30, 2014	6%
July 1, 2014–September 30, 2014	5%
October 1, 2014–December 31, 2014	6%
Beginning January 1, 2015	5%

Additional information

- Visit www.irs.gov/cp501
- For tax forms, instructions, and publications, visit www.irs.gov or call 1-800-TAX-FORM (1-800-829-3676).
- Paying online is convenient, secure, and ensures timely receipt of your payment. To pay your taxes online or for more information, go to www.irs.gov/directpay.
- Keep this notice for your records.

We're required to send a copy of this notice to both you and your spouse. Each copy contains the same information about your joint account. Please note: Only pay the amount due once.
If you need assistance, please don't hesitate to contact us.

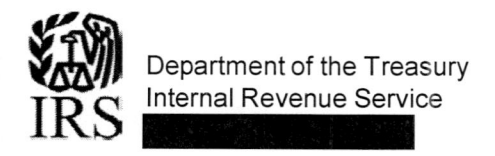

Notice	CP503
Tax Year	2014
Notice date	December 16, 2016
Social Security number	
To contact us	Phone
Your Caller ID	
Page 1 of 5	

Department of the Treasury
Internal Revenue Service

Second reminder: You have unpaid taxes for 2014

Amount due:

As we notified you before, our records show you have unpaid taxes for the tax year ending December 31, 2014 (Form 1040). If you don't pay ▮▮▮ by February 26, 2006, interest will increase and additional penalties may apply.

Billing Summary

Amount you owed
Failure-to-pay penalty
Interest charges
Amount due by January 26, 2015

What you need to do immediately

Pay immediately

- Pay the amount due of ▮▮▮ by January 26, 2015 to avoid additional penalty and interest charges. **You can pay online now at www.irs.gov/directpay.**

Continued on back...

Payment

Notice	CP503
Notice date	December 16, 2016
Social Security Number	

- Make your check or money order payable to the United States Treasury.
- Write your Social Security number ▮▮▮, the tax year (2014), and the form number (1040) on your payment and any correspondence.

Amount due by January 26, 2015

INTERNAL REVENUE SERVICE

EXHIBIT 4

Notice	CP503
Tax Year	2014
Notice date	December 16, 2016
Social Security number	

What you need to do immediately—continued

Pay immediately—**continued**

- If you can't pay the amount due, pay as much as you can now and make payment arrangements that allow you to pay off the rest over time. Visit www.irs.gov/payments for more information about:
  -- Credit and debit card payments
  -- Electronic payments
  -- Installment and payment plans:
    - Automatic deductions from your bank account
    - Payroll deductions

    - [Apply online or mail Form 9465, Installment Agreement Request.]

  -- Offer in Compromise- To see if you qualify for an offer, visit the Offer in Compromise Pre-Qualifier tool at www.irs.gov/Individuals/Offer-in-Compromise-1

  Or, call us at 1-800-XXX-XXXX to discuss your options

If you need to pay your tax debt over time, we encourage you to apply for
a Direct Debit Installment Agreement. These agreements save you time
and money by having your monthly payment automatically withdrawn from your bank account. There are no checks to write and mail and these agreements have a reduced user fee.

[Apply for a payment plan using the Online Payment Agreement application at: www.irs.gov and search "online-payment.".]
Apply for a payment plan by completing Form 433-F prior to calling us at 1-800-XXX-XXXX. This will assist us in handling your call more efficiently.]

[By setting up an agreement online now, you may be able to avoid the
filing of a Notice of Federal Tax Lien, if one hasn't already been filed. If a
Notice of Federal Tax Lien has been filed, certain taxpayers may request
the notice be withdrawn after establishing a Direct Debit Installment Agreement. For more information on liens, visit: www.irs.gov and search
"federal tax lien"].

If you already paid your balance in full within the past 14 days or made payment arrangements, please disregard this notice.

	Notice	CP503
	Tax Year	2014
	Notice date	December 16, 2016
	Social Security number	
	Page 3 of 5	

If we don't hear from you

- If you don't pay ▮▮▮▮ by January 26, 2015, interest will increase and additional penalties may apply.
- If you don't pay the amount due or call us to make payment arrangements, we can file a Notice of Federal Tax Lien on your property at any time, if we haven't already done so.
- If the lien is in place, you may find it difficult to sell or borrow against your property. The tax lien would also appear on your credit report—which may harm your credit rating--and your creditors would also be publicly notified that the IRS has priority to seize your property.
- If you don't pay your tax debt, we have the right to seize ("levy") your property.

Penalties

We are required by law to charge any applicable penalties.

Failure-to-pay

Description	Amount
Total failure-to-pay	▮▮▮▮

When you pay your taxes after the due date, we charge a penalty of 0.5% of the unpaid amount due per month, up to 25% of the amount due. We count part of a month as a full month. (Internal Revenue Code Section 6651)

For a detailed calculation of your penalty charges, call 1-800-829-0922.

IRS

Notice	CP503
Notice date	December 16, 2016
Social Security Number	

Contact information

If your address has changed, please call 1-800-829-0922 or visit www.irs.gov.

☐ Please check here if you've included any correspondence. Write your Social Security number ▮▮▮▮, the tax year (2014), and the form number (1040) on any correspondence.

☐ a.m.		☐ a.m.	
☐ p.m.		☐ p.m.	
Primary phone	Best time to call	Secondary phone	Best time to call

Notice	CP503
Tax Year	2014
Notice date	December 16, 2016
Social Security number	

Removal of penalties due to erroneous written advice from the IRS

If you were penalized based on written advice from the IRS, we will remove the penalty if you meet the following criteria:
- If you sent a written request to the IRS for written advice on a specific issue
- You gave us complete and accurate information
- You received written advice from us
- You reasonably relied on our written advice and were penalized based on that advice

To request removal of penalties based on erroneous written advice from us, submit a completed Claim for Refund and Request for Abatement (Form 843) to the IRS service center where you filed your tax return. For a copy of the form or to find your IRS service center, go to www.irs.gov or call 1-800-829-0922.

Removal or reduction of penalties

We understand that circumstances—such as serious illness or injury, a family member's death, or loss of financial records due to natural disaster—may make it difficult for you to meet your taxpayer responsibility in a timely manner.

If you would like us to consider removing or reducing any of your penalty charges, please do the following:
- Identify which penalty charges you would like us to remove or reduce (e.g., 2005 late filing penalty).
- For each penalty charge, explain why you believe removal or reduction is appropriate.
- Sign your statement, and mail it to us along with any supporting documents.

We will review your statement and let you know whether we accept your explanation as reasonable cause to reduce or remove the penalty charge(s).

Notice	CP503
Tax Year	2014
Notice date	December 16, 2016
Social Security number	

Interest charges

We are required by law to charge interest on unpaid tax from the date the tax return was due to the date the tax is paid in full. The interest is charged as long as there is an unpaid amount due, including penalties, if applicable. (Internal Revenue Code section 6601)

Description	Amount
Total interest	

The table below shows the rates used to calculate the interest on your unpaid amount due. For a detailed calculation of your interest, call 1-800-829-0922.

Period	Interest rate
July 1, 2013–December 31, 2013	8%
January 1, 2014–March 31, 2014	7%
April 1, 2014–June 30, 2014	6%
July 1, 2014–September 30, 2014	5%
October 1, 2014 December 31, 2014	6%
Beginning January 1, 2015	5%

Additional information

- Visit www.irs.gov/cp503.
- For tax forms, instructions, and publications, visit www.irs.gov or call 1-800-TAX-FORM (1-800-829-3676).
- Paying online is convenient, secure, and ensures timely receipt of your payment. To pay your taxes online or for more information, go to www.irs.gov/directpay.
- Keep this notice for your records.

We're required to send a copy of this notice to both you and your spouse. Each copy contains the same information about your joint account. Please note: Only pay the amount due once.
If you need assistance, please don't hesitate to contact us.

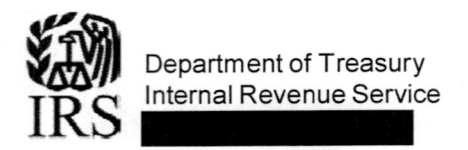

Notice	CP504
Tax Year	2014
Notice date	December 16, 2016
Social Security number	
To contact us	Phone
Your Caller ID	
Page 1 of 5	

Department of Treasury
Internal Revenue Service

Notice of Intent to Levy

Amount due immediately:

This is a notice of intent to seize ("levy") your state tax refund or other property. As we notified you before, our records show you have unpaid taxes for the tax year ending December 31, 2014 (Form 1040). If you don't call us immediately or pay the amount due, we may seize ("levy") your property or rights to property (including any state tax refunds) and apply it to the ▇ you owe.

Billing Summary

Tax you owe
Failure-to-pay penalty
Interest charges
Amount due immediately

What you need to do immediately

Pay immediately

- Pay the amount due of ▇. If you fail to pay by January 26, 2015, interest will increase and additional penalties may apply. If you don't pay by January 26, 2015, we may seize ("levy") your property or rights to property (including any state tax refunds). **You can pay online now at www.irs.gov/directpay.**

Continued on back..

Notice	CP504
Notice date	December 16, 2016
Social Security Number	

Payment

- Make your check or money order payable to the United States Treasury.
- Write your Social Security number ▇, the tax year (2014), and the form number (1040) on your payment and any correspondence.

Amount due immediately

INTERNAL REVENUE SERVICE

EXHIBIT 5

Notice	CP504
Tax Year	2014
Notice date	December 16, 2016
Social Security number	

What you need to do immediately—continued

Pay immediately—**continued**

- If you can't pay the amount due, pay as much as you can now and make payment arrangements that allow you to pay off the rest over time. Visit www.irs.gov/Payments for more information about:
  -- Credit and debit card payments
  -- Electronic payments
  -- Installment and payment plans:
    - Automatic deductions from your bank account
    - Payroll deductions
    - [Apply online or mail Form 9465, Installment Agreement Request.]

  -- Offer in Compromise- To see if you qualify for an offer, visit the Offer in Compromise Pre-Qualifier tool at www.irs.gov/Individuals/Offer-in-Compromise-1.

Or, call us at 1-800-XXX-XXXX to discuss your options.]

If you need to pay your tax debt over time, we encourage you to apply for a Direct Debit Installment Agreement. These agreements save you time and money by having your monthly payment automatically withdrawn from your bank account. There are no checks to write and mail and these agreements have a reduced user fee.

[Apply for a payment plan using the Online Payment Agreement application at:www.irs.gov and search "online-payment.".

[Apply for a payment plan by completing Form 433-F prior to calling us at 1-800-XXX-XXXX. This will assist us in handling your call more efficiently.]

[By setting up an agreement online now, you may be able to avoid the filing of a Notice of Federal Tax Lien, if one hasn't already been filed. If a Notice of Federal Tax Lien has been filed, certain taxpayers may request the notice be withdrawn after establishing a Direct Debit Installment Agreement. For more information on liens, visit: www.irs.gov and search "federal tax lien".]

If you already paid your balance in full or believe we haven't credited a payment to your account, please call 1-800-XXX-XXXX, and have your payment information available to review with us. You can also contact us by mail. Fill out the Contact information section, detach, and send it to us with any correspondence or documentation, including proof of payment.

If we don't hear from you	• If you don't pay or make payment arrangements by ▮▮▮ we may seize ("levy") your property (including any state tax refund).
• Property and your rights to property include:
-Wages, real estate commissions, and other income
-Bank Accounts
-Personal assets (e.g., your car and home)
-Social Security Benefits
• This is your **Notice of Intent to Levy**. (Internal Revenue Code section 6331(d)).
• If you don't pay the amount due or call us to make payment arrangements, we may file a notice of Federal Tax Lien in your property at any time, if we haven't already done so.
• If the lien is filed, you may find it difficult to sell or borrow against your property. The Notice of federal Tax Lien would also appear on your credit report—which may harm your credit rating—and your creditors would also be publicly notified that the IRS has priority to seize your property.
Penalties	We are required by law to charge any applicable penalties.
Failure-to-pay	Description Amount
Total failure-to-pay
When you pay your taxes after the due date, we charge a penalty of 0.5% of the unpaid amount due per month, up to 25% of the amount due. Beginning 10 days after we issue this notice, the penalty increases to 1.0% for each month the amount remains unpaid. We count part of a month as a full month. (Internal Revenue Code section 6651)
For a detailed calculation of your penalty charges, call 1-800-829-0922.

Contact information

Notice CP504
Notice date December 16, 2016
Social Security Number ▮▮▮▮

If your address has changed, please call 1-800-829-0922 or visit www.irs.gov.

☐ Please check here if you've included any correspondence. Write your Social Security number ▮▮▮▮, the tax year (2014), and the form number (1040) on any correspondence.

Primary phone	Best time to call	Secondary phone	Best time to call
	☐ a.m. ☐ p.m.		☐ a.m. ☐ p.m.

Notice	CP504
Tax Year	2014
Notice date	December 16, 2016
Social Security number	

Removal or reduction of penalties

We understand that circumstances—such as serious illness or injury, a family member's death, or loss of financial records due to natural disaster—may make it difficult for you to meet your taxpayer responsibility in a timely manner.

If you would like us to consider removing or reducing any of your penalty charges, please do the following:

- Identify which penalty charges you would like us to remove or reduce (e.g., 2005 late filing penalty).
- For each penalty charge, explain why you believe removal or reduction is appropriate.
- Sign your statement, and mail it to us with any supporting documents. We will review your statement and let you know whether we accept your explanation as reasonable cause to reduce or remove the penalty charge(s).

Removal of penalties due to erroneous written advice from the IRS

If you were penalized based on written advice from the IRS, we will remove the penalty if you meet the following criteria:

- If you sent a written request to the IRS for written advice on a specific issue
- You gave us complete and accurate information
- You received written advice from us
- You reasonably relied on our written advice and were penalized based on that advice

To request removal of penalties based on erroneous written advice from us, submit a completed Claim for Refund and Request for Abatement (Form 843) to the IRS service center where you filed your tax return. For a copy of the form or to find your IRS service center, go to www.irs.gov or call 1-800-829-8374.

Notice	CP504
Tax Year	2014
Notice date	December 16, 2016
Social Security number	

Page 5 of 5

Interest charges

We are required by law to charge interest on unpaid tax from the date the tax return was due to the date the tax is paid in full. The interest is charged as long as there is an unpaid amount due, including penalties, if applicable. (Internal Revenue Code section 6601)

Description	Amount
Total interest	

The table below shows the rates used to calculate the interest on your unpaid amount due. For a detailed calculation of your interest, call 1-800-829-0922.

Period	Interest rate
October 1, 2013–June 30, 2013	7%
July 1, 2013–December 31, 2013	8%
January 1, 2014–March 31, 2014	7%
April 1, 2014–June 30, 2014	6%
July 1, 2014–September 30, 2014	5%
October 1, 2014–December 31, 2014	6%
Beginning January 1, 2015	5%

Additional information

- Visit www.irs.gov/cp504.
- For tax forms, instructions, and publications, visit www.irs.gov or call 1-800-TAX-FORM (1-800-829-3676).
- Paying online is convenient, secure, and ensures timely receipt of your payment. To pay your taxes online or for more information, go to www.irs.gov/directpay.
- Review the enclosed document: IRS Collection Process (Publication 594)
- Generally, we deal directly with taxpayers or their authorized representatives. Sometimes, however, it's necessary for us to speak with other people, such as employees, employers, banks, or neighbors to gather the information we need about a taxpayer's account. You have the right to request a list of individuals we've contacted in connection with your account at any time.
- Keep this notice for your records.

[We're required to send a copy of this notice to both you and your spouse. Each copy contains the same information about your joint account. Please note: Only pay the amount due once.]
If you need assistance, please don't hesitate to contact us.

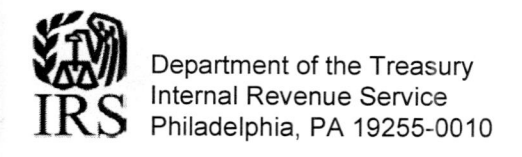

Department of the Treasury Internal Revenue Service Philadelphia, PA 19255-0010	Notice **CP90** Notice date **January 23, 2019** Social Security number **999-99-9999** To contact us **Phone 800-829-1040** Your Caller ID **9999** Page 1 of 5

JAMES & KAREN Q. SPARROW
22 BOULDER STREET
HANSON, CT 00000-7253

Intent to seize your assets and notice of your right to a hearing

Amount due immediately: $5,947.81

We haven't received full payment despite sending you several notices about your unpaid federal taxes. The IRS may seize (levy) your property. However, you can appeal the proposed seizure (levy) of your assets by requesting a Collection Due Process hearing (Internal Revenue Code Section 6330) by **February 22, 2019.**

Billing Summary

Amount you owed	$5,947.81
Additional failure-to-pay penalty	0.00
Additional interest charges	0.00
Amount due immediately	**$5,947.81**

Continued on back...

Payment

James & Karen Q. Sparrow
22 Boulder Street
Hanson, CT 00000-7253

Notice **CP90**
Notice date **January 23, 2019**
Social Security number **999-99-9999**

- Make your check or money order payable to the United States Treasury.
- Write your Social Security number (999-99-9999) and tax period(s) on your payment and any correspondence.

Amount due immediately	$5,947.81

INTERNAL REVENUE SERVICE
PHILADELPHIA, PA 19255-0010

0000 0000000 0000000000 0000000 0000

EXHIBIT 6

Notice	CP90
Notice date	January 23, 2019
Social Security number	999-99-9999

What you need to do immediately

Pay immediately

- Send us the amount due of **$5,947.81**, or we may seize (levy) your property on or after **February 22, 2019**.
- If you can't pay the amount due, pay as much as you can now and ma[ke] payment arrangements that allow you to pay off the rest over time. Vis[it] www.irs.gov/payments for more information about:
  - Installment and payment agreements—download required forms or save time and money by applying online if you qualify
  - Automatic deductions from your bank account
  - Payroll deductions
  - Credit card payments

  Or, call us at 1-800-xxx-xxxx to discuss your options.
- If you've already paid your balance in full or think we haven't credited a payment to your account, please send proof of that payment.

Right to request a Collection Due Process hearing

If you wish to appeal this proposed levy action, complete and mail the enclosed Form 12153, Request for a Collection Due Process or Equivale[nt] Hearing, by **February 22, 2019**. Send the form to us at the address liste[d] at the top of page 1. Be sure to include the reason you are requesting a hearing (see section 8 of, and the instructions to, Form 12153) as well as other information requested by the form. If you don't file Form 12153 by **February 22, 2019**, you will lose the ability to contest Appeals' decision the U.S. Tax Court.

About Federal Tax Liens

The tax lien is a claim against all of your property that arises once you h[ave] not paid your bill. If you don't pay the amount due or call us to make payment arrangements, we can file a Notice of Federal Tax Lien at any time, if we haven't already done so. The Notice of Federal Tax Lien publically notifies your creditors that the IRS has a lien (or claim) agains[t] your property, including property acquired by you after the Notice of Federal Tax Lien is filed. Once the lien's notice to creditors has been file[d] it may appear on your credit report and may harm your credit rating

Notice	CP90
Notice date	January 23, 2019
Social Security number	999-99-9999

Contact information

If your address has changed, please call 1-800-xxx-xxxx or visit www.irs.gov.

☐ Please check here if you've included any correspondence. Write your Social Security number (999-99-9999) and tax period(s) on any correspondence.

	☐ a.m. ☐ p.m.		☐ a.m. ☐ p.m.
Primary phone	Best time to call	Secondary phone	Best time to call

Notice	CP90
Notice date	January 23, 2019
Social Security number	999-99-9999

What you need to do immediately-continued

or make it difficult for you to get credit (such as a loan or credit card). It cannot be released until your bill, including interest, penalties, and fees, is paid in full, we accept a bond guaranteeing payment of the amount owed, or we determine that you don't owe or the liability is reduced to zero. The lien's notice to creditors may be withdrawn under certain circumstances. You can find additional information about tax liens, including helpful videos, at http://www.irs.gov/Businesses/Small-Businesses-&-Self-Employed/Understanding-a-Federal-Tax-Lien or by typing lien in the IRS.gov search box.

Denial or revocation of United States passport

On December 4, 2015, as part of the Fixing America's Surface Transportation (FAST) Act, Congress enacted section 7345 of the Internal Revenue Code, which requires the Internal Revenue Service to notify the State Department of taxpayers certified as owing a seriously delinquent tax debt. The FAST Act generally prohibits the State Department from issuing or renewing a passport to a taxpayer with seriously delinquent tax debt.

Seriously delinquent tax debt means an unpaid, legally enforceable federal tax debt of an individual totaling more than $52,000 for which, a Notice of Federal Tax lien has been filed and all administrative remedies under IRC § 6320 have lapsed or been exhausted, or a levy has been issued. If you are individually liable for tax debt (including penalties and interest) totaling more than $52,000 and you do not pay the amount you owe or make alternate arrangements to pay, we may notify the State Department that your tax debt is seriously delinquent. The State Department generally will not issue or renew a passport to you after we make this notification. If you currently have a valid passport, the State Department may revoke your passport or limit your ability to travel outside the United States. Additional information on passport certification is available at www.irs.gov/passports.

If we don't hear from you

If you don't call us immediately, pay the amount due, or request a hearing by **February 22, 2019**, we may seize (levy) your property or your rights to property. Property includes:
- Wages and other income
- Bank accounts
- Business assets
- Personal assets (including your car and home)
- State tax refund
- Social Security benefits

Your billing details

Tax period ending	Form number	Amount you owed	Additional interest	Additional penalty	Total
12-31-2007	1040	$9,999.99	$9,999.99	$9,999.99	$9,999.99
9999	9999	$9,999.99	$9,999.99	$9,999.99	$9,999.99

Notice	CP90
Notice date	January 23, 2019
Social Security number	999-99-9999

Penalties

We are required by law to charge any applicable penalties.

Failure-to-pay

We assess a 1/2% monthly penalty for not paying the tax you owe by the due date. We base the monthly penalty for paying late on the net unpaid tax at the beginning of each penalty month following the payment due date for that tax. This penalty applies even if you filed the return on time.

We charge the penalty for each month or part of a month the payment is late; however, the penalty can't be more than 25% in total.

- The due date for payment of the tax shown on a return generally is the return due date, without regard to extensions.
- The due date for paying increases in tax is within 21 days of the date of our notice demanding payment (10 business days if the amount in the notice is $100,000 or more).

If we issue a Notice of Intent to Levy and you don't pay the balance due within 10 days of the date of the notice, the penalty for paying late increases to 1% per month.

For individuals who filed on time, the penalty decreases to 1/4% per month while an approved installment agreement with the IRS is in effect for payment of that tax.

For a detailed computation of the penalty call 1-800-xxx-xxxx.

(Internal Revenue Code Section 6651)

Removal or reduction of penalties

We understand that circumstances—such as serious illness or injury, a family member's death, or loss of financial records due to natural disaster—may make it difficult for you to meet your taxpayer responsibility in a timely manner.

We can generally process your request for penalty removal or reduction quicker if you contact us at the number listed above with the following information:
- Identify which penalty charges you would like us to reconsider (e.g., 2016 late filing penalty).
- For each penalty charge, explain why you believe it should be reconsidered.

If you write us, include a signed statement and supporting documentation for penalty abatement request.

We'll review your statement and let you know whether we accept your explanation as reasonable cause to reduce or remove the penalty charge(s).

Removal of penalties due to erroneous written advice from the IRS

If you were penalized based on written advice from the IRS, we will remove the penalty if you meet the following criteria:
- You wrote us for written advice on a specific issue
- You gave us adequate and accurate information
- You received written advice from us
- You reasonably relied on our written advice and were penalized based on that advice

Notice	CP90
Notice date	January 23, 2019
Social Security number	999-99-9999

Removal of penalties due to erroneous written advice from the IRS - **continued**	To request removal of penalties based on erroneous written advice from us, submit a completed Claim for Refund and Request for Abatement (Form 843) to the address shown above. For a copy of the form, go to www.irs.gov or call 1-800-TAX-FORM (1-800-829-3676).
Interest charges	We are required by law to charge interest when you don't pay your liability on time. Generally, we calculate interest from the due date of your return (regardless of extensions) until you pay the amount you owe in full, including accrued interest and any penalty charges. Interest on some penalties accrues from the date we notify you of the penalty until it is paid in full. Interest on other penalties, such as failure to file a tax return, starts from the due date or extended due date of the return. Interest rates are variable and may change quarterly. (Internal Revenue Code Section 6601) For a detailed calculation of your interest, call 1-800-xxx-xxxx.

Additional information	- Visit www.irs.gov/cp90
	- For tax forms, instructions, and publications, visit www.irs.gov or call 1-800-TAX-FORM (1-800-829-3676).
	- Review the enclosed documents:
	  – IRS Collection Process (Publication 594)
	  – Collection Appeal Rights (Publication 1660)
	  – Request for a Collection Due Process Hearing (Form 12153)
	- Keep this notice for your records.
	
	We're required to send a copy of this notice to both you and your spouse. Each copy contains the information you are authorized to receive. Please note: Only pay the amount due once.
	
	If you need assistance, please don't hesitate to contact us

Form **12153**
(Rev. 12-2013)

Request for a Collection Due Process or Equivalent Hearing

Use this form to request a Collection Due Process (CDP) or equivalent hearing with the IRS Office of Appeals if you have been issued one of the following lien or levy notices:

- Notice of Federal Tax Lien Filing and Your Right to a Hearing under IRC 6320,
- Notice of Intent to Levy and Notice of Your Right to a Hearing,
- Notice of Jeopardy Levy and Right of Appeal,
- Notice of Levy on Your State Tax Refund,
- Notice of Levy and Notice of Your Right to a Hearing.

Complete this form and send it to the address shown on your lien or levy notice. Include a copy of your lien or levy notice to ensure proper handling of your request.

Call the phone number on the notice or 1-800-829-1040 if you are not sure about the correct address or if you want to fax your request.

You can find a section explaining the deadline for requesting a Collection Due Process hearing in this form's instructions. If you've missed the deadline for requesting a CDP hearing, you must check line 7 (Equivalent Hearing) to request an equivalent hearing.

1. Taxpayer Name: (Taxpayer 1) _____

   Taxpayer Identification Number _____

   Current Address _____

   City _____ State _____ Zip Code _____

2. Telephone Number and Best Time to Call During Normal Business Hours
   - Home (___) ___ - _____ ☐ am. ☐ pm.
   - Work (___) ___ - _____ ☐ am. ☐ pm.
   - Cell (___) ___ - _____ ☐ am. ☐ pm.

3. Taxpayer Name: (Taxpayer 2) _____

   Taxpayer Identification Number _____

   Current Address _____
   (If Different from Address Above)

   City _____ State _____ Zip Code _____

4. Telephone Number and Best Time to Call During Normal Business Hours
   - Home (___) ___ - _____ ☐ am. ☐ pm.
   - Work (___) ___ - _____ ☐ am. ☐ pm.
   - Cell (___) ___ - _____ ☐ am. ☐ pm.

5. Tax Information as Shown on the Lien or Levy Notice (*If possible, attach a copy of the notice*)

Type of Tax (Income, Employment, Excise, etc. or Civil Penalty)	Tax Form Number (1040, 941, 720, etc)	Tax Period or Periods

Form **12153** (Rev. 12-2013)　　Catalog Number 26685D　　www.irs.gov　　Department of the Treasury - **Internal Revenue Service**

EXHIBIT 7

Form **12153**
(Rev. 12-2013)

Request for a Collection Due Process or Equivalent Hearing

6. Basis for Hearing Request (Both boxes can be checked if you have received both a lien and levy notice)

☐ Filed Notice of Federal Tax Lien   ☐ Proposed Levy or Actual Levy

7. Equivalent Hearing (See the instructions for more information on Equivalent Hearings)

☐ I would like an Equivalent Hearing - I would like a hearing equivalent to a CDP Hearing if my request for a CDP hearing does not meet the requirements for a timely CDP Hearing.

8. Check the most appropriate box for the reason you disagree with the filing of the lien or the levy. **See page 4 of this form for examples.** You can add more pages if you don't have enough space. If, during your CDP Hearing, you think you would like to discuss a Collection Alternative to the action proposed by the Collection function it is recommended you submit a completed Form 433A (Individual) and/or Form 433B (Business), as appropriate, with this form. See www.irs.gov for copies of the forms. Generally, the Office of Appeals will ask the Collection Function to review, verify and provide their opinion on any new information you submit. We will share their comments with you and give you the opportunity to respond.

Collection Alternative   ☐ Installment Agreement   ☐ Offer in Compromise   ☐ I Cannot Pay Balance

Lien   ☐ Subordination   ☐ Discharge   ☐ Withdrawal
Please explain:

My Spouse Is Responsible   ☐ Innocent Spouse Relief (Please attach Form 8857, *Request for Innocent Spouse Relief,* to your request.)

Other (*For examples, see page 4*)   ☐

Reason (*You must provide a reason for the dispute or your request for a CDP hearing will not be honored. Use as much space as you need to explain the reason for your request. Attach extra pages if necessary.*):

---

9. Signatures   I understand the CDP hearing and any subsequent judicial review will suspend the statutory period of limitations for collection action. I also understand my representative or I must sign and date this request before the IRS Office of Appeals can accept it. If you are signing as an officer of a company add your title (*president, secretary, etc.*) behind your signature.

SIGN HERE

Taxpayer 1's Signature	Date
Taxpayer 2's Signature (*if a joint request, both must sign*)	Date

☐ I request my CDP hearing be held with my authorized representative (*attach a copy of Form 2848*)

Authorized Representative's Signature	Authorized Representative's Name	Telephone Number

IRS Use Only

IRS Employee (Print)	Employee Telephone Number	IRS Received Date

Form **12153** (Rev. 12-2013)   Catalog Number 26685D   www.irs.gov   Department of the Treasury - **Internal Revenue Service**

Information You Need To Know When Requesting A Collection Due Process Hearing

What Is the Deadline for Requesting a Timely Collection Due Process (CDP) Hearing?

- Your request for a CDP hearing about a Federal Tax Lien filing must be postmarked by the date indicated in the *Notice of Federal Tax Lien Filing and Your Right to a Hearing under IRC 6320* (lien notice).

- Your request for a CDP hearing about a levy must be postmarked within 30 days after the date of the *Notice of Intent to Levy and Notice of Your Right to a Hearing* (levy notice) or Notice of Your Right to a Hearing After an Actual Levy.

Your timely request for a CDP hearing will prohibit levy action in most cases. A timely request for CDP hearing will also suspend the 10-year period we have, by law, to collect your taxes. Both the prohibition on levy and the suspension of the 10-year period will last until the determination the IRS Office of Appeals makes about your disagreement is final. The amount of time the suspension is in effect will be added to the time remaining in the 10-year period. For example, if the 10-year period is suspended for six months, the time left in the period we have to collect taxes will be extended by six months.

You can go to court to appeal the CDP determination the IRS Office of Appeals makes about your disagreement.

What Is an Equivalent Hearing?

If you still want a hearing with the IRS Office of Appeals after the deadline for requesting a timely CDP hearing has passed, you can use this form to request an equivalent hearing. You must check the Equivalent Hearing box on line 7 of the form to request an equivalent hearing. **An equivalent hearing request does not prohibit levy or suspend the 10-year period for collecting your taxes; also, you cannot go to court to appeal the IRS Office of Appeals' decision about your disagreement.** You must request an equivalent hearing within the following timeframe:

- Lien Notice—one year plus five business days from the filing date of the Notice of Federal Tax Lien.
- Levy Notice—one year from the date of the levy notice.
- Your request for a CDP levy hearing, whether timely or Equivalent, does not prohibit the Service from filing a Notice of Federal Tax Lien.

Where Should You File Your CDP or Equivalent Hearing Request?

File your request by mail at the address on your lien notice or levy notice. You may also fax your request. Call the telephone number on the lien or levy notice to ask for the fax number. **Do not send your CDP or equivalent hearing request directly to the IRS Office of Appeals, it must be sent to the address on the lien or levy notice. If you send your request directly to Appeals it may result in your request not being considered a timely request. Depending upon your issue the originating function may contact you in an attempt to resolve the issue(s) raised in your request prior to forwarding your request to Appeals.**

Where Can You Get Help?

You can call the telephone number on the lien or levy notice with your questions about requesting a hearing. The contact person listed on the notice or other representative can access your tax information and answer your questions.

In addition, you may qualify for representation by a low-income taxpayer clinic for free or nominal charge. Our Publication 4134, Low Income Taxpayer Clinic List, provides information on clinics in your area.

If you are experiencing economic harm, the Taxpayer Advocate Service (TAS) may be able to help you resolve your problems with the IRS. TAS cannot extend the time you have to request a CDP or equivalent hearing. See Publication 594, *The IRS Collection Process*, or visit www.irs.gov/advocate/index-html. You also can call 1-877-777-4778 for TAS assistance.

Note–The IRS Office of Appeals will not consider frivolous requests. You can find examples of frivolous reasons for requesting a hearing or disagreeing with a tax assessment in Publication 2105, *Why do I have to Pay Taxes?*, or at **www.irs.gov** by typing "frivolous" into the search engine.

> **You can get copies of tax forms, schedules, instructions, publications, and notices at www.irs.gov, at your local IRS office, or by calling toll-free *1-800-TAX-FORM (829-3676).***

Form **12153** (Rev. 12-2013)   Catalog Number 26685D   www.irs.gov   Department of the Treasury - **Internal Revenue Service**

Information You Need To Know When Requesting A Collection Due Process Hearing

What Are Examples of Reasons for Requesting a Hearing?

You will have to explain your reason for requesting a hearing when you make your request. Below are examples of reasons for requesting a hearing.

You want a collection alternative— "I would like to propose a different way to pay the money I owe." Common collection alternatives include:

- Full payment—you pay your taxes by personal check, cashier's check, money order, or credit card.
- Installment Agreement—you pay your taxes fully or partially by making monthly payments.
- Offer in Compromise—you offer to make a payment or payments to settle your tax liability for less than the full amount you owe.

"I cannot pay my taxes." Some possible reasons why you cannot pay your taxes are: (1) you have a terminal illness or excessive medical bills; (2) your only source of income is Social Security payments, welfare payments, or unemployment benefit payments; (3) you are unemployed with little or no income; (4) you have reasonable expenses exceeding your income; or (5) you have some other hardship condition. The IRS Office of Appeals may consider freezing collection action until your circumstances improve. Penalty and interest will continue to accrue on the unpaid balance.

You want action taken about the filing of the tax lien against your property—You can get a Federal Tax Lien released if you pay your taxes in full. You also may request a lien subordination, discharge, or withdrawal. See www.irs.gov for more information.

When you request **lien subordination**, you are asking the IRS to make a Federal Tax Lien secondary to a non-IRS lien. For example, you may ask for a subordination of the Federal Tax Lien to get a refinancing mortgage on your house or other real property you own. You would ask to make the Federal Tax Lien secondary to the mortgage, even though the mortgage came after the tax lien filing. The IRS Office of Appeals would consider lien subordination, in this example, if you used the mortgage proceeds to pay your taxes.

When you request a **lien discharge**, you are asking the IRS to remove a Federal Tax Lien from a specific property. For example, you may ask for a discharge of the Federal Tax Lien in order to sell your house if you use all of the sale proceeds to pay your taxes even though the sale proceeds will not fully pay all of the tax you owe.

When you request a **lien withdrawal**, you are asking the IRS to remove the Notice of Federal Tax Lien (NFTL) information from public records because you believe the NFTL should not have been filed. For example, you may ask for a withdrawal of the filing of the NFTL if you believe the IRS filed the NFTL prematurely or did not follow procedures, or you have entered into an installment agreement and the installment agreement does not provide for the filing of the NFTL. A withdrawal does not remove the lien from your IRS records.

Your spouse is responsible—"My spouse (or former spouse) is responsible for all or part of the tax liability." You may believe that your spouse or former spouse is the only one responsible for all or a part of the tax liability. If this is the case, you are requesting a hearing so you can receive relief as an innocent spouse. You should complete and attach Form 8857, *Request for Innocent Spouse Relief*, to your hearing request.

Other Reasons—"I am not liable for (I don't owe) all or part of the taxes." You can raise a disagreement about the amount you owe only if you did not receive a deficiency notice for the liability (a notice explaining why you owe taxes—it gives you the right to challenge in court, within a specific timeframe, the additional tax the IRS says you owe), or if you have not had another prior opportunity to disagree with the amount you owe.

"I do not believe I should be responsible for penalties." The IRS Office of Appeals may remove all or part of the penalties if you have a reasonable cause for not paying or not filing on time. See Notice 746, Information About Your Notice, Penalty and Interest for what is reasonable cause for removing penalties.

"I have already paid all or part of my taxes." You disagree with the amount the IRS says you haven't paid if you think you have not received credit for payments you have already made.

See Publication 594, *The IRS Collection Process*, for more information on the following topics: Installment Agreements and Offers in Compromise; Lien Subordination, Discharge, and Withdrawal; Innocent Spouse Relief; Temporarily Delay Collection; and belief that tax bill is wrong.

Form **12153** (Rev. 12-2013)   Catalog Number 26685D   www.irs.gov   Department of the Treasury - **Internal Revenue Service**

Internal Revenue Service
United States Department of the Treasury

This Product Contains Sensitive Taxpayer Data

Account Transcript

Request Date: 03-23-2020
Response Date: 03-23-2020
Tracking Number: 100514376791

FORM NUMBER: CIVIL PENALTY

TAX PERIOD: Jun. 30, 2014

TAXPAYER IDENTIFICATION NUMBER: XXX-XX-xxxx

<<<<POWER OF ATTORNEY/TAX INFORMATION AUTHORIZATION (POA/TIA) ON FILE>>>>

--- ANY MINUS SIGN SHOWN BELOW SIGNIFIES A CREDIT AMOUNT ---

ACCOUNT BALANCE: 0.00
ACCRUED INTEREST: 0.00   AS OF: Apr. 06, 2020

ACCOUNT BALANCE PLUS ACCRUALS
(this is not a payoff amount): 0.00

** INFORMATION FROM THE RETURN OR AS ADJUSTED **

TRANSACTIONS

CODE	EXPLANATION OF TRANSACTION	CYCLE	DATE	AMOUNT
240	Miscellaneous penalty IRC 6672 Trust Fund Recovery Penalty 08-24-2025	20153105	08-24-2015	$31,351.75
n/a	83254-612-52026-5			

EXHIBIT 8

Code	Description	Cycle	Date	Amount
290	Additional tax assessed 00-00-0000	20153105	08-24-2015	$0.00
n/a	83254-612-52026-5			
960	Appointed representative		07-31-2015	$0.00
971	Notice issued CP 015B		08-24-2015	$0.00
971	Collection due process Notice of Intent to Levy -- issued		09-09-2015	$0.00
582	Lien placed on assets due to balance owed		09-18-2015	$0.00
360	Fees and other expenses for collection		10-12-2015	$106.00
971	Issued notice of lien filing and right to Collection Due Process hearing		09-22-2015	$0.00
971	Unclaimed notice of lien filing and right to Collection Due Process hearing		10-20-2015	$0.00
971	Collection due process Notice of Intent to Levy -- refused or unclaimed		10-28-2015	$0.00
240	Miscellaneous penalty IRC 6672 Trust Fund Recovery Penalty 05-23-2026	20161805	05-23-2016	$22,283.24
n/a	85254-524-52095-6			
290	Additional tax assessed 00-00-0000	20161805	05-23-2016	$0.00
n/a	85254-524-52095-6			
971	Notice issued CP 015B		05-23-2016	$0.00
530	Balance due account currently not collectable		10-28-2016	$0.00
537	Account currently considered collectable		10-16-2017	$0.00
241	Reduced or removed miscellaneous penalty IRC 6672 Trust Fund Recovery Penalty Balance Due to Payment by Related Business Entity		06-14-2017	-$22,283.24
n/a	13254-429-53168-8			
241	Reduced or removed miscellaneous penalty IRC 6672 Trust Fund Recovery Penalty Balance Due to Payment by Related Business Entity		06-14-2017	-$963.78
n/a	13254-429-53189-8			
670	Payment Levy		05-13-2019	-$841.83
670	Payment Levy		05-20-2019	-$898.01
670	Payment Levy		05-28-2019	-$898.01
670	Payment Levy		06-03-2019	-$898.01
670	Payment		06-10-2019	-$898.01

Code	Description	Date	Amount
	Levy		
670	Payment Levy	06-17-2019	-$895.32
670	Payment Levy	06-24-2019	-$895.32
530	Balance due account currently not collectable	07-03-2019	$0.00
670	Payment Levy	07-01-2019	-$895.32
670	Payment Levy	07-09-2019	-$769.82
670	Payment Levy	07-16-2019	-$895.32
670	Payment Levy	07-22-2019	-$895.31
670	Payment Levy	07-31-2019	-$895.32
670	Payment Levy	08-05-2019	-$895.32
670	Payment Levy	08-12-2019	-$895.32
670	Payment Levy	08-19-2019	-$895.32
670	Payment Levy	08-26-2019	-$895.32
670	Payment Levy	09-03-2019	-$895.32
670	Payment Levy	09-09-2019	-$895.31
670	Payment Levy	09-16-2019	-$895.32
537	Account currently considered collectable	10-14-2019	$0.00
670	Payment Levy	09-23-2019	-$895.33
670	Payment Levy	09-30-2019	-$895.32
670	Payment Levy	10-07-2019	-$895.31
670	Payment Levy	10-15-2019	-$895.32

670	Payment Levy			10-21-2019	-$895.32
670	Payment Levy			10-28-2019	-$895.31
670	Payment Levy			11-04-2019	-$895.32
670	Payment Levy			11-12-2019	-$895.33
670	Payment Levy			11-18-2019	-$895.32
670	Payment Levy			11-25-2019	-$895.31
670	Payment Levy			12-02-2019	-$895.32
670	Payment Levy			12-09-2019	-$895.32
670	Payment Levy			12-16-2019	-$895.32
670	Payment Levy			12-23-2019	-$895.31
670	Payment Levy			12-30-2019	-$346.86
670	Payment Levy			01-07-2020	-$895.32
670	Payment Levy			01-13-2020	-$896.64
196	Interest charged for late payment		20200405	02-10-2020	$1,022.14
670	Payment Levy			01-21-2020	-$897.48
196	Interest charged for late payment		20200505	02-17-2020	$897.48
670	Payment Levy			01-27-2020	-$897.49
196	Interest charged for late payment		20200605	02-24-2020	$897.49
670	Payment Levy			02-03-2020	-$897.50
196	Interest charged for late payment		20200705	03-02-2020	$897.50
670	Payment Levy			02-10-2020	-$897.49
196	Interest charged for late payment		20200805	03-09-2020	$897.49

670	Payment Levy		02-18-2020	-$897.48
196	Interest charged for late payment	20200905	03-16-2020	$897.48
670	Payment Levy		02-24-2020	-$897.49
196	Interest charged for late payment	20201005	03-23-2020	$897.49
670	Payment Levy		03-02-2020	-$707.43
196	Interest charged for late payment	20201105	03-30-2020	$707.43

This Product Contains Sensitive Taxpayer Data

Form **433-B**
(February 2019)
Department of the Treasury
Internal Revenue Service

Collection Information Statement for Businesses

Note: *Complete all entry spaces with the current data available or "N/A" (not applicable). Failure to complete all entry spaces may result in rejection of your request or significant delay in account resolution.* **Include attachments if additional space is needed to respond completely to any question.**

Section 1: Business Information

1a Business Name	2a Employer Identification No. (EIN)
1b Business Street Address	2b Type of entity *(Check appropriate box below)*
Mailing Address	☐ Partnership ☐ Corporation ☐ Other
City ____ State ____ ZIP ____	☐ Limited Liability Company (LLC) classified as a corporation
1c County	☐ Other LLC - Include number of members ____
1d Business Telephone ( )	2c Date Incorporated/Established ____ *mmddyyyy*
1e Type of Business	3a Number of Employees
	3b Monthly Gross Payroll
	3c Frequency of Tax Deposits
1f Business Website (web address)	3d Is the business enrolled in Electronic Federal Tax Payment System (EFTPS) ☐ Yes ☐ No

4 Does the business engage in e-Commerce *(Internet sales)* If yes, complete 5a and 5b.   ☐ Yes   ☐ No

PAYMENT PROCESSOR *(e.g., PayPal, Authorize.net, Google Checkout, etc.)* Include virtual currency wallet, exchange or digital currency exchange.

Name and Address *(Street, City, State, ZIP code)*	Payment Processor Account Number
5a	
5b	

CREDIT CARDS ACCEPTED BY THE BUSINESS

Type of Credit Card *(e.g., Visa, Mastercard, etc.)*	Merchant Account Number	Issuing Bank Name and Address *(Street, City, State, ZIP code)*
6a		Phone
6b		Phone
6c		Phone

Section 2: Business Personnel and Contacts

PARTNERS, OFFICERS, LLC MEMBERS, MAJOR SHAREHOLDERS (Foreign and Domestic), ETC.

7a Full Name	Taxpayer Identification Number
Title	Home Telephone ( )
Home Address	Work/Cell Phone ( )
City ____ State ____ ZIP ____	Ownership Percentage & Shares or Interest
Responsible for Depositing Payroll Taxes ☐ Yes ☐ No	Annual Salary/Draw
7b Full Name	Taxpayer Identification Number
Title	Home Telephone ( )
Home Address	Work/Cell Phone ( )
City ____ State ____ ZIP ____	Ownership Percentage & Shares or Interest
Responsible for Depositing Payroll Taxes ☐ Yes ☐ No	Annual Salary/Draw
7c Full Name	Taxpayer Identification Number
Title	Home Telephone ( )
Home Address	Work/Cell Phone ( )
City ____ State ____ ZIP ____	Ownership Percentage & Shares or Interest
Responsible for Depositing Payroll Taxes ☐ Yes ☐ No	Annual Salary/Draw
7d Full Name	Taxpayer Identification Number
Title	Home Telephone ( )
Home Address	Work/Cell Phone ( )
City ____ State ____ ZIP ____	Ownership Percentage & Shares or Interest
Responsible for Depositing Payroll Taxes ☐ Yes ☐ No	Annual Salary/Draw

Catalog Number 16649P

EXHIBIT 9

Form 433-B (Rev. 2-2019) Page **2**

Section 3: Other Financial Information *(Attach copies of all applicable documents)*

| 8 | Does the business use a Payroll Service Provider or Reporting Agent *(If yes, answer the following)* | ☐ Yes ☐ No |

Name and Address *(Street, City, State, ZIP code)* | Effective dates *(mmddyyyy)*

| 9 | Is the business a party to a lawsuit *(If yes, answer the following)* | ☐ Yes ☐ No |

☐ Plaintiff ☐ Defendant | Location of Filing | Represented by | Docket/Case No.

Amount of Suit $ | Possible Completion Date *(mmddyyyy)* | Subject of Suit

| 10 | Has the business ever filed bankruptcy *(If yes, answer the following)* | ☐ Yes ☐ No |

Date Filed *(mmddyyyy)* | Date Dismissed *(mmddyyyy)* | Date Discharged *(mmddyyyy)* | Petition No. | District of Filing

| 11 | Do any related parties *(e.g., officers, partners, employees)* have outstanding amounts owed to the business *(If yes, answer the following)* | ☐ Yes ☐ No |

Name and Address *(Street, City, State, ZIP code)* | Date of Loan | Current Balance As of _____ *mmddyyyy* $ | Payment Date | Payment Amount $

| 12 | Have any assets been transferred, in the last 10 years, from this business for less than full value *(If yes, answer the following)* | ☐ Yes ☐ No |

List Asset | Value at Time of Transfer $ | Date Transferred *(mmddyyyy)* | To Whom or Where Transferred

| 13 | Does this business have other business affiliations *(e.g., subsidiary or parent companies)* *(If yes, answer the following)* | ☐ Yes ☐ No |

Related Business Name and Address *(Street, City, State, ZIP code)* | Related Business EIN:

| 14 | Any increase/decrease in income anticipated *(If yes, answer the following)* | ☐ Yes ☐ No |

Explain *(Use attachment if needed)* | How much will it increase/decrease $ | When will it increase/decrease

| 15 | Is the business a Federal Government Contractor *(Include Federal Government contracts in #18, Accounts/Notes Receivable)* | ☐ Yes ☐ No |

Section 4: Business Asset and Liability Information (Foreign and Domestic)

| 16a | **CASH ON HAND** *Include cash that is not in the bank* | **Total Cash on Hand** $ |

| 16b | Is there a safe on the business premises ☐ Yes ☐ No | Contents |

BUSINESS BANK ACOUNTS Include online and mobile accounts *(e.g., PayPal)*, money market accounts, savings accounts, checking accounts and stored value cards *(e.g., payroll cards, government benefit cards, etc.)*
List safe deposit boxes including location, box number and value of contents. Attach list of contents.

	Type of Account	Full Name and Address *(Street, City, State, ZIP code)* of Bank, Savings & Loan, Credit Union or Financial Institution	Account Number	Account Balance As of _____ *mmddyyyy*
17a				$
17b				$
17c				$
17d	Total Cash in Banks *(Add lines 17a through 17c and amounts from any attachments)*			$

Form 433-B (Rev. 2-2019) Page **3**

ACCOUNTS/NOTES RECEIVABLE Include e-payment accounts receivable and factoring companies, and any bartering or online auction accounts. *(List all contracts separately including contracts awarded, but not started).* **Include Federal, state and local government grants and contracts.**

Name & Address *(Street, City, State, ZIP code)*	Status *(e.g., age, factored, other)*	Date Due *(mmddyyyy)*	Invoice Number or Government Grant or Contract Number	**Amount Due**
18a Contact Name Phone				$
18b Contact Name Phone				$
18c Contact Name Phone				$
18d Contact Name Phone				$
18e Contact Name Phone				$

18f Outstanding Balance *(Add lines 18a through 18e and amounts from any attachments)* $

INVESTMENTS List all investment assets below. Include stocks, bonds, mutual funds, stock options, certificates of deposit, commodities (e.g., gold, silver, copper, etc.) and virtual currency (e.g., Bitcoin, Ripple and Litecoin).

Name of Company & Address *(Street, City, State, ZIP code)*	Used as collateral on loan	Current Value	Loan Balance	**Equity** Value Minus Loan
19a Phone	☐ Yes ☐ No	$	$	$
19b Phone	☐ Yes ☐ No	$	$	$

19c Total Investments *(Add lines 19a, 19b, and amounts from any attachments)* $

AVAILABLE CREDIT Include all lines of credit and credit cards.

Full Name & Address *(Street, City, State, ZIP code)*	Credit Limit	Amount Owed As of _____ *mmddyyyy*	**Available Credit** As of _____ *mmddyyyy*
20a Account No.	$	$	$
20b Account No.	$	$	$

20c Total Credit Available *(Add lines 20a, 20b, and amounts from any attachments)* $

Catalog Number 16649P www.irs.gov Form **433-B** (Rev. 2-2019)

Form 433-B (Rev. 2-2019) Page **4**

REAL PROPERTY Include all real property and land contracts the business owns/leases/rents.

	Purchase/Lease Date (mmddyyyy)	Current Fair Market Value (FMV)	Current Loan Balance	Amount of Monthly Payment	Date of Final Payment (mmddyyyy)	**Equity** FMV Minus Loan
21a Property Description		$	$	$		$
Location (Street, City, State, ZIP code) and County		Lender/Lessor/Landlord Name, Address, (Street, City, State, ZIP code) and Phone Phone				
21b Property Description		$	$	$		$
Location (Street, City, State, ZIP code) and County		Lender/Lessor/Landlord Name, Address, (Street, City, State, ZIP code) and Phone Phone				
21c Property Description		$	$	$		$
Location (Street, City, State, ZIP code) and County		Lender/Lessor/Landlord Name, Address, (Street, City, State, ZIP code) and Phone Phone				
21d Property Description		$	$	$		$
Location (Street, City, State, ZIP code) and County		Lender/Lessor/Landlord Name, Address, (Street, City, State, ZIP code) and Phone Phone				

21e Total Equity (Add lines 21a through 21d and amounts from any attachments) $

VEHICLES, LEASED AND PURCHASED Include boats, RVs, motorcycles, all-terrain and off-road vehicles, trailers, mobile homes, etc.

		Purchase/Lease Date (mmddyyyy)	Current Fair Market Value (FMV)	Current Loan Balance	Amount of Monthly Payment	Date of Final Payment (mmddyyyy)	**Equity** FMV Minus Loan
22a Year	Make/Model		$	$	$		$
Mileage	License/Tag Number	Lender/Lessor Name, Address, (Street, City, State, ZIP code) and Phone					
Vehicle Identification Number (VIN)		Phone					
22b Year	Make/Model		$	$	$		$
Mileage	License/Tag Number	Lender/Lessor Name, Address, (Street, City, State, ZIP code) and Phone					
Vehicle Identification Number (VIN)		Phone					
22c Year	Make/Model		$	$	$		$
Mileage	License/Tag Number	Lender/Lessor Name, Address, (Street, City, State, ZIP code) and Phone					
Vehicle Identification Number (VIN)		Phone					
22d Year	Make/Model		$	$	$		$
Mileage	License/Tag Number	Lender/Lessor Name, Address, (Street, City, State, ZIP code) and Phone					
Vehicle Identification Number (VIN)		Phone					

22e Total Equity (Add lines 22a through 22d and amounts from any attachments) $

Catalog Number 16649P   www.irs.gov   Form **433-B** (Rev. 2-2019)

Form 433-B (Rev. 2-2019) Page **5**

BUSINESS EQUIPMENT AND INTANGIBLE ASSETS Include all machinery, equipment, merchandise inventory, and other assets in 23a through 23d. List intangible assets in 23e through 23g (*licenses, patents, logos, domain names, trademarks, copyrights, software, mining claims, goodwill and trade secrets.*)

	Purchase/ Lease Date (*mmddyyyy*)	Current Fair Market Value (FMV)	Current Loan Balance	Amount of Monthly Payment	Date of Final Payment (*mmddyyyy*)	**Equity** FMV Minus Loan
23a Asset Description		$	$	$		$
Location of asset (*Street, City, State, ZIP code*) and County			Lender/Lessor Name, Address, (*Street, City, State, ZIP code*) and Phone			
			Phone			
23b Asset Description		$	$	$		$
Location of asset (*Street, City, State, ZIP code*) and County			Lender/Lessor Name, Address, (*Street, City, State, ZIP code*) and Phone			
			Phone			
23c Asset Description		$	$	$		$
Location of asset (*Street, City, State, ZIP code*) and County			Lender/Lessor Name, Address, (*Street, City, State, ZIP code*) and Phone			
			Phone			
23d Asset Description		$	$	$		$
Location of asset (*Street, City, State, ZIP code*) and County			Lender/Lessor Name, Address, (*Street, City, State, ZIP code*) and Phone			
			Phone			
23e Intangible Asset Description						$
23f Intangible Asset Description						$
23g Intangible Asset Description						$
23h Total Equity (*Add lines 23a through 23g and amounts from any attachments*)						$

BUSINESS LIABILITIES Include notes and judgements not listed previously on this form.

Business Liabilities	Secured/ Unsecured	Date Pledged (*mmddyyyy*)	Balance Owed	Date of Final Payment (*mmddyyyy*)	Payment Amount
24a Description:	☐ Secured ☐ Unsecured		$		$
Name Street Address City/State/ZIP code			Phone		
24b Description:	☐ Secured ☐ Unsecured		$		$
Name Street Address City/State/ZIP code			Phone		
24c Total Payments (*Add lines 24a and 24b and amounts from any attachments*)					$

Catalog Number 16649P www.irs.gov Form **433-B** (Rev. 2-2019)

Form 433-B (Rev. 2-2019) — Page 6

Section 5: Monthly Income/Expenses Statement for Business

Accounting Method Used: ☐ Cash ☐ Accrual

Use the prior 3, 6, 9 or 12 month period to determine your typical business income and expenses.

Income and Expenses during the period (mmddyyyy) _____ to (mmddyyyy) _____

Provide a breakdown below of your average monthly income and expenses, based on the period of time used above.

Total Monthly Business Income		Total Monthly Business Expenses	
Income Source	Gross Monthly	Expense items	Actual Monthly
25 Gross Receipts from Sales/Services	$	36 Materials Purchased [1]	$
26 Gross Rental Income	$	37 Inventory Purchased [2]	$
27 Interest Income	$	38 Gross Wages & Salaries	$
28 Dividends	$	39 Rent	$
29 Cash Receipts (Not included in lines 25-28)	$	40 Supplies [3]	$
Other Income (Specify below)		41 Utilities/Telephone [4]	$
30	$	42 Vehicle Gasoline/Oil	$
31	$	43 Repairs & Maintenance	$
32	$	44 Insurance	$
33	$	45 Current Taxes [5]	$
34	$	46 Other Expenses (Specify)	$
35 **Total Income** (Add lines 25 through 34)	$	47 IRS Use Only-Allowable Installment Payments	$
		48 **Total Expenses** (Add lines 36 through 47)	$
		49 **Net Income** (Line 35 minus Line 48)	$

1 **Materials Purchased:** Materials are items directly related to the production of a product or service.

2 **Inventory Purchased:** Goods bought for resale.

3 **Supplies:** Supplies are items used to conduct business and are consumed or used up within one year. This could be the cost of books, office supplies, professional equipment, etc.

4 **Utilities/Telephone:** Utilities include gas, electricity, water, oil, other fuels, trash collection, telephone, cell phone and business internet.

5 **Current Taxes:** Real estate, state, and local income tax, excise, franchise, occupational, personal property, sales and the employer's portion of employment taxes.

Certification: *Under penalties of perjury, I declare that to the best of my knowledge and belief this statement of assets, liabilities, and other information is true, correct, and complete.*

Signature	Title	Date

Print Name of Officer, Partner or LLC Member

After we review the completed Form 433-B, you may be asked to provide verification for the assets, encumbrances, income and expenses reported. Documentation may include previously filed income tax returns, profit and loss statements, bank and investment statements, loan statements, financing statements, bills or statements for recurring expenses, etc.

IRS USE ONLY (Notes)

Privacy Act: The information requested on this Form is covered under Privacy Acts and Paperwork Reduction Notices which have already been provided to the taxpayer.

Form 433-A
(February 2019)
Department of the Treasury
Internal Revenue Service

Collection Information Statement for Wage Earners and Self-Employed Individuals

Wage Earners Complete Sections 1, 2, 3, 4, and 5 including the signature line on page 4. *Answer all questions or write N/A if the question is not applicable.*
Self-Employed Individuals Complete Sections 1, 3, 4, 5, 6 and 7 and the signature line on page 4. *Answer all questions or write N/A if the question is not applicable.*
For Additional Information, refer to Publication 1854, "How To Prepare a Collection Information Statement."
Include attachments if additional space is needed to respond completely to any question.

Name on Internal Revenue Service (IRS) Account	SSN or ITIN on IRS Account	Employer Identification Number EIN

Section 1: Personal Information

1a	Full Name of Taxpayer and Spouse *(if applicable)*		1c Home Phone ( )	1d Cell Phone ( )
1b	Address *(Street, City, State, ZIP code) (County of Residence)*		1e Business Phone ( )	1f Business Cell Phone ( )
			2b Name, Age, and Relationship of dependent(s)	
2a	Marital Status: ☐ Married ☐ Unmarried *(Single, Divorced, Widowed)*			

	SSN or ITIN	Date of Birth *(mmddyyyy)*	Driver's License Number and State
3a Taxpayer			
3b Spouse			

Section 2: Employment Information for Wage Earners

If you or your spouse have self-employment income instead of, or in addition to wage income, complete Business Information in Sections 6 and 7.

Taxpayer			Spouse		
4a Taxpayer's Employer Name			5a Spouse's Employer Name		
4b Address *(Street, City, State, and ZIP code)*			5b Address *(Street, City, State, and ZIP code)*		
4c Work Telephone Number ( )	4d Does employer allow contact at work ☐ Yes ☐ No		5c Work Telephone Number ( )	5d Does employer allow contact at work ☐ Yes ☐ No	
4e How long with this employer *(years) (months)*	4f Occupation		5e How long with this employer *(years) (months)*	5f Occupation	
4g Number of withholding allowances claimed on Form W-4	4h Pay Period: ☐ Weekly ☐ Bi-weekly ☐ Monthly ☐ Other		5g Number of withholding allowances claimed on Form W-4	5h Pay Period: ☐ Weekly ☐ Bi-weekly ☐ Monthly ☐ Other	

Section 3: Other Financial Information *(Attach copies of applicable documentation)*

6	Are you a party to a lawsuit *(If yes, answer the following)*			☐ Yes ☐ No
	☐ Plaintiff ☐ Defendant	Location of Filing	Represented by	Docket/Case No.
	Amount of Suit $	Possible Completion Date *(mmddyyyy)*	Subject of Suit	

7	Have you ever filed bankruptcy *(If yes, answer the following)*				☐ Yes ☐ No
	Date Filed *(mmddyyyy)*	Date Dismissed *(mmddyyyy)*	Date Discharged *(mmddyyyy)*	Petition No.	Location Filed

8	In the past 10 years, have you lived outside of the U.S for 6 months or longer *(If yes, answer the following)*		☐ Yes ☐ No
	Dates lived abroad: from *(mmddyyyy)*	To *(mmddyyyy)*	

9a	Are you the beneficiary of a trust, estate, or life insurance policy *(If yes, answer the following)*		☐ Yes ☐ No
	Place where recorded:		EIN:
	Name of the trust, estate, or policy	Anticipated amount to be received $	When will the amount be received

9b	Are you a trustee, fiduciary, or contributor of a trust		☐ Yes ☐ No
	Name of the trust:		EIN:

10	Do you have a safe deposit box (business or personal) *(If yes, answer the following)*		☐ Yes ☐ No
	Location *(Name, address and box number(s))*	Contents	Value $

11	In the past 10 years, have you transferred any assets for less than their full value *(If yes, answer the following)*			☐ Yes ☐ No
	List Asset(s)	Value at Time of Transfer $	Date Transferred *(mmddyyyy)*	To Whom or Where was it Transferred

Catalog Number 20312N www.irs.gov Form **433-A** (Rev. 2-2019)

Form 433-A (Rev. 2-2019) Page **2**

Section 4: Personal Asset Information for all Individuals (Foreign and Domestic)

12 CASH ON HAND Include cash that is not in a bank   **Total Cash on Hand** $

PERSONAL BANK ACCOUNTS Include all checking, online and mobile (e.g., PayPal) accounts, money market accounts, savings accounts, and stored value cards (e.g., payroll cards, government benefit cards, etc.).

Type of Account	Full Name & Address (Street, City, State, ZIP code) of Bank, Savings & Loan, Credit Union, or Financial Institution	Account Number	Account Balance As of _____ mmddyyyy
13a			$
13b			$
13c Total Cash (Add lines 13a, 13b, and amounts from any attachments)			$

INVESTMENTS Include stocks, bonds, mutual funds, stock options, certificates of deposit, and retirement assets such as IRAs, Keogh, 401(k) plans and commodities (e.g., gold, silver, copper, etc.). Include all corporations, partnerships, limited liability companies, or other business entities in which you are an officer, director, owner, member, or otherwise have a financial interest. Include attachment(s) if additional space is needed to respond.

Type of Investment or Financial Interest	Full Name & Address (Street, City, State, ZIP code) of Company	Current Value	Loan Balance (if applicable) As of _____ mmddyyyy	Equity Value minus Loan
14a				
	Phone	$	$	$
14b				
	Phone	$	$	$

VIRTUAL CURRENCY (CRYPTOCURRENCY) List all virtual currency you own or in which you have a financial interest. (e.g., Bitcoin, Ethereum, Litecoin, Ripple, etc.) If applicable, attach a statement with each virtual currency's public key.

Type of Virtual Currency	Name of Virtual Currency Wallet, Exchange or Digital Currency Exchange (DCE)	Email Address Used to Set-up With the Virtual Currency Exchange or DCE	Location(s) of Virtual Currency (Mobile Wallet, Online, and/or External Hardware storage)	Virtual Currency Amount and Value in US dollars as of today (e.g., 10 Bitcoins $64,600.00 USD)
14c				$
14d				$
14e Total Equity (Add lines 14a through 14d and amounts from any attachments)				$

AVAILABLE CREDIT Include all lines of credit and bank issued credit cards.

Full Name & Address (Street, City, State, ZIP code) of Credit Institution	Credit Limit	Amount Owed As of _____ mmddyyyy	Available Credit As of _____ mmddyyyy
15a			
Acct. No	$	$	$
15b			
Acct. No	$	$	$
15c Total Available Credit (Add lines 15a, 15b and amounts from any attachments)			$

16a LIFE INSURANCE Do you own or have any interest in any life insurance policies with cash value (Term Life insurance does not have a cash value)
☐ Yes   ☐ No   If yes, complete blocks 16b through 16f for each policy.

16b	Name and Address of Insurance Company(ies):				
16c	Policy Number(s)				
16d	Owner of Policy				
16e	Current Cash Value	$	$	$	
16f	Outstanding Loan Balance	$	$	$	
16g	Total Available Cash (Subtract amounts on line 16f from line 16e and include amounts from any attachments)				$

Form 433-A (Rev. 2-2019) Page **3**

REAL PROPERTY Include all real property owned or being purchased

	Purchase Date (mmddyyyy)	Current Fair Market Value (FMV)	Current Loan Balance	Amount of Monthly Payment	Date of Final Payment (mmddyyyy)	**Equity** FMV Minus Loan
17a Property Description		$	$	$		$
Location *(Street, City, State, ZIP code)* and County			Lender/Contract Holder Name, Address *(Street, City, State, ZIP code)*, and Phone			
			Phone			
17b Property Description		$	$	$		$
Location *(Street, City, State, ZIP code)* and County			Lender/Contract Holder Name, Address *(Street, City, State, ZIP code)*, and Phone			
			Phone			

17c Total Equity *(Add lines 17a, 17b and amounts from any attachments)* $

PERSONAL VEHICLES LEASED AND PURCHASED Include boats, RVs, motorcycles, all-terrain and off-road vehicles, trailers, etc.

Description (Year, Mileage, Make/Model, Tag Number, Vehicle Identification Number)		Purchase/ Lease Date (mmddyyyy)	Current Fair Market Value (FMV)	Current Loan Balance	Amount of Monthly Payment	Date of Final Payment (mmddyyyy)	**Equity** FMV Minus Loan
18a Year	Make/Model		$	$	$		$
Mileage	License/Tag Number	Lender/Lessor Name, Address *(Street, City, State, ZIP code)*, and Phone					
Vehicle Identification Number					Phone		
18b Year	Make/Model		$	$	$		$
Mileage	License/Tag Number	Lender/Lessor Name, Address *(Street, City, State, ZIP code)*, and Phone					
Vehicle Identification Number					Phone		

18c Total Equity *(Add lines 18a, 18b and amounts from any attachments)* $

PERSONAL ASSETS Include all furniture, personal effects, artwork, jewelry, collections *(coins, guns, etc.)*, antiques or other assets. Include intangible assets such as licenses, domain names, patents, copyrights, mining claims, etc.

	Purchase/ Lease Date (mmddyyyy)	Current Fair Market Value (FMV)	Current Loan Balance	Amount of Monthly Payment	Date of Final Payment (mmddyyyy)	**Equity** FMV Minus Loan
19a Property Description		$	$	$		$
Location *(Street, City, State, ZIP code)* and County			Lender/Lessor Name, Address *(Street, City, State, ZIP code)*, and Phone			
			Phone			
19b Property Description		$	$	$		$
Location *(Street, City, State, ZIP code)* and County			Lender/Lessor Name, Address *(Street, City, State, ZIP code)*, and Phone			
			Phone			

19c Total Equity *(Add lines 19a, 19b and amounts from any attachments)* $

Form 433-A (Rev. 2-2019) Page 4

If you are self-employed, sections 6 and 7 must be completed before continuing.

Section 5: Monthly Income and Expenses

Monthly Income/Expense Statement *(For additional information, refer to Publication 1854.)*

Total Income			Total Living Expenses		IRS USE ONLY
Source	Gross Monthly		Expense Items [6]	Actual Monthly	Allowable Expenses
20 Wages (Taxpayer) [1]	$	35	Food, Clothing and Misc. [7]	$	
21 Wages (Spouse) [1]	$	36	Housing and Utilities [8]	$	
22 Interest - Dividends	$	37	Vehicle Ownership Costs [9]	$	
23 Net Business Income [2]	$	38	Vehicle Operating Costs [10]	$	
24 Net Rental Income [3]	$	39	Public Transportation [11]	$	
25 Distributions (K-1, IRA, etc.) [4]	$	40	Health Insurance	$	
26 Pension (Taxpayer)	$	41	Out of Pocket Health Care Costs [12]	$	
27 Pension (Spouse)	$	42	Court Ordered Payments	$	
28 Social Security (Taxpayer)	$	43	Child/Dependent Care	$	
29 Social Security (Spouse)	$	44	Life Insurance	$	
30 Child Support	$	45	Current year taxes (Income/FICA) [13]	$	
31 Alimony	$	46	Secured Debts (Attach list)	$	
Other Income (Specify below) [5]		47	Delinquent State or Local Taxes	$	
32	$	48	Other Expenses (Attach list)	$	
33	$	49	Total Living Expenses (add lines 35-48)	$	
34 Total Income (add lines 20-33)	$	50	Net difference (Line 34 minus 49)	$	

1. **Wages, salaries, pensions, and social security**: Enter gross monthly wages and/or salaries. Do not deduct tax withholding or allotments taken out of pay, such as insurance payments, credit union deductions, car payments, etc. To calculate the gross monthly wages and/or salaries:

   If paid weekly - multiply weekly gross wages by 4.3. Example: $425.89 x 4.3 = $1,831.33

   If paid biweekly (every 2 weeks) - multiply biweekly gross wages by 2.17. Example: $972.45 x 2.17 = $2,110.22

   If paid semimonthly (twice each month) - multiply semimonthly gross wages by 2. Example: $856.23 x 2 = $1,712.46

2. **Net Income from Business**: Enter monthly net business income. This is the amount earned after ordinary and necessary monthly business expenses are paid. **This figure is the amount from page 6, line 89.** If the net business income is a loss, enter "0". Do not enter a negative number. If this amount is more or less than previous years, attach an explanation.

3. **Net Rental Income**: Enter monthly net rental income. This is the amount earned after ordinary and necessary monthly rental expenses are paid. Do not include deductions for depreciation or depletion. If the net rental income is a loss, enter "0." Do not enter a negative number.

4. **Distributions**: Enter the total distributions from partnerships and subchapter S corporations reported on Schedule K-1, and from limited liability companies reported on Form 1040, Schedule C, D or E. Enter total distributions from IRAs if not included under pension income.

5. **Other Income**: Include agricultural subsidies, unemployment compensation, gambling income, oil credits, rent subsidies, etc.

6. **Expenses not generally allowed**: We generally do not allow tuition for private schools, public or private college expenses, charitable contributions, voluntary retirement contributions or payments on unsecured debts. However, we may allow the expenses if proven that they are necessary for the health and welfare of the individual or family or the production of income. See Publication 1854 for exceptions.

7. **Food, Clothing and Miscellaneous**: Total of food, clothing, housekeeping supplies, and personal care products for one month. The miscellaneous allowance is for expenses incurred that are not included in any other allowable living expense items. Examples are credit card payments, bank fees and charges, reading material, and school supplies.

8. **Housing and Utilities**: For principal residence: Total of rent or mortgage payment. Add the average monthly expenses for the following: property taxes, homeowner's or renter's insurance, maintenance, dues, fees, and utilities. Utilities include gas, electricity, water, fuel, oil, other fuels, trash collection, telephone, cell phone, cable television and internet services.

9. **Vehicle Ownership Costs**: Total of monthly lease or purchase/loan payments.

10. **Vehicle Operating Costs**: Total of maintenance, repairs, insurance, fuel, registrations, licenses, inspections, parking, and tolls for one month.

11. **Public Transportation**: Total of monthly fares for mass transit *(e.g., bus, train, ferry, taxi, etc.)*

12. **Out of Pocket Health Care Costs**: Monthly total of medical services, prescription drugs and medical supplies *(e.g., eyeglasses, hearing aids, etc.)*

13. **Current Year Taxes**: Include state and Federal taxes withheld from salary or wages, or paid as estimated taxes.

Certification: *Under penalties of perjury, I declare that to the best of my knowledge and belief this statement of assets, liabilities, and other information is true, correct, and complete.*

Taxpayer's Signature	Spouse's signature	Date

After we review the completed Form 433-A, you may be asked to provide verification for the assets, encumbrances, income and expenses reported. Documentation may include previously filed income tax returns, pay statements, self-employment records, bank and investment statements, loan statements, bills or statements for recurring expenses, etc.

IRS USE ONLY *(Notes)*

Form 433-A (Rev. 2-2019) — Page 5

Sections 6 and 7 must be completed only if you are SELF-EMPLOYED.

Section 6: Business Information

51. Is the business a sole proprietorship *(filing Schedule C)* ☐ **Yes**, Continue with Sections 6 and 7. ☐ **No**, Complete Form 433-B.
All other business entities, including limited liability companies, partnerships or corporations, must complete Form 433-B.

52. Business Name & Address *(if different than 1b)*

53. Employer Identification Number

54. Type of Business

55. Is the business a Federal Contractor ☐ Yes ☐ No

56. Business Website (web address)

57. Total Number of Employees

58. Average Gross Monthly Payroll

59. Frequency of Tax Deposits

60. Does the business engage in e-Commerce *(Internet sales)* If yes, complete *lines 61a and 61b* ☐ Yes ☐ No

PAYMENT PROCESSOR *(e.g., PayPal, Authorize.net, Google Checkout, etc.)* Include virtual currency wallet, exchange or digital currency exchange.

	Name & Address *(Street, City, State, ZIP code)*. Name & Address *(Street, City, State, ZIP code)*	Payment Processor Account Number
61a		
61b		

CREDIT CARDS ACCEPTED BY THE BUSINESS

	Credit Card	Merchant Account Number	Issuing Bank Name & Address *(Street, City, State, ZIP code)*
62a			
62b			
62c			

63. **BUSINESS CASH ON HAND** Include cash that is not in a bank. **Total Cash on Hand** $

BUSINESS BANK ACCOUNTS Include checking accounts, online and mobile *(e.g., PayPal)* accounts, money market accounts, savings accounts, and stored value cards *(e.g., payroll cards, government benefit cards, etc.)*. Report Personal Accounts in Section 4.

	Type of Account	Full name & Address *(Street, City, State, ZIP code)* of Bank, Savings & Loan, Credit Union or Financial Institution.	Account Number	Account Balance As of _____ *mmddyyyy*
64a				$
64b				$
64c	Total Cash in Banks *(Add lines 64a, 64b and amounts from any attachments)*			$

ACCOUNTS/NOTES RECEIVABLE Include e-payment accounts receivable and factoring companies, and any bartering or online auction accounts. *(List all contracts separately, including contracts awarded, but not started.)* Include Federal, state and local government grants and contracts.

	Accounts/Notes Receivable & Address *(Street, City, State, ZIP code)*	Status *(e.g., age, factored, other)*	Date Due *(mmddyyyy)*	Invoice Number or Government Grant or Contract Number	Amount Due
65a					$
65b					$
65c					$
65d					$
65e					$
65f	Total Outstanding Balance *(Add lines 65a through 65e and amounts from any attachments)*				$

Form 433-A (Rev. 2-2019) Page 6

BUSINESS ASSETS Include all tools, books, machinery, equipment, inventory or other assets used in trade or business. Include a list and show the value of all intangible assets such as licenses, patents, domain names, copyrights, trademarks, mining claims, etc.

	Purchase/Lease Date (mmddyyyy)	Current Fair Market Value (FMV)	Current Loan Balance	Amount of Monthly Payment	Date of Final Payment (mmddyyyy)	**Equity** FMV Minus Loan
66a Property Description		$	$	$		$
Location (Street, City, State, ZIP code) and Country			Lender/Lessor/Landlord Name, Address (Street, City, State, ZIP code), and Phone Phone			
66b Property Description		$	$	$		$
Location (Street, City, State, ZIP code) and Country			Lender/Lessor/Landlord Name, Address (Street, City, State, ZIP code), and Phone Phone			
66c Total Equity (Add lines 66a, 66b and amounts from any attachments)						$

Section 7 should be completed only if you are SELF-EMPLOYED

Section 7: Sole Proprietorship Information (lines 67 through 87 should reconcile with business Profit and Loss Statement)

Accounting Method Used: ☐ Cash ☐ Accrual
Use the prior 3, 6, 9 or 12 month period to determine your typical business income and expenses.

Income and Expenses during the period (mmddyyyy) _____ to (mmddyyyy) _____

Provide a breakdown below of your average monthly income and expenses, based on the period of time used above.

Total Monthly Business Income		**Total Monthly Business Expenses** (Use attachments as needed)		
Source	Gross Monthly		Expense Items	Actual Monthly
67 Gross Receipts	$	77	Materials Purchased [1]	$
68 Gross Rental Income	$	78	Inventory Purchased [2]	$
69 Interest	$	79	Gross Wages & Salaries	$
70 Dividends	$	80	Rent	$
71 Cash Receipts not included in lines 67-70	$	81	Supplies [3]	$
Other Income (Specify below)		82	Utilities/Telephone [4]	$
72	$	83	Vehicle Gasoline/Oil	$
73	$	84	Repairs & Maintenance	$
74	$	85	Insurance	$
75	$	86	Current Taxes [5]	$
		87	Other Expenses, including installment payments (Specify)	$
76 Total Income (Add lines 67 through 75)	$	88	Total Expenses (Add lines 77 through 87)	$
		89	Net Business Income (Line 76 minus 88) [6]	$

Enter the monthly net income amount from line 89 on line 23, section 5. If line 89 is a loss, enter "0" on line 23, section 5.
Self-employed taxpayers must return to page 4 to sign the certification.

1. **Materials Purchased:** Materials are items directly related to the production of a product or service.
2. **Inventory Purchased:** Goods bought for resale.
3. **Supplies:** Supplies are items used in the business that are consumed or used up within one year. This could be the cost of books, office supplies, professional equipment, etc.
4. **Utilities/Telephone:** Utilities include gas, electricity, water, oil, other fuels, trash collection, telephone, cell phone and business internet.
5. **Current Taxes:** Real estate, excise, franchise, occupational, personal property, sales and employer's portion of employment taxes.
6. **Net Business Income:** Net profit from Form 1040, Schedule C may be used if duplicated deductions are eliminated (e.g., expenses for business use of home already included in housing and utility expenses on page 4). Deductions for depreciation and depletion on Schedule C are not cash expenses and must be added back to the net income figure. In addition, interest cannot be deducted if it is already included in any other installment payments allowed.

IRS USE ONLY (Notes)

Privacy Act: The information requested on this Form is covered under Privacy Acts and Paperwork Reduction Notices which have already been provided to the taxpayer.

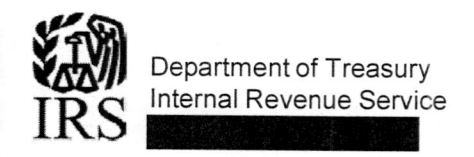

Notice	CP523
Tax period	2014
Notice date	December 16, 2016
Social Security number	
To contact us	
Your Caller ID	
Page 1 of 5	

Department of Treasury
Internal Revenue Service

Notice of intent to levy

Intent to terminate your Installment Agreement
Amount due immediately:

The monthly payment for your installment agreement is overdue. Because we didn't receive one or more payments from you, as your installment agreement requires, we will terminate your installment agreement on [Month DD, YYYY].

In addition, we can seize (levy) any state tax refund you're entitled to and apply it to your ▮▮▮▮ in overdue taxes on or after [Month DD, YYYY].

Billing Summary

Amount you owed	
Failure-to-pay penalty	
Interest charges	
Amount due immediately	

Continued on back...

Notice	CP523
Notice date	December 16, 2016
Social Security number	

ayment

- Make your check or money order payable to the United States Treasury.
- Write your Social Security number ▮▮▮▮▮, the tax year (2014), and form number (1040) on your payment.

TERNAL REVENUE SERVICE

- **Amount due immediately**

Exhibit 5-6
EXHIBIT 11

Notice	CP523
Tax Year	2014
Notice date	December 16, 2016
Social Security number	

What you need to do immediately

If you agree with the amount due
- Pay the past due amount or we will terminate your installment agreement under Internal Revenue Code Section 6159(b) and the full amount you owe will be due immediately.
- Pay online or send us a check or money order with the attached payment stub. **You can pay online now at www.irs.gov/payments.**

If you agree but can't pay the amount due
- Call 1-800-829-0922 to discuss the reason for default and provide us with your updated financial statement (Form 433-F). We may be able to restructure your installment agreement. If we agree, you'll have to pay an additional fee of $50.

If you disagree with the amount due
Call us at [1-800-xxx-xxx] to review your account with a representative. Be sure to have your account information available when you call.

We'll assume you agree with the information in this notice if we don't hear from you.

What you need to know

Notice of Intent to Levy
This notice is your Notice of Intent to Levy (Internal Revenue Code Section 6331(d)).

If you don't pay the amount due by [Month DD, YYYY], we can levy your state tax refund. If you still have an outstanding balance after we levy your state refund, we may send you a notice giving you the right to a hearing before the IRS Office of Appeals, if you have not already received one. At that time, we can (levy your other property or rights to property, which includes:

Notice	CP523
Tax Year	2014
Notice date	December 16, 2016
Social Security number	

What you need to know - continued

Notice of Intent to Levy - continued

- Wages, real estate commissions, and other income
- Bank accounts
- Business assets
- Personal assets (including your car and home)
- Social security benefits

Right to request an appeal
If you don't agree, you have the right to request an appeal under the Collection Appeals Program. Please call 1-800-829-0115 or send us a Collection Appeals Request (Form 9423) to the address at the top of the notice by [Month DD, YYYY].

Payment options

Pay now electronically or by phone
The Electronic Federal Tax Payment System (EFTPS) is a free payment service for paying taxes online or by phone. TO use EFTPS, you must enroll online at www.eftps.gov (registration may take up to 7 business days to take effect . When you use the EFTPS website, you can:

- Receive instant confirmation of your payment
- Access payment history to review previous payments
- Schedule payments up to 365 days in advance
- Cancel a payment before the scheduled date
- Make a payment 24 hours a day, 7 days a week
- Authorize your financial institution or authorized third party (such as an accountant or payroll provider) to schedule payments for you

You may also be able to pay by debit or credit card for a small fee, depending on the type of tax you owe. To see all of our payment options, visit www.irs.gov/payments.

Payment history
If you made payments through EFTPS, you can log on to your EFTPS account online to review payments you made by phone or online.

If you already paid your balance in full within the past 21 days or made payment arrangements, please disregard this notice.

If you think we made a mistake, call 1-[xxx-xxx-xxxx] to review your account.

If we don't hear from you

If you don't pay the amount due immediately or call us to make payment arrangements, we can file a Notice of Federal Tax Lien on your property at any time, if we haven't already done so.

If a lien is in place, it may be difficult to sell or borrow against your property. A tax lien will also appear on your credit report – which may harm your credit rating – and your creditors will be publicly notified that the IRS has priority to seize your property.

	Notice	CP523
	Tax Year	2014
	Notice date	December 16, 2016
	Social Security number	

Penalties

We are required by law to charge any applicable penalties.

Failure-to-pay

Description	Amount
Total failure-to-pay	

When you pay your taxes after the due date, we charge a penalty of 0.5% of the unpaid amount due per month, up to 25% of the amount due. We count part of a month as a full month. (Internal Revenue Code Section 6651)

For a detailed calculation of your penalty charges, call 1-800-829-0922.

Removal of penalties due to erroneous written advice from the IRS

If you were penalized based on written advice from the IRS, we will remove the penalty if you meet the following criteria:
- If you sent a written request to the IRS for written advice on a specific issue
- You gave us complete and accurate information
- You received written advice from us
- You reasonably relied on our written advice and were penalized based on that advice

To request removal of penalties based on erroneous written advice from us, submit a completed Claim for Refund and Request for Abatement (Form 843) to the IRS service center where you filed your tax return.

For a copy of the form or to find your IRS service center, go to www.irs.gov or call 1-800-829-0922.

Removal or reduction of penalties

We understand that circumstances—such as serious illness or injury, a family member's death, or loss of financial records due to natural disaster—may make it difficult for you to meet your taxpayer responsibility in a timely manner.

If you would like us to consider removing or reducing any of your penalty charges, please do the following:
- Identify which penalty charges you would like us to remove or reduce (e.g., 2005 late filing penalty).
- For each penalty charge, explain why you believe removal or reduction is appropriate.
- Sign your statement, and mail it to us along with any supporting documents.

We will review your statement and let you know whether we accept your explanation as reasonable cause to reduce or remove the penalty charge(s).

Notice	CP523
Tax Year	2014
Notice date	December 16, 2016
Social Security number	

Interest

We are required by law to charge interest on unpaid tax from the date the tax return was due to the date the tax is paid in full. The interest is charged as long as there is an unpaid amount due, including penalties, if applicable. (Internal Revenue Code section 6601)

Period	Interest rate
October 1, 2013 – December 31, 2013	3%
January 1, 2014 – March 31, 2014	3%
April 1, 2014 – June 30, 2014	3%
July 1, 2014 – September 30, 2014	3%
October 1, 2014 – December 31, 2014	3%
Beginning January 1, 2015	5%

Additional information

- Visit www.irs.gov/cp523.
- For tax forms, instructions, and publications, visit www.irs.gov or call 1-800-TAX-FORM (1-800-829-3676).
- Paying online is convenient, secure, and ensures timely receipt of your payment. To pay your taxes online or for more information, go to www.irs.gov/payments.
- You can contact us by mail at the address at the top of the first page of this notice. Be sure to include your social security number and the tax year and form number you are writing about.
- Review the enclosed IRS Collection Process (Publication 594).
- Generally, we deal directly with taxpayers or their authorized representatives. Sometimes, however, it's necessary for us to speak with other people, such as employees, employers, banks, or neighbors to gather the information we need about a taxpayer's account. You have the right to request a list of individuals we've contacted in connection with your account at any time.
- Keep this notice for your records.

If you need assistance, please don't hesitate to contact us.

Department of the Treasury - Internal Revenue Service

Collection Appeal Request

Form **9423**
(August 2014)

(Instructions are on the reverse side of this form)

1. Taxpayer's name	2. Representative *(Attach a copy of Form 2848, Power of Attorney)*		
3. SSN/EIN	4. Taxpayer's business phone	5. Taxpayer's home phone	6. Representative's phone

7. Taxpayer's street address

8. City	9. State	10. ZIP code
11. Type of tax *(Tax form)*	12. Tax periods being appealed	13. Tax due

Collection Action(s) Appealed

14. Check the Collection action(s) you are appealing

- [ ] Federal Tax Lien
- [ ] Levy or Proposed Levy
- [ ] Seizure
- [ ] Rejection of Installment Agreement
- [ ] Termination of Installment Agreement
- [ ] Modification of Installment Agreement

Explanation

15. Explain why you disagree with the collection action(s) you checked above and explain how you would resolve your tax problem. Attach additional pages if needed. Attach copies of any documents that you think will support your position. Generally, the Office of Appeals will ask the Collection Function to review, verify and provide their opinion on any new information you submit. We will share their comments with you and give you the opportunity to respond.

Under penalties of perjury, I declare that I have examined this request and any accompanying documents, and to the best of my knowledge and belief, they are true, correct and complete. A submission by a representative, other than the taxpayer, is based on all information of which the representative has any knowledge.

16. ☐ Taxpayer's or ☐ Authorized Representative's signature *(Only check one box)*	17. Date signed

IRS USE ONLY

18. Revenue Officer's name	19. Revenue Officer's signature	20. Date signed
21. Revenue Officer's phone	22. Revenue Officer's email address	23. Date received
24. Collection Manager's name	25. Collection Manager's signature	26. Date signed
27. Collection Manager's phone	28. Collection Manager's email address	29. Date received

Form **9423** (Rev. 8-2014) Catalog Number 14169I   www.irs.gov   Department of the Treasury - Internal Revenue Service

EXHIBIT 12

Instructions for Form 9423, Collection Appeal Request

For Liens, Levies, Seizures, and Rejection, Modification or Termination of Installment Agreements

A taxpayer, or third party whose property is subject to a collection action, may appeal the following actions under the Collection Appeals Program (CAP):
  a. Levy or seizure action that has been or will be taken.
  b. A Notice of Federal Tax Lien (NFTL) that has been or will be filed.
  c. The filing of a notice of lien against an alter-ego or nominee's property.
  d. Denials of requests to issue lien certificates, such as subordination, withdrawal, discharge or non-attachment.
  e. Rejected, proposed for modification or modified, or proposed for termination or terminated installment agreements.
  f. Disallowance of taxpayer's request to return levied property under IRC 6343(d).
  g. Disallowance of property owner's claim for return of property under IRC 6343(b).

How to Appeal If You Disagree With a Lien, Levy, or Seizure Action

1. If you disagree with the decision of the IRS employee, and wish to appeal, you must first request a conference with the employee's manager. If you do not resolve your disagreement with the Collection manager, submit Form 9423 to request consideration by Appeals. Let the Collection office know within two (2) business days after the conference with the Collection manager that you plan to submit Form 9423. The Form 9423 must be received or postmarked within three (3) business days of the conference with the Collection manager or collection action may resume.

   NOTE: If you request an appeal after IRS makes a seizure, you must appeal to the Collection manager within 10 business days after the Notice of Seizure is provided to you or left at your home or business.

2. If you request a conference and are not contacted by a manager or his/her designee within two (2) business days of making the request, you can contact Collection again or submit Form 9423. If you submit Form 9423, note the date of your request for a conference in Block 15 and indicate that you were not contacted by a manager. The Form 9423 should be received or postmarked within four (4) business days of your request for a conference as collection action may resume.

3. On the Form 9423, check the collection action(s) you disagree with and explain why you disagree. You must also explain your solution to resolve your tax problem. Submit Form 9423 to the Collection office involved in the lien, levy or seizure action.

4. In situations where the IRS action(s) are creating an economic harm or you want help because your tax problem has not been resolved through normal channels, you can reach the Taxpayer Advocate Service at 877-777-4778.

How to Appeal An Installment Agreement Which Has Been Rejected, Proposed for Modification or Modified, or Proposed for Termination or Terminated

1. If you disagree with the decision regarding your installment agreement, you should appeal by completing a Form 9423, Collection Appeal Request.
2. You should provide it to the office or revenue officer who took the action regarding your installment agreement, within 30 calendar days.

   NOTE: A managerial conference is not required. However, it is strongly recommended a conference be held with the manager whenever possible.

   IMPORTANT: Never forward your request for an Appeals conference directly to Appeals. It must be submitted to the office which took the action on your installment agreement.

What Will Happen When You Appeal Your Case

Normally, we will stop the collection action(s) you disagree with until your appeal is settled, unless we have reason to believe that collection or the amount owed is at risk.

You May Have a Representative

You may represent yourself at your Appeals conference or you may be represented by an attorney, certified public accountant or a person enrolled to practice before the IRS. If you want your representative to appear without you, you must provide a properly completed Form 2848, Power of Attorney and Declaration of Representative. You can obtain Form 2848 from your local IRS office, by calling 1-800-829-3676, or by going to www.irs.gov.

Decision on the Appeal

Once Appeals makes a decision regarding your case, that decision is binding on both you and the IRS. You cannot obtain a judicial review of Appeals' decision following a CAP. However, there may be other opportunities to obtain administrative or judicial review of the issue raised in the CAP hearing. For example, a third party may contest a wrongful levy by filing an action in district court. See Publication 4528, *Making an Administrative Wrongful Levy Claim Under Internal Revenue Code (IRC) Section 6343(b)*.

   Note: Providing false information, failing to provide all pertinent information or fraud will void Appeals' decision.

Refer to Publication 594, *The IRS Collection Process*, and Publication 1660, *Collection Appeal Rights*, for more information regarding the Collection Appeals Program. Copies of these publications can be obtained online at www.irs.gov.

Privacy Act

The information requested on this Form is covered under Privacy Acts and Paperwork Reduction Notices which have already been provided to the taxpayer.

POA Copy

Department of the Treasury
Internal Revenue Service
Small Business / Self-Employed Division
STREET ADDRESS
CITY, STATE ZIP

Date:
03/18/2019
Person to contact:
  Name: RO NAME
  Employee ID number: 1000XXXXX
  Telephone: (203)XXX-XXX
  Fax: (855)XXX-XXXX
Taxpayer ID number:
XXX-XX-XXXX

TAXPAYER NAME
STREET ADDRESS
CITY, STATE ZIP

Case Closed -- Currently Not Collectible

We temporarily closed your collection case for the tax types and periods listed below. We determined you don't have the ability to pay the money you owe at this time.

Although we have temporarily closed your case, you still owe the money to the IRS. We may re-open your case in the future if your financial situation improves. Because you still owe money, we will continue to add penalties and interest to your account and it will be subject to other adjustments and offsets, such as applying future tax refunds to the amount you owe.

You don't need to take any action at this time. However, it is very important that you file all future tax returns and pay any amounts you owe on time. It is to your advantage to make voluntary payments towards the amount you owe, if possible, to minimize additional penalties and interest.

You owe a shared responsibility payment (SRP) because one or more members of your tax household didn't have minimum essential health coverage, per Internal Revenue Code Section 5000A. The SRP amount that you owe is not subject to a Notice of Federal Tax Lien filing, a levy on your property, or the failure-to-pay penalty. However, we charge interest on unpaid SRP balances. We may also apply your federal tax refunds to the SRP balance until it is paid in full. If you need health coverage, visit healthcare.gov to learn about health insurance options that are available for you and your family, how to purchase health insurance, and how you might qualify to get financial assistance with the cost of insurance.

If you have any questions you can call us at 1-800-829-1040 (individuals) or 1-800-829-4933 (businesses). For non-case-related questions, you can visit our website at www.irs.gov.

Thank you for your cooperation.

Sincerely,

EXHIBIT 13

Letter 4223 (Rev. 1-2017)
Catalog Number: 50072A

Form 656 Booklet
Offer in Compromise

CONTENTS

- What you need to know 1
- Paying for your offer 3
- How to apply 4
- Completing the application package 5
- Important information 6
- Removable Forms - Form 433-A (OIC), Collection Information Statement for Wage Earners and Self-Employed; Form 433-B (OIC), Collection Information Statement for Businesses; Form 656, Offer in Compromise 7
- Application Checklist 29

IRS contact information

If you want to see if you qualify for an offer in compromise before filling out the paperwork, you may use the Offer in Compromise Pre-Qualifier tool. The questionnaire format assists in gathering the information needed and provides instant feedback as to your eligibility based on the information you provided. The tool will also assist you in determining a preliminary offer amount for consideration of an acceptable offer. The Pre-Qualifier tool is located on our website at www.irs.gov.

If you have questions regarding qualifications for an offer in compromise, please call our toll-free number at 1-800-829-1040. You can get forms and publications by calling 1-800-TAX-FORM (1-800-829-3676), by visiting your local IRS office, or at www.irs.gov.

Taxpayer resources

The Taxpayer Advocate Service (TAS) is an independent organization within the Internal Revenue Service that helps taxpayers and protects taxpayer rights. TAS helps taxpayers whose problems with the IRS are causing financial difficulties, who've tried but haven't been able to resolve their problems with the IRS, or believe an IRS system or procedure isn't working as it should. And the service is free. Your local advocate's number is in your local directory and at taxpayeradvocate.irs.gov. You can also call us at 1-877-777-4778. For more information about TAS and your rights under the Taxpayer Bill of Rights, go to taxpayeradvocate.irs.gov. TAS is your voice at the IRS.

Low-Income Taxpayer Clinics (LITCs) are independent from the IRS. LITCs serve individuals whose income is below a certain level and who need to resolve a tax problem with the IRS. LITCs provide professional representation before the IRS or in court on audits, appeals, tax collection disputes, and other issues for free or for a small fee. For more information and to find a LITC near you, see the LITC page at www.taxpayeradvocate.irs.gov/litcmap or IRS Publication 4134, Low-Income Taxpayer Clinic List. This Publication is also available by calling the IRS toll-free at 1-800-829-3676 or visiting your local IRS office.

EXHIBIT 14

WHAT YOU NEED TO KNOW

What is an Offer?

An Offer in Compromise (offer) is an agreement between you (the taxpayer) and the IRS that settles a tax debt for less than the full amount owed. The offer program provides eligible taxpayers with a path toward paying off their tax debt and getting a fresh start. The ultimate goal is a compromise that suits the best interest of both the taxpayer and the IRS. To be considered, generally you must make an appropriate offer based on what the IRS considers your true ability to pay.

Submitting an application does not ensure that the IRS will accept your offer. It begins a process of evaluation and verification by the IRS, taking into consideration any special circumstances that might affect your ability to pay.

This booklet will lead you through a series of steps to help you calculate an appropriate offer based on your assets, income, expenses, and future earning potential. The application requires you to describe your financial situation in detail, so before you begin, make sure you have the necessary information and documentation.

Are You Eligible?

Before your offer can be considered, you must (1) file all tax returns you are legally required to file, (2) have received a bill for at least one tax debt included on your offer, (3) make all required estimated tax payments for the current year, and (4) make all required federal tax deposits for the current quarter if you are a business owner with employees. Your offer will be immediately returned without further consideration if you have not filed all tax returns you are legally required to file.

Note: If it is determined you have not filed all tax returns you are legally required to file, the IRS will apply any initial payment you sent with your offer to your tax debt and return both your offer and application fee to you. You cannot appeal this decision.

Bankruptcy, Open Audit or Innocent Spouse Claim

If you or your business is currently in an open bankruptcy proceeding, you are not eligible to apply for an offer. Any resolution of your outstanding tax debts generally must take place within the context of your bankruptcy proceeding.

If you are not sure of your bankruptcy status, contact the Centralized Insolvency Operation at 1-800-973-0424. Be prepared to provide your bankruptcy case number and/or Taxpayer Identification Number.

If you currently have any open audit or outstanding innocent spouse claim, wait for those issues to be resolved before you submit an offer.

For any additional questions see www.irs.gov. Offer in Compromise FAQs.

Can You Pay in Full?

Generally, the IRS will not accept an offer if you can pay your tax debt in full or through an installment agreement and/or equity in assets.

Note: Adjustments or exclusions, which may be considered during the offer investigation, such as allowance of $1,000 to a bank balance or $3,450 against the value of a car, are only applied after it is determined that you cannot pay your tax debt in full.

Your Future Tax Refunds

The IRS will keep any refund, including interest, for tax periods extending through the calendar year that the IRS accepts the offer. For example, if your offer is accepted in 2019 and you file your 2019 Form 1040 on April 15, 2020 showing a refund, the IRS will apply your refund to your tax debt. **The refund is not considered as a payment toward your offer.**

Doubt as to Liability

If you have a legitimate doubt that you owe part or all of the tax debt, complete and submit a **Form 656-L, Offer in Compromise (Doubt as to Liability)**. The Form 656-L is not included as part of this package. To request a Form 656-L, visit www.irs.gov or a local IRS office or call toll-free 1-800-TAX-FORM (1-800-829-3676).

Note: Do not submit both a Doubt as to Liability offer and an offer under Doubt as to Collectibility or Effective Tax Administration at the same time. Any doubt you owe part or all of the tax debt must be resolved before sending in an offer based on your ability to pay.

Notice of Federal Tax Lien

A lien is a legal claim against all your current and future property. When you don't pay your first bill for taxes due, a lien is created by law and attaches to your property. A Notice of Federal Tax Lien (NFTL) provides public notice to creditors and is filed to establish priority of the IRS claim versus the claims of other creditors. The IRS may file a NFTL while your offer is being considered. You may be entitled to file an appeal under the Collection Appeal Program (CAP) before this occurs or request a Collection Due Process hearing after this occurs.

Note: A Notice of Federal Tax Lien (NFTL) will not be filed on any individual shared responsibility payment under the Affordable Care Act.

Trust Fund Taxes

If your business owes trust fund taxes, responsible individuals may be held liable for the trust fund portion of the tax. Trust fund taxes are the money withheld from an employee's wages, such as income tax, Social Security, and Medicare taxes. You are not eligible for consideration of an offer unless the trust fund portion of the tax is paid or the Trust Fund Recovery Penalty determination(s) has/have been made on all potentially responsible individual(s). However, if you are submitting the offer as a victim of payroll service provider fraud or failure, the trust fund assessment discussed above is not required prior to submitting the offer.

Other Important Facts

Each and every taxpayer has a set of fundamental rights they should be aware of when dealing with the IRS. Explore your rights and our obligations to protect them. For more information on your rights as a taxpayer, go to http://www.irs.gov/Taxpayer-Bill-of-Rights.

Penalties and interest will continue to accrue during consideration of your offer.

After you submit your offer, you must continue to timely file and pay all required tax returns, estimated tax payments, and federal tax payments. Failure to meet your filing and payment responsibilities during consideration of your offer will result in your offer being returned. If your offer is accepted, you must continue to stay current with all tax filing and payment obligations through the fifth year after your offer is accepted (including any extensions).

Note: If you have filed your tax returns but you have not received a bill for at least one tax debt included on your offer, your offer and application fee may be returned and any initial payment sent with your offer will be applied to your tax debt. Include a complete copy of any tax return filed within 60 days prior to this offer submission.

An offer cannot be accepted for processing if the IRS has referred your case, or cases, involving all of the liabilities identified in the offer to the Department of Justice. In addition, the IRS cannot compromise any tax liability arising from a restitution amount ordered by a court or a tax debt that has been reduced to judgment.

The law requires the IRS to make certain information from accepted offers available for public inspection and review. Instructions to request a public inspection file can be found on www.irs.gov.

The IRS may levy your assets up to the time the IRS official signs and acknowledges your offer as pending. In addition, the IRS may keep any proceeds received from the levy. If your assets are levied after your offer is submitted and pending evaluation, immediately contact the IRS person whose name and phone number are listed on the levy.

If you currently have an approved installment agreement, you will not be required to make your installment agreement payments while your offer is being considered. If your offer is not accepted and you have not incurred any additional tax debt, your installment agreement with the IRS will be reinstated with no additional fee.

PAYING FOR YOUR OFFER

Application Fee

Offers require a $186 application fee.

Exception: If you are an individual and meet the Low-Income Certification guidelines, you are not required to send any money with your offer. You are considered an individual if you are seeking compromise of a liability for which you are personally responsible, including any liability you incurred as a sole proprietor or any Form 941 liability incurred prior to January 1, 2009 as a disregarded single member LLC.

Payment Options

You must select a payment option and include the payment with your offer. The amount of the initial payment and subsequent payments will depend on the total amount of your offer and which of the following payment options you choose:

Lump Sum Cash: This option requires 20% of the total offer amount to be paid with the offer and the remaining balance paid in 5 or fewer payments within 5 or fewer months of the date your offer is accepted.

Periodic Payment: This option requires the first payment to be paid with the offer and the remaining balance paid in monthly payments within 6 to 24 months, in accordance with your proposed offer terms.

Note: Under this option, you must continue to make monthly payments while the IRS is evaluating your offer. Failure to make these payments, until you have received a final decision letter, will cause your offer to be returned. There is no appeal. Total payments must equal the total offer amount.

Exception: If you are an individual and meet the Low-Income Certification guidelines, you will not be required to send the initial payment or make the required monthly payments while your offer is being considered.

Generally, payments made on an offer will not be returned. You may make a deposit, as described in Form 656, Section 5, which may be returned if the offer is not accepted. If your offer is accepted, your payments made during the offer process, including any money designated as a deposit, will be applied to your offer amount.

If you do not have sufficient cash to pay for your offer, you may need to consider borrowing money from a bank, friends, and/or family. Other options may include borrowing against or selling other assets. **If you are an individual, use the OIC Pre-Qualifier tool located on our website at www.irs.gov to assist in determining a starting point for your offer amount.**

Note: You may not pay your offer amount with an expected or current tax refund, money already paid, funds attached by any collection action, or anticipated benefits from a capital or net operating loss. If you are planning to use your retirement savings from an IRA or 401k plan, you may have future tax debt as a result. Contact the IRS or your tax advisor before taking this action.

HOW TO APPLY

Application Process

The application must include:

- **Form 656**, Offer in Compromise
- **Completed** and signed **Form 433-A (OIC)**, Collection Information Statement for Wage Earners and Self-Employed Individuals, if applicable
- **Completed** and signed **Form 433-B (OIC)**, Collection Information Statement for Businesses, if applicable
- **$186 application fee**, unless you meet Low-Income Certification
- **Initial offer payment** based on the payment option you choose, unless you meet Low-Income Certification

Note: Your offer(s) cannot be considered without the completed and signed Form 433-A (OIC) and/or 433-B (OIC) and supporting documentation.

If You and Your Spouse Owe Joint and Separate Tax Debts

If you and your spouse have joint tax debt(s) and you and/or your spouse are also responsible for separate tax debt(s), you will each need to send in a separate Form 656. You will complete one Form 656 for yourself listing all your joint and any separate tax debts and your spouse will complete one Form 656 listing all his or her joint tax debt(s) plus any separate tax debt(s), for a total of two Forms 656.

If you and your spouse or ex-spouse have a joint tax debt and your spouse or ex-spouse does not want to be part of the offer, you on your own may submit a Form 656 to compromise your responsibility for the joint tax debt.

Each Form 656 will require the $186 application fee and initial payment unless you are an individual and meet the Low-Income Certification guidelines. You are considered an individual if you are seeking compromise of a liability for which you are personally responsible, including any liability you incurred as a sole proprietor, or any Form 941 liability incurred prior to January 1, 2009 as a disregarded single member LLC.

If You Owe Individual and Business Tax Debt

If you have individual and business tax debt that you wish to compromise, you will need to send in two Forms 656. Complete one Form 656 for your individual tax debts and one Form 656 for your business tax debts. **Each Form 656 will require the $186 application fee and initial payment.**

Note: A business is defined as a corporation, partnership, or any business that is operated as other than a sole-proprietorship. An individual's share of a partnership debt will not be compromised. The partnership must submit its own offer based on the partnership's and partners' ability to pay.

If You Have Tax Debt From a Limited Liability Company (LLC)

Individuals or individuals operating as a disregarded single member LLC taxed as a sole proprietor with tax debts (including employment taxes) incurred before January 1, 2009 may be included on your individual Form 656. However, in those instances where an LLC incurred employment taxes on or after January 1, 2009 or excise taxes on or after January 1, 2008, **two Forms 656 must be sent with a separate application fee and initial payment for each offer**, even if the tax debts were reported under the same Tax Identification Number. One Form 656 will be for the individual tax debts while the second Form 656 will be for the LLC employment tax debts incurred on or after January 1, 2009 and excise tax debts on or after January 1, 2008.

COMPLETING THE APPLICATION PACKAGE

Step 1 – Gather Your Information

To calculate an offer amount, you will need to gather information about your financial situation, including cash, investments, available credit, assets, income, and debt.

You will also need to gather information about your household's average gross monthly income and actual expenses. The entire household includes all those in addition to yourself who contribute money to pay expenses relating to the household such as, rent, utilities, insurance, groceries, etc. This is necessary for the IRS to accurately evaluate your offer. It may also be used to determine your share of the total household income and expenses.

In general, the IRS will not consider expenses for tuition for private schools, college expenses, charitable contributions, and other unsecured debt payments as part of the expense calculation.

Step 2 – Fill out Form 433-A (OIC), Collection Information Statement for Wage Earners and Self-Employed Individuals

Fill out Form 433-A (OIC) if you are an individual wage earner, or operate or operated as a sole proprietor, a disregarded single member LLC taxed as a sole proprietor prior to 2009 or are authorized to submit an offer on behalf of the estate of a deceased individual. If you are married but living separately from your spouse then you each must submit a Form 433-A (OIC). This will be used to calculate an appropriate offer amount based on your assets, income, expenses, and future earning potential. You will have the opportunity to provide a written explanation of any special circumstances that affect your financial situation.

Step 3 – Fill out Form 433-B (OIC), Collection Information Statement for Businesses

Fill out Form 433-B (OIC) if the business is a Corporation, Partnership, LLC classified as a corporation, single member LLC taxed as a corporation, or other multi-owner/multi-member LLC. This will be used to calculate an appropriate offer amount based on the business assets, income, expenses, and future earning potential. If the business has assets that are used to produce income (for example, a tow truck used in the business for towing vehicles), the business may be allowed to exclude equity in these assets.

Step 4 – Attach Required Documentation

You will need to attach supporting documentation with Form(s) 433-A (OIC) and 433-B (OIC). A list of the documents required will be found at the end of each form. Include copies of all required attachments. **Do not send original documents.**

Step 5 – Fill out Form 656, Offer in Compromise

Fill out Form 656. The Form 656 identifies the tax years and type of tax you would like to compromise. It also identifies your offer amount and the payment terms.

Step 6 – Include Initial Payment and $186 Application Fee

Include a personal check, cashier's check, or money order for your initial payment based on the payment option you selected (20% of the offer amount for a lump sum cash offer or the first month's payment for a periodic payment offer). Generally, initial payments will not be returned but will be applied to your tax debt if your offer is not accepted.

Include a separate personal check, cashier's check, or money order for the application fee ($186).

Make both payments payable to the "United States Treasury". All payments must be made in U.S. dollars.

Reminder: If you meet the Low-Income Certification guidelines DO NOT send any money with your offer since the initial payment and application fee are not required.

Step 7 – Mail the Application Package

Make a copy of your application package and keep it for your records.

Mail the completed application package to the appropriate IRS facility. See page 29, Application Checklist, for details.

Note: If you are working with an IRS employee, let him or her know you are sending or have sent an offer to compromise your tax debt(s).

IMPORTANT INFORMATION

After You Mail Your Application:
We will contact you after we receive and review your offer application. Promptly reply to any requests for additional information within the time frame specified. Failure to reply timely will result in the return of your offer without appeal rights.

If you selected the Periodic Payment option, you must continue to make the payments during consideration of your offer, unless you meet the Low-Income Certification. Failure to make monthly payments (until you have received a final decision letter) will result in the return of your offer without appeal rights.

If your offer is accepted, you must continue to timely file all required tax returns and timely pay all estimated tax payments and federal tax payments that become due in the future. If you fail to timely file and timely pay any tax obligations that become due within the five years after your offer is accepted (including any extensions) your offer may be defaulted. If your offer is defaulted, you will be liable for the original tax debt, less payments made, and all accrued interest and penalties. An offer does not stop the accrual of interest and penalties. Please note that if your final payment is more than the agreed amount by $50 or less, the money will not be returned but will be applied to your tax debt. If your final payment is more than $50 over the agreed amount, then the overpayment will be returned to you.

In addition, your offer may be defaulted if you fail to promptly pay any tax debts assessed after acceptance of your offer for any tax years prior to acceptance that were not included in your original offer.

Form 433-A (OIC)
(March 2019)

Department of the Treasury — Internal Revenue Service

Collection Information Statement for Wage Earners and Self-Employed Individuals

Use this form if you are
- An individual who owes income tax on a Form 1040, U.S. Individual Income Tax Return
- An individual with a personal liability for Excise Tax
- An individual responsible for a Trust Fund Recovery Penalty
- An individual who is self-employed or has self-employment income. You are considered to be self-employed if you are in business for yourself, or carry on a trade or business.
- An individual who is personally responsible for a partnership liability (only if the partnership is submitting an offer)
- An individual who operated as a disregarded single member Limited Liability Company (LLC) taxed as a sole proprietor prior to 2009
- An individual who is submitting an offer on behalf of the estate of a deceased person

Note: Include attachments if additional space is needed to respond completely to any question. This form should only be used with the Form 656, Offer in Compromise.

Section 1 — Personal and Household Information

Last name

First name

Date of birth (mm/dd/yyyy)

Social Security Number - -

Marital status
☐ Unmarried   ☐ Married

If married, date of marriage (mm/dd/yyyy)

Home physical address (street, city, state, ZIP code)

Do you
☐ Own your home   ☐ Rent
☐ Other (specify e.g., share rent, live with relative, etc.)

County of residence

Primary phone
( ) -

Home mailing address (if different from above or post office box number)

Secondary phone
( ) -

FAX number
( ) -

Provide information about your spouse.

Spouse's last name

Spouse's first name

Date of birth (mm/dd/yyyy)

Social Security Number - -

Provide information for all other persons in the household or claimed as a dependent.

Name	Age	Relationship	Claimed as a dependent on your Form 1040	Contributes to household income
			☐ Yes ☐ No	☐ Yes ☐ No
			☐ Yes ☐ No	☐ Yes ☐ No
			☐ Yes ☐ No	☐ Yes ☐ No
			☐ Yes ☐ No	☐ Yes ☐ No

Section 2 — Employment Information for Wage Earners

Complete this section if you or your spouse are wage earners and receive a Form W-2. If you or your spouse have self-employment income (that is you file a Schedule C, E, F, etc.) instead of, or in addition to wage income, you must also complete Business Information in Sections 4, 5, and 6.

Your employer's name

Pay period ☐ Weekly ☐ Bi-weekly ☐ Monthly ☐ Other

Employer's address (street, city, state, ZIP code)

Do you have an ownership interest in this business
☐ Yes   ☐ No

If yes, check the business interest that applies ☐ Partner ☐ Officer ☐ Sole proprietor

Your occupation

How long with this employer
(years)   (months)

Spouse's employer's name

Pay period ☐ Weekly ☐ Bi-weekly ☐ Monthly ☐ Other

Employer's address (street, city, state, ZIP code)

Does your spouse have an ownership interest in this business
☐ Yes   ☐ No

If yes, check the business interest that applies ☐ Partner ☐ Officer ☐ Sole proprietor

Spouse's occupation

How long with this employer
(years)   (months)

Page 2

Section 3 — **Personal Asset Information**

Use the most current statement for each type of account, such as checking, savings, money market and online accounts, stored value cards *(such as a payroll card from an employer)*, investment, retirement accounts *(IRAs, Keogh, 401(k) plans, stocks, bonds, mutual funds, certificates of deposit)* and virtual currency *(such as Bitcoin, Ripple, Ethereum, etc.)*, life insurance policies that have a cash value, and safe deposit boxes. Asset value is subject to adjustment by IRS based on individual circumstances. Enter the total amount available for each of the following *(if additional space is needed include attachments).*

Round to the nearest dollar. Do not enter a negative number. If any line item is a negative number, enter "0".

Cash and Investments (domestic and foreign)

☐ Cash ☐ Checking ☐ Savings ☐ Money Market Account/CD ☐ Online Account ☐ Stored Value Card

Bank name _____ Account number _____

(1a) $ _____

☐ Checking ☐ Savings ☐ Money Market Account/CD ☐ Online Account ☐ Stored Value Card

Bank name _____ Account number _____

(1b) $ _____

Total of bank accounts from attachment (1c) $ _____

Add lines (1a) through (1c) minus ($1,000) = **(1) $** _____

Investment account ☐ Stocks ☐ Bonds ☐ Other

Name of Financial Institution _____ Account number _____

Current market value   Minus loan balance

$ _____ X .8 = $ _____   − $ _____   = (2a) $ _____

Investment account ☐ Stocks ☐ Bonds ☐ Other

Name of Financial Institution _____ Account number _____

Current market value   Minus loan balance

$ _____ X .8 = $ _____   − $ _____   = (2b) $ _____

☐ Virtual currency | Name of virtual currency wallet, exchange or digital currency exchange (DCE) | Email address used to set-up with the virtual currency exchange or DCE | Location(s) of virtual currency

Type of virtual currency _____

Current market value in U.S. dollars as of today

$ _____ X .8 = $ _____ = (2c) $ _____

Total investment accounts from attachment. [current market value minus loan balance(s)] (2d) $ _____

Add lines (2a) through (2d) = **(2) $** _____

Retirement account ☐ 401K ☐ IRA ☐ Other

Name of Financial Institution _____ Account number _____

Current market value   Minus loan balance

$ _____ X .8 = $ _____   − $ _____   = (3a) $ _____

Total of retirement accounts from attachment. [current market value X .8 minus loan balance(s)] (3b) $ _____

Add lines (3a) through (3b) = **(3) $** _____

Note: Your reduction from current market value may be greater than 20% due to potential tax consequences/withdrawal penalties.

Cash value of Life Insurance Policies

Name of Insurance Company _____ Policy number _____

Current cash value   Minus loan balance

$ _____   − $ _____   = (4a) $ _____

Total cash value of life insurance policies from attachment   Minus loan balance(s)

$ _____   − $ _____   = (4b) $ _____

Add lines (4a) through (4b) = **(4) $** _____

Catalog Number 55896Q   www.irs.gov   Form **433-A (OIC)** (Rev. 3-2019)

Section 3 (Continued) — Personal Asset Information

Real property *(enter information about any house, condo, co-op, time share, etc. that you own or are buying)*

Property description *(indicate if personal residence)*	Purchase/Lease date *(mm/dd/yyyy)*	
Amount of mortgage/rent payment	Date of final payment	How title is held *(joint tenancy, etc.)*
Location *(street, city, state, ZIP code, county, and country)*	Lender/Lessor/Landlord name, address *(street, city, state, ZIP code) and phone*	

Current market value
$ _____ X .8 = $ _____ − $ _____ (total value of real estate) = (5a) $

Property description *(indicate if personal residence)*	Purchase/Lease date *(mm/dd/yyyy)*	
Amount of mortgage/rent payment	Date of final payment	How title is held *(joint tenancy, etc.)*
Location *(street, city, state, ZIP code, county, and country)*	Lender/Lessor/Landlord name, address *(street, city, state, ZIP code) and phone*	

Current market value
$ _____ X .8 = $ _____ − $ _____ (total value of real estate) = (5b) $

Total value of property(s) from attachment [current market value X .8 minus any loan balance(s)] (5c) $

Add lines (5a) through (5c) = (5) $

Vehicles *(enter information about any cars, boats, motorcycles, etc. that you own or lease)*

Vehicle make & model	Year	Date purchased	Mileage
☐ Lease ☐ Loan Name of creditor		Date of final payment	Monthly lease/loan amount $

Current market value
$ _____ X .8 = $ _____ − $ _____ Total value of vehicle *(if the vehicle is leased, enter 0 as the total value)* = (6a) $

Subtract $3,450 from line (6a)
(If line (6a) minus $3,450 is a negative number, enter "0") (6b) $

Vehicle make & model	Year	Date purchased	Mileage
☐ Lease ☐ Loan Name of creditor		Date of final payment	Monthly lease/loan amount $

Current market value
$ _____ X .8 = $ _____ − $ _____ Total value of vehicle *(if the vehicle is leased, enter 0 as the total value)* = (6c) $

If you are filing a joint offer, subtract $3,450 from line (6c)
(If line (6c) minus $3,450 is a negative number, enter "0")
If you are not filing a joint offer, enter the amount from line (6c) (6d) $

Total value of vehicles listed from attachment [current market value X .8 minus any loan balance(s)] (6e) $

Total lines (6b), (6d), and (6e) = (6) $

Catalog Number 55896Q www.irs.gov Form **433-A (OIC)** (Rev. 3-2019)

Page 4

Section 3 (Continued) — Personal Asset Information

Other valuable items *(artwork, collections, jewelry, items of value in safe deposit boxes, interest in a company or business that is not publicly traded, etc.)*

Description of asset(s)

Current market value   Minus loan balance
$ _____ X .8 = $ _____   – $ _____   =   (7a) $ _____

Value of remaining furniture and personal effects *(not listed above)*

Description of asset

Current market value   Minus loan balance
$ _____ X .8 = $ _____   – $ _____   =   (7b) $ _____

Total value of valuable items listed from attachment [current market value X .8 minus any loan balance(s)]   (7c) $ _____

Add lines (7a) through (7c) minus IRS deduction of $9,540 =   (7) $ _____

Do not include amount on the lines with a letter beside the number. Round to the nearest whole dollar.
Do not enter a negative number. If any line item is a negative, enter "0" on that line.
Add lines (1) through (7) and enter the amount in Box A =

Box A
Available Individual Equity in Assets
$ _____

NOTE: If you or your spouse are self-employed, Sections 4, 5, and 6 must be completed before continuing with Sections 7 and 8.

Section 4 — Self-Employed Information

If you or your spouse are self-employed (e.g., files Schedule(s) C, E, F, etc.), complete this section.

Is your business a sole proprietorship
☐ Yes   ☐ No

Name of business

Address of business *(if other than personal residence)*

Business telephone number
( ) -

Employer Identification Number

Business website address

Trade name or DBA

Description of business

Total number of employees

Frequency of tax deposits

Average gross monthly payroll $

Do you or your spouse have any other business interests? Include any interest in an LLC, LLP, corporation, partnership, etc.

☐ Yes *(percentage of ownership: ____)* Title
☐ No

Business name

Business address *(street, city, state, ZIP code)*

Business telephone number
( ) -

Employer Identification Number

Type of business *(select one)*
☐ Partnership   ☐ LLC   ☐ Corporation   ☐ Other _____

Section 5 — Business Asset Information *(for Self-Employed)*

List business assets such as bank accounts, virtual currency (cryptocurrency), tools, books, machinery, equipment, business vehicles and real property that is owned/leased/rented. If additional space is needed, attach a list of items. Do not include personal assets listed in Section 3.

Round to the nearest whole dollar. Do not enter a negative number. If any line item is a negative number, enter "0".

☐ Cash   ☐ Checking   ☐ Savings   ☐ Money Market Account/CD   ☐ Online Account   ☐ Stored Value Card

Bank name   Account number
                                                                            (8a) $ _____

☐ Cash   ☐ Checking   ☐ Savings   ☐ Money Market Account/CD   ☐ Online Account   ☐ Stored Value Card

Bank name   Account number
                                                                            (8b) $ _____

☐ Virtual currency
Type of virtual currency

Name of virtual currency wallet, exchange or digital currency exchange (DCE)

Email address used to set-up with the virtual currency exchange or DCE

Location(s) of virtual currency

Current market value in U.S. dollars as of today
$ _____ X .8 = $ _____   =   (8c) $ _____

Total bank accounts from attachment   (8d) $ _____

Add lines (8a) through (8d) =   (8) $ _____

Catalog Number 55896Q   www.irs.gov   Form **433-A (OIC)** (Rev. 3-2019)

Page 5

Section 5 (Continued) — Business Asset Information (for Self-Employed)

Description of asset

Current market value		Minus loan balance	Total value (if leased or used in the production of income, enter 0 as the total value)	
$	X .8 = $	– $	=	(9a) $

Description of asset:

Current market value		Minus Loan Balance	Total value (if leased or used in the production of income, enter 0 as the total value)	
$	X .8 = $	– $	=	(9b) $

Total value of assets listed from attachment [current market value X .8 minus any loan balance(s)]	(9c) $
Add lines (9a) through (9c) =	**(9) $**
IRS allowed deduction for professional books and tools of trade –	(10) $ [4,770]
Enter the value of line (9) minus line (10). If less than zero enter zero. =	**(11) $**

Notes Receivable

Do you have notes receivable ☐ Yes ☐ No

If yes, attach current listing that includes name(s) and amount of note(s) receivable

Accounts Receivable

Do you have accounts receivable, including e-payment, factoring companies, and any bartering or online auction accounts ☐ Yes ☐ No

If yes, you may be asked to provide a list of your account(s) receivable

Do not include amounts from the lines with a letter beside the number [for example: (9c)].
Round to the nearest whole dollar.
Do not enter a negative number. If any line item is a negative, enter "0" on that line.
Add lines (8) and (11) and enter the amount in Box B =

Box B
Available Business Equity in Assets
$

Section 6 — Business Income and Expense Information (for Self-Employed)

If you provide a current profit and loss (P&L) statement for the information below, enter the total gross monthly income on line 17 and your monthly expenses on line 29 below. Do not complete lines (12) - (16) and (18) - (28). You may use the amounts claimed for income and expenses on your most recent Schedule C; however, if the amount has changed significantly within the past year, a current P&L should be submitted to substantiate the claim.

Round to the nearest whole dollar. Do not enter a negative number. If any line item is a negative number, enter "0".

Business income *(you may average 6-12 months income/receipts to determine your gross monthly income/receipts)*

Gross receipts	(12) $
Gross rental income	(13) $
Interest income	(14) $
Dividends	(15) $
Other income	(16) $
Add lines (12) through (16) =	**(17) $**

Business expenses *(you may average 6-12 months expenses to determine your average expenses)*

Materials purchased *(e.g., items directly related to the production of a product or service)*	(18) $
Inventory purchased *(e.g., goods bought for resale)*	(19) $
Gross wages and salaries	(20) $
Rent	(21) $
Supplies *(items used to conduct business and used up within one year, e.g., books, office supplies, professional equipment, etc.)*	(22) $
Utilities/telephones	(23) $
Vehicle costs *(gas, oil, repairs, maintenance)*	(24) $
Business insurance	(25) $
Current business taxes *(e.g., real estate, excise, franchise, occupational, personal property, sales and employer's portion of employment taxes)*	(26) $
Secured debts *(not credit cards)*	(27) $
Other business expenses *(include a list)*	(28) $
Add lines (18) through (28) =	**(29) $**

Round to the nearest whole dollar.
Do not enter a negative number. If any line item is a negative, enter "0" on that line.
Subtract line (29) from line (17) and enter the amount in Box C =

Box C
Net Business Income
$

Catalog Number 55896Q   www.irs.gov   Form **433-A (OIC)** (Rev. 3-2019)

Page 6

Section 7 — Monthly Household Income and Expense Information

Enter your household's gross monthly income. The information below is for yourself, your spouse, and anyone else who contributes to your household's income. The entire household includes spouse, non-liable spouse, significant other, children, and others who contribute to the household. This is necessary for the IRS to accurately evaluate your offer.

Monthly Household Income

Note: Entire household income should also include income that is considered not taxable and may not be included on your tax return.

Round to the nearest whole dollar.

Primary taxpayer
Gross wages $ _____ + Social Security $ _____ + Pension(s) $ _____ + Other income (e.g. unemployment) $ _____ = Total primary taxpayer income (30) $ _____

Spouse
Gross wages $ _____ + Social Security $ _____ + Pension(s) $ _____ + Other Income (e.g. unemployment) $ _____ = Total spouse income (31) $ _____

Additional sources of income used to support the household, e.g., non-liable spouse, or anyone else who may contribute to the household income, etc. List source(s) _____	(32) $
Interest and dividends	(33) $
Distributions (e.g., income from partnerships, sub-S Corporations, etc.)	(34) $
Net rental income	(35) $
Net business income from Box C	(36) $
Child support received	(37) $
Alimony received	(38) $
Round to the nearest whole dollar. Do not enter a negative number. If any line item is a negative, enter "0" on that line. Add lines (30) through (38) and enter the amount in Box D =	**Box D** Total Household Income $

Monthly Household Expenses

Enter your average monthly expenses.

Note: For expenses claimed in boxes (39) and (45) only, you should list the full amount of the allowable standard even if the actual amount you pay is less. For the other boxes input your actual expenses. You may find the allowable standards at http://www.irs.gov/Businesses/Small-Businesses-&-Self-Employed/Collection-Financial-Standards.

Round to the nearest whole dollar.

Food, clothing, and miscellaneous (e.g., housekeeping supplies, personal care products, minimum payment on credit card). A reasonable estimate of these expenses may be used	(39) $
Housing and utilities (e.g., rent or mortgage payment and average monthly cost of property taxes, home insurance, maintenance, dues, fees and utilities including electricity, gas, other fuels, trash collection, water, cable television and internet, telephone, and cell phone)	(40) $
Vehicle loan and/or lease payment(s)	(41) $
Vehicle operating costs (e.g., average monthly cost of maintenance, repairs, insurance, fuel, registrations, licenses, inspections, parking, tolls, etc.). A reasonable estimate of these expenses may be used	(42) $
Public transportation costs (e.g., average monthly cost of fares for mass transit such as bus, train, ferry, taxi, etc.). A reasonable estimate of these expenses may be used	(43) $
Health insurance premiums	(44) $
Out-of-pocket health care costs (e.g. average monthly cost of prescription drugs, medical services, and medical supplies like eyeglasses, hearing aids, etc.)	(45) $
Court-ordered payments (e.g., monthly cost of any alimony, child support, etc.)	(46) $
Child/dependent care payments (e.g., daycare, etc.)	(47) $
Term life insurance premiums	(48) $
Current monthly taxes (e.g., monthly cost of federal, state, and local tax, personal property tax, etc.)	(49) $
Secured debts (e.g., any loan where you pledged an asset as collateral not previously listed, government guaranteed student loan) List debt(s) _____	(50) $
Enter the amount of your monthly delinquent state and/or local tax payment(s)	(51) $
Round to the nearest whole dollar. Do not enter a negative number. If any line item is a negative, enter "0" on that line. Add lines (39) through (51) and enter the amount in Box E =	**Box E** Total Household Expenses $
Round to the nearest whole dollar. Do not enter a negative number. If any line item is a negative, enter "0" on that line. Subtract Box E from Box D and enter the amount in Box F =	**Box F** Remaining Monthly Income $

Catalog Number 55896Q   www.irs.gov   Form **433-A (OIC)** (Rev. 3-2019)

Section 8 — Calculate Your Minimum Offer Amount

The next steps calculate your minimum offer amount. The amount of time you take to pay your offer in full will affect your minimum offer amount. Paying over a shorter period of time will result in a smaller minimum offer amount.

Note: The multipliers below (12 and 24) and the calculated offer amount (which included the amount(s) allowed for vehicles and bank accounts) do not apply if the IRS determines you have the ability to pay your tax debt in full within the legal period to collect.

Round to the nearest whole dollar.

If you will pay your offer in 5 or fewer payments within 5 months or less, multiply "Remaining Monthly Income" (Box F) by 12 to get "Future Remaining Income" (Box G). Do not enter a number less than $0.

Enter the total from Box F		Box G Future Remaining Income
$	X 12 =	$

If you will pay your offer in 6 to 24 months, multiply "Remaining Monthly Income" (Box F) by 24 to get "Future Remaining Income" (Box H). Do not enter a number less than $0.

Enter the total from Box F		Box H Future Remaining Income
$	X 24 =	$

Determine your minimum offer amount by adding the total available assets from Box A and Box B (if applicable) to the amount in either Box G or Box H.

Enter the amount from Box A plus Box B (if applicable)		Enter the amount from either Box G or Box H		Offer Amount — Your offer must be more than zero ($0). Do not leave blank. Use whole dollars only.
$	+	$	=	$

If you cannot pay the Offer Amount shown above due to special circumstances, explain on the Form 656, Offer in Compromise, Section 3, Reason for Offer, Explanation of Circumstances. You must offer an amount more than $0.

Section 9 — Other Information

Additional information IRS needs to consider settlement of your tax debt. If you or your business are currently in a bankruptcy proceeding, you are not eligible to apply for an offer.

Are you a party to or involved in litigation *(if yes, answer the following)* ☐ Yes ☐ No

Plaintiff / Defendant	Location of filing	Represented by	Docket/Case number
☐ Plaintiff ☐ Defendant			

Amount of dispute	Possible completion date *(mmddyyyy)*	Subject of litigation
$		

Have you filed bankruptcy in the past 7 years *(if yes, answer the following)* ☐ Yes ☐ No

Date filed *(mmddyyyy)*	Date dismissed *(mmddyyyy)*	Date discharged *(mmddyyyy)*	Petition no.	Location filed

In the past 10 years, have you lived outside of the U.S. for 6 months or longer *(if yes, answer the following)* ☐ Yes ☐ No

Dates lived abroad: From *(mmddyyyy)* _____ To *(mmddyyyy)* _____

Are you or have you ever been party to any litigation involving the IRS/United States *(including any tax litigation)* ☐ Yes ☐ No

If yes and the litigation included tax debt, provide the types of tax and periods involved

Are you the beneficiary of a trust, estate, or life insurance policy *(if yes, answer the following)* ☐ Yes ☐ No

Place where recorded	EIN

Name of the trust, estate, or policy	Anticipated amount to be received	When will the amount be received
	$	

Are you a trustee, fiduciary, or contributor of a trust ☐ Yes ☐ No

Name of the trust	EIN

Do you have a safe deposit box *(business or personal)* *(if yes, answer the following)* ☐ Yes ☐ No

Location *(name, address and box number(s))*	Contents	Value
		$

In the past 10 years, have you transferred any assets, including real property, for less than their full value *(if yes, answer the following)* ☐ Yes ☐ No

List asset(s)	Value at time of transfer	Date transferred *(mmddyyyy)*	To whom or where was it transferred
	$		

Catalog Number 55896Q   www.irs.gov   Form **433-A (OIC)** (Rev. 3-2019)

Page 8

Section 9 (Continued) — Other Information

Do you have any assets or own any real property outside the U.S. ☐ Yes ☐ No

If yes, provide description, location, and value

Do you have any funds being held in trust by a third party ☐ Yes ☐ No

If yes, how much $ _____ Where _____

Section 10 — Signatures

Under penalties of perjury, I declare that I have examined this offer, including accompanying documents, and to the best of my knowledge it is true, correct, and complete.

▶ Signature of Taxpayer   Date (mm/dd/yyyy)

▶ Signature of Spouse   Date (mm/dd/yyyy)

Remember to include all applicable attachments listed below.

- ☐ Copies of the most recent pay stub, earnings statement, etc., from each employer.
- ☐ Copies of the most recent statement for each investment and retirement account.
- ☐ Copies of the most recent statement, etc., from all other sources of income such as pensions, Social Security, rental income, interest and dividends (including any received from a related partnership, corporation, LLC, LLP, etc.), court order for child support, alimony, and rent subsidies.
- ☐ Copies of individual bank statements for the three most recent months. If you operate a business, copies of the six most recent statements for each business bank account.
- ☐ Copies of the most recent statement from lender(s) on loans such as mortgages, second mortgages, vehicles, etc., showing monthly payments, loan payoffs, and balances.
- ☐ List of Notes Receivable, if applicable.
- ☐ Verification of delinquent State/Local Tax Liability showing total delinquent state/local taxes and amount of monthly payments, if applicable.
- ☐ Documentation to support any special circumstances described in the "Explanation of Circumstances" on Form 656, if applicable.
- ☐ Attach a Form 2848, *Power of Attorney*, if you would like your attorney, CPA, or enrolled agent to represent you and you do not have a current form on file with the IRS.
- ☐ Completed and signed current Form 656.

Form **433-B (OIC)**
(March 2019)

Department of the Treasury — Internal Revenue Service

Collection Information Statement for Businesses

Complete this form if your business is a

▶ Corporation

▶ Partnership

▶ Limited Liability Company (LLC) classified as a corporation

▶ Other LLC

Note: If your business is a sole proprietorship or was a disregarded single member LLC taxed as a sole proprietor (filing Schedule C, D, E, F, etc.) prior to 2009, do not use this form. Instead, complete Form 433-A (OIC) Collection Information Statement for Wage Earners and Self-Employed Individuals. This form should only be used with the Form 656, Offer in Compromise.

Include attachments if additional space is needed to respond completely to any question.

Section 1 — Business Information

Business name

Employer Identification Number

Business physical address (street, city, state, ZIP code)

County of business location

Description of business and DBA or "Trade Name"

Primary phone ( ) -

Secondary phone ( ) -

Business mailing address (if different from above or post office box number)

Business website address

FAX number ( ) -

Does the business outsource its payroll processing and tax return preparation for a fee
☐ Yes ☐ No   If yes, list provider name and address in box below (street, city, state, ZIP code)

Federal contractor ☐ Yes ☐ No

Total number of employees

Frequency of tax deposits

Average gross monthly payroll $

Provide information about all partners, officers, LLC members, major shareholders (foreign and domestic), etc., associated with the business. Include attachments if additional space is needed.

Last name	First name	Title
Percent of ownership and annual salary	Social Security Number - -	Home address (street, city, state, ZIP code)
Primary phone ( ) -	Secondary phone ( ) -	
Last name	First name	Title
Percent of ownership and annual salary	Social Security Number - -	Home address (street, city, state, ZIP code)
Primary phone ( ) -	Secondary phone ( ) -	
Last name	First name	Title
Percent of ownership and annual salary	Social Security Number - -	Home address (street, city, state, ZIP code)
Primary phone ( ) -	Secondary phone ( ) -	

Catalog Number 55897B

www.irs.gov

Form **433-B (OIC)** (Rev. 3-2019)

Page 2

Section 2 — Business Asset Information

Gather the most current statement from banks, lenders on loans, mortgages *(including second mortgages)*, monthly payments, loan balances, and accountant's depreciation schedules, if applicable. Also, include make/model/year/mileage of vehicles and current value of business assets. To estimate the current value, you may consult resources like Kelley Blue Book *(www.kbb.com)*, NADA *(www.nada.com)*, local real estate postings of properties similar to yours, and any other websites or publications that show what the business assets would be worth if you were to sell them. Asset value is subject to adjustment by IRS. Enter the total amount available for each of the following *(if additional space is needed, please include attachments)*.

Round to the nearest dollar. Do not enter a negative number. If any line item is a negative number, enter "0".

Cash and investments *(domestic and foreign)*

☐ Cash ☐ Checking ☐ Savings ☐ Money Market Account/CD ☐ Online Account ☐ Stored Value Card
Bank name | Account number
(1a) $

☐ Cash ☐ Checking ☐ Savings ☐ Money Market Account/CD ☐ Online Account ☐ Stored Value Card
Bank name | Account number
(1b) $

☐ Cash ☐ Checking ☐ Savings ☐ Money Market Account/CD ☐ Online Account ☐ Stored Value Card
Bank name | Account number
(1c) $

Total bank accounts from attachment (1d) $

Add lines (1a) through (1d) = **(1) $**

Investment account ☐ Stocks ☐ Bonds ☐ Other
Name of Financial Institution | Account number
Current market value | Minus loan balance
$ _____ X .8 = $ _____ − $ _____ = (2a) $

Investment Account: ☐ Stocks ☐ Bonds ☐ Other
Name of Financial Institution | Account number
Current market value | Minus loan balance
$ _____ X .8 = $ _____ − $ _____ = (2b) $

☐ Virtual currency | Name of virtual currency wallet, exchange or digital currency exchange (DCE) | Email address used to set-up with the virtual currency exchange or DCE | Location(s) of virtual currency
Type of virtual currency

Current market value in U.S. dollars as of today
$ _____ X .8 = $ _____ = (2c) $

Total investment accounts from attachment. [current market value minus loan balance(s)] (2d) $

Add lines (2a) through (2d) = **(2) $**

Notes Receivable

Do you have notes receivable ☐ Yes ☐ No
If yes, attach current listing which includes name, age, and amount of note(s) receivable

Accounts Receivable

Do you have accounts receivable, including e-payment, factoring companies, and any bartering or online auction accounts ☐ Yes ☐ No
If yes, you may be asked to provide a list of name, age, and amount of the account(s) receivable

Catalog Number 55897B | www.irs.gov | Form **433-B (OIC)** (Rev. 3-2019)

Page 3

Section 2 (Continued) — Business Asset Information

If the business owns more properties, vehicles, or equipment than shown in this form, please list on a separate attachment.

Real estate (buildings, lots, commercial property, etc.)

Property address (street address, city, state, ZIP code, county, and country)	Property description	Date purchased	
	Monthly mortgage/rent payment	Date of final payment	
	Name of creditor		
Current market value $ _____ X .8 = $ _____	Minus loan balance (mortgages, etc.) − $ _____	Total value of real estate =	(3a) $
Property address (street address, city, state, ZIP code, county, and country)	Property description	Date purchased	
	Monthly mortgage/rent payment	Date of final payment	
	Name of creditor		
Current market value $ _____ X .8 = $ _____	Minus loan balance (mortgages, etc.) − $ _____	Total value of real estate =	(3b) $
Total value of property(s) listed from attachment [current market value X .8 minus any loan balance(s)]			(3c) $
		Add lines (3a) through (3c) =	**(3) $**

Business vehicles (cars, boats, motorcycles, trailers, etc.). If additional space is needed, list on an attachment

Vehicle make & model	Year	Date purchased	Mileage or use hours	
☐ Lease ☐ Loan / Monthly lease/loan amount $		Name of creditor	Date of final payment	
Current market value $ _____ X .8 = $ _____		Minus loan balance − $ _____	Total value of vehicle (if the vehicle is leased, enter 0 as the total value) =	(4a) $
Vehicle make & model	Year	Date purchased	Mileage or use hours	
☐ Lease ☐ Loan / Monthly lease/loan amount $		Name of creditor	Date of final payment	
Current market value $ _____ X .8 = $ _____		Minus loan balance − $ _____	Total value of vehicle (if the vehicle is leased, enter 0 as the total value) =	(4b) $
Vehicle make & model	Year	Date purchased	Mileage or use hours	
☐ Lease ☐ Loan / Monthly lease/loan amount $		Name of creditor	Date of final payment	
Current market value $ _____ X .8 = $ _____		Minus loan balance − $ _____	Total value of vehicle (if the vehicle is leased, enter 0 as the total value) =	(4c) $
Total value of vehicles listed from attachment [current market value X .8 minus any loan balance(s)]				(4d) $
			Add lines (4a) through (4d) =	**(4) $**

Catalog Number 55897B www.irs.gov Form **433-B (OIC)** (Rev. 3-2019)

Page 4

Section 2 (Continued) — Business Asset Information

Other business equipment
[If you have more than one piece of equipment, please list on a separate attachment and put the total of all equipment in box (5b)]

Type of equipment

Current market value   Minus loan balance   Total value of equipment
(if leased or used in the production of income enter 0 as the total value) =

$ _____ X .8 = $ _____ – $ _____   (5a) $

Total value of equipment listed from attachment [current market value X .8 minus any loan balance(s)]	(5b) $
Total value of all business equipment **Add lines (5a) and (5b)** =	(5) $
Do not include amount on the lines with a letter beside the number. Round to the nearest dollar. Do not enter a negative number. If any line item is a negative number, enter "0" on that line. **Add lines (1) through (5) and enter the amount in Box A** =	**Box A** Available Equity in Assets $

Section 3 — Business Income Information

Enter the average gross monthly income of your business. To determine your gross monthly income use the most recent 6-12 months documentation of commissions, invoices, gross receipts from sales/services, etc.; most recent 6-12 months earnings statements, etc., from every other source of income (such as rental income, interest and dividends, or subsidies); or you may use the most recent 6-12 months Profit and Loss (P&L) to provide the information of income and expenses.

Note: If you provide a current profit and loss statement for the information below, enter the total gross monthly income in Box B below. Do not complete lines (6) - (10). Entire household income should also include income that is considered as not taxable and may not be included on your tax return.

Gross receipts	(6) $
Gross rental income	(7) $
Interest income	(8) $
Dividends	(9) $
Other income *(specify on attachment)*	(10) $
Round to the nearest dollar. Do not enter a negative number. If any line item is a negative number, enter "0" on that line. **Add lines (6) through (10) and enter the amount in Box B** =	**Box B** Total Business Income $

Section 4 — Business Expense Information

Enter the average gross monthly expenses for your business using your most recent 6-12 months statements, bills, receipts, or other documents showing monthly recurring expenses.

Note: If you provide a current profit and loss statement for the information below, enter the total monthly expenses in Box C below. Do not complete lines (11) - (20).

Materials purchased *(e.g., items directly related to the production of a product or service)*	(11) $
Inventory purchased *(e.g., goods bought for resale)*	(12) $
Gross wages and salaries	(13) $
Rent	(14) $
Supplies *(items used to conduct business and used up within one year, e.g., books, office supplies, professional equipment, etc.)*	(15) $
Utilities/telephones	(16) $
Vehicle costs *(gas, oil, repairs, maintenance)*	(17) $
Insurance *(other than life)*	(18) $
Current taxes *(e.g., real estate, state, and local income tax, excise franchise, occupational, personal property, sales and employer's portion of employment taxes, etc.)*	(19) $
Other expenses *(e.g., secured debt payments. Specify on attachment. Do not include credit card payments)*	(20) $
Round to the nearest dollar. Do not enter a negative number. If any line item is a negative number, enter "0" on that line. **Add lines (11) through (20) and enter the amount in Box C** =	**Box C** Total Business Expenses $
Round to the nearest dollar. Do not enter a negative number. If any line item is a negative number, enter "0" on that line. **Subtract Box C from Box B and enter the amount in Box D** =	**Box D** Remaining Monthly Income $

Catalog Number 55897B   www.irs.gov   Form **433-B (OIC)** (Rev. 3-2019)

Page 5

Section 5 — Calculate Your Minimum Offer Amount

The next steps calculate your minimum offer amount. The amount of time you take to pay your offer in full will affect your minimum offer amount. Paying over a shorter period of time will result in a smaller minimum offer amount.

If you will pay your offer in 5 or fewer payments within 5 months or less, multiply "Remaining Monthly Income" (Box D) by 12 to get "Future Remaining Income." Do not enter a number less than zero.

Note: The multipliers below (12 and 24) and the calculated offer amount do not apply if IRS determines you have the ability to pay your tax debt in full within the legal period to collect.

Round to the nearest whole dollar.

Enter the total from Box D		Box E Future Remaining Income
$	X 12 =	$

If you will pay your offer in 6 to 24 months, multiply "Remaining Monthly Income" (Box D) by 24 to get "Future Remaining Income". Do not enter a number less than zero.

Enter the total from Box D		Box F Future Remaining Income
$	X 24 =	$

Determine your minimum offer amount by adding the total available assets from Box A to the amount in either Box E or Box F. Your offer amount must be more than zero.

Enter the amount from Box A*		Enter the amount from either Box E or Box F		Offer Amount
$	+	$	=	Your offer must be more than zero ($0). Do not leave blank. Use whole dollars only. $

You must offer an amount more than $0.

*You may exclude any equity in income producing assets (except real estate) shown in Section 2 of this form.

Section 6 — Other Information

Additional information IRS needs to consider settlement of your tax debt. If this business is currently in a bankruptcy proceeding, the business is not eligible to apply for an offer.

Is the business currently in bankruptcy

☐ Yes ☐ No

Has the business filed bankruptcy in the past 10 years

☐ Yes ☐ No

If yes, provide

Date filed (mm/dd/yyyy) _____   Date dismissed or discharged (mm/dd/yyyy) _____

Petition no. _____   Location filed _____

Does this business have other business affiliations (e.g., subsidiary or parent companies)

☐ Yes ☐ No

If yes, list the name and Employer Identification Number

Do any related parties (e.g., partners, officers, employees) owe money to the business

☐ Yes ☐ No

Is the business currently, or in the past, party to litigation

☐ Yes ☐ No

If yes, answer the following

☐ Plaintiff ☐ Defendant	Location of filing	Represented by	Docket/Case number
Amount in dispute $	Possible completion date (mmddyyyy)	Subject of litigation	

Are you or have you been party to litigation involving the IRS/United States (including any tax litigation)

☐ Yes ☐ No

If yes and the litigation included tax debt, provide the types of tax and periods involved.

Catalog Number 55897B   www.irs.gov   Form **433-B (OIC)** (Rev. 3-2019)

Page 6

Section 6 (Continued) — Other Information

In the past 10 years, has the business transferred any assets for less than their full value
☐ Yes ☐ No
If yes, provide date, value, and type of asset transferred

In the past 3 years have you transferred any real property *(land, house, etc.)*
☐ Yes ☐ No
If yes, list the type of property, value, and date of the transfer

Has the business been located outside the U.S. for 6 months or longer in the past 10 years
☐ Yes ☐ No

Do you have any assets or own any real property outside the U.S.
☐ Yes ☐ No
If yes, please provide description, location, and value

Does the business have any funds being held in trust by a third party
☐ Yes ☐ No   If yes, how much $ _____   Where _____

Does the business have any lines of credit
☐ Yes ☐ No   If yes, credit limit $ _____   Amount owed $ _____
What property secures the line of credit _____

Section 7 — Signatures

Under penalties of perjury, I declare that I have examined this offer, including accompanying documents, and to the best of my knowledge it is true, correct, and complete.

▶ **Signature of Taxpayer** | Title | Date *(mm/dd/yyyy)*

Remember to include all applicable attachments from the list below.

- ☐ A current Profit and Loss statement covering at least the most recent 6–12 month period, if appropriate.
- ☐ Copies of the six most recent bank statements for each business account and copies of the three most recent statements for each investment and retirement accounts.
- ☐ If an asset is used as collateral on a loan, include copies of the most recent statement from lender(s) on loans, monthly payments, loan payoffs, and balances.
- ☐ Copies of the most recent statement of outstanding notes receivable.
- ☐ Copies of the most recent statements from lenders on loans, mortgages (including second mortgages), monthly payments, loan payoffs, and balances.
- ☐ Copies of relevant supporting documentation of the special circumstances described in the "Explanation of Circumstances" on Form 656, if applicable.
- ☐ Attach a Form 2848, Power of Attorney, if you would like your attorney, CPA, or enrolled agent to represent you and you do not have a current form on file with the IRS. Make sure the current tax year is included.
- ☐ Completed and current signed Form 656.

Catalog Number 55897B   www.irs.gov   Form **433-B (OIC)** (Rev. 3-2019)

Form **656**
(August 2019)

Department of the Treasury — Internal Revenue Service

Offer in Compromise

IRS Received Date

▶ **To: Commissioner of Internal Revenue Service**

In the following agreement, the pronoun "we" may be assumed in place of "I" when there are joint liabilities and both parties are signing this agreement.

I submit this offer to compromise the tax liabilities plus any interest, penalties, additions to tax, and additional amounts required by law for the tax type and period(s) marked in Section 1 or Section 2 below.

Did you use the Pre-Qualifier tool located on our website at http://irs.treasury.gov/oic_pre_qualifier/ prior to filling out this form
☐ Yes   ☐ No

Note: The use of the Pre-Qualifier tool is not mandatory before sending in your offer. However, it is recommended.

Include the $186 application fee and initial payment *(personal check, cashier's check, or money order)* with your Form 656 unless you qualify for the low-income certification. You must also include the completed Form 433-A (OIC) and/or 433-B (OIC) and supporting documentation. You should fill out either Section 1 or Section 2, but not both, depending on the tax debt you are offering to compromise.

Section 1 — Individual Information (Form 1040 filers)

If you are a 1040 filer, an individual with personal liability for Excise tax, individual responsible for Trust Fund Recovery Penalty, self-employed individual, individual personally responsible for partnership liabilities, and/or an individual who operated as a disregarded single member Limited Liability Company (LLC) taxed as a sole proprietor prior to 2009 you should fill out Section 1.

Your first name, middle initial, last name _____
Social Security Number (SSN) ___ - ___ - ___

If a joint offer, spouse's first name, middle initial, last name _____
Social Security Number (SSN) ___ - ___ - ___

Your home physical address *(street, city, state, ZIP code, county of residence)*

Your home mailing address *(if different from above or post office box number)*

Is this a new address ☐ Yes ☐ No
If yes, would you like us to update our records to this address ☐ Yes ☐ No

Your Employer Identification Number *(if applicable)* ___ - ___

Individual Tax Periods *(If Your Offer is for Individual Tax Debt Only)*

☐ 1040 Income Tax-Year(s) _____

☐ Trust Fund Recovery Penalty as a responsible person of *(enter business name)* _____
for failure to pay withholding and Federal Insurance Contributions Act taxes (Social Security taxes), for period(s) ending _____

☐ 941 Employer's Quarterly Federal Tax Return - Quarterly period(s) _____

☐ 940 Employer's Annual Federal Unemployment (FUTA) Tax Return - Year(s) _____

☐ Other Federal Tax(es) [specify type(s) and period(s)] _____

Note: If you need more space, use attachment and title it "Attachment to Form 656 dated _____." Make sure to sign and date the attachment.

Warning: The IRS will not compromise any amounts of restitution assessed by the IRS. Any liability arising from restitution is excluded from this offer.

Catalog Number 16728N   www.irs.gov   Form **656** (Rev. 8-2019)

Low-Income Certification (Individuals and Sole Proprietors Only)

Do you qualify for Low-Income Certification? You qualify if your adjusted gross income, as determined by your most recently filed Individual Income Tax return (Form 1040) or your household's gross monthly income from Form 433-A(OIC) x 12, is equal to or less than the amount shown in the chart below based on your family size and where you live. If you qualify, you are not required to submit any payments or the application fee upon submission or during the consideration of your offer. If your business is other than a sole proprietor or disregarded single member LLC taxed as a sole proprietor and you owe employment taxes on or after January 1, 2009, you cannot qualify for the waiver. The IRS will verify whether you qualify for low-income certification.

☐ I qualify for the low-income certification because my adjusted gross income is equal to or less than the amount shown in the table below.

☐ I qualify for the low-income certification because my household's size and gross monthly income x 12 is equal to or less than the income shown in the table below.

Note: By checking one of the boxes you are certifying that your adjusted gross income or your household's gross monthly income x 12 and size of your family qualify you for the Low-Income Certification.

IF YOU QUALIFY FOR THE LOW-INCOME CERTIFICATION DO NOT INCLUDE ANY PAYMENTS WITH YOUR OFFER. However, if you elect to send in money and the Low-Income Certification box is checked, you MUST check ONE of the options listed below.

☐ **Payment** - By checking this box I am requesting all money to be applied to my tax debt

☐ **Deposit** - By checking this box I am requesting all money to be treated as a deposit and returned if my offer is not accepted

Please note that failure to check either box or checking both boxes above will result in all payments being applied to your tax debt and not returned to you.

Size of family unit	48 contiguous states and D.C.	Hawaii	Alaska
1	$30,348	$34,896	$37,956
2	$41,148	$47,328	$51,456
3	$51,948	$59,748	$64,956
4	$62,748	$72,180	$78,456
5	$73,548	$84,600	$91,956
6	$84,348	$97,020	$105,456
7	$95,148	$109,452	$118,956
8	$105,948	$121,872	$132,456
For each additional person, add	$10,800	$12,420	$13,500

Section 2 — Business Information (Form 1120, 1065, etc., filers)

If your business is a Corporation, Partnership, LLC, or LLP and you want to compromise those tax debts, you must complete this section. You must also include all required documentation including the Form 433-B (OIC), and a separate $186 application fee, and initial payment.

Business name

Business physical address *(street, city, state, ZIP code)*

Business mailing address *(street, city, state, ZIP code)*

Employer Identification Number (EIN)	Name and title of primary contact	Telephone number
-		( ) -

Business Tax Periods *(If Your Offer is for Business Tax Debt Only)*

☐ 1120 Income Tax-Year(s) _____

☐ 941 Employer's Quarterly Federal Tax Return - Quarterly period(s) _____

☐ 940 Employer's Annual Federal Unemployment (FUTA) Tax Return - Year(s) _____

☐ Other Federal Tax(es) [specify type(s) and period(s)] _____

Note: If you need more space, use attachment and title it "Attachment to Form 656 dated _____." Make sure to sign and date the attachment.

Catalog Number 16728N   www.irs.gov   Form **656** (Rev. 8-2019)

Page 3

Section 3 — Reason for Offer

☐ **Doubt as to Collectibility** - I do not have enough in assets and income to pay the full amount

☐ **Exceptional Circumstances (Effective Tax Administration)** - I owe this amount and have enough in assets and income to pay the full amount, but due to my exceptional circumstances, requiring full payment would cause an economic hardship or collection of the full liability would undermine public confidence that the tax laws are being administered in a fair and equitable manner. I am submitting a written narrative explaining my circumstances

Explanation of Circumstances *(Add additional pages, if needed)* – The IRS understands that there are unplanned events or special circumstances, such as serious illness, where paying the full amount or the minimum offer amount might impair your ability to provide for yourself and your family. If this is the case and you can provide documentation to prove your situation, then your offer may be accepted despite your financial profile. If applicable, describe your special circumstances below and attach appropriate documents to this offer application

_____
_____
_____
_____
_____
_____
_____

Section 4 — Payment Terms

▼ Check one of the payment options below to indicate how long it will take you to pay your offer in full. You must offer more than $0. The offer amount should be in whole dollars only. ▼

Lump Sum Cash

☐ Check here if you will pay your offer in 5 or fewer payments within 5 or fewer months from the date of acceptance:

Enclose a check for 20% of the offer amount (waived if you met the requirements for Low-Income Certification) and fill in the amount(s) of your future payment(s).

Total offer amount	-	20% initial payment	=	Remaining balance
$	-	$	=	$

You may pay the remaining balance in one payment after acceptance of the offer or up to five payments, but cannot exceed 5 months.

Amount of payment	$	payable within	1	Month after acceptance
Amount of payment	$	payable within	2	Months after acceptance
Amount of payment	$	payable within	3	Months after acceptance
Amount of payment	$	payable within	4	Months after acceptance
Amount of payment	$	payable within	5	Months after acceptance

Periodic Payment

☐ Check here if you will pay your offer in full in 6 to 24 months

Enter the amount of your offer $ _____

Note: The total months may not exceed a total of 24, including the first payment. Your first payment is considered to be month 1; therefore, the remainder of the payments must be made within 23 months for a total of 24.

Enclose a check for the first month's payment *(waived if you met the requirements for the Low-Income Certification)*.

The first monthly payment of $ _____ is included with this offer then $ _____ will be sent in on the _____

day of each month thereafter for a total of _____ months with a final payment of $ _____ to be paid on the _____ day

of the _____ month.

You must continue to make these monthly payments while the IRS is considering the offer *(waived if you met the requirements for Low-Income Certification)*. Failure to make regular monthly payments until you have received a final decision letter will cause your offer to be returned with no appeal rights.

IRS Use Only

☐ Attached is an addendum dated (insert date) _____ setting forth the amended offer amount and payment terms.

Catalog Number 16728N   www.irs.gov   Form **656** (Rev. 8-2019)

Page 4

Section 5 — Designation of Payment, Electronic Federal Tax Payment System (EFTPS), and Deposit

Designation of Payment

If you want your payment to be applied to a specific tax year and a specific tax debt, such as a Trust Fund Recovery Penalty, please tell us the tax year/quarter _____. If you do not designate a preference, we will apply any money you send to the government's best interest. If you want to designate any payments not included with this offer, you must designate a preference for each payment at the time the payment is made. However, you cannot designate the application fee or any payment after the IRS accepts the offer.

Note: Payments submitted with your offer cannot be designated as estimated tax payments for a current or past tax year.

Electronic Federal Tax Payment System (EFTPS)

Did you make your payment through the Electronic Federal Tax Payment System (EFTPS)

☐ Yes ☐ No

If yes, provide the amount of your payment(s) $ _____, the date paid _____,

and the 15 digit Electronic Funds Transfer (EFT) Number _____.

Note: Any initial payments paid through the EFTPS system must be made the same date your offer is mailed.

Deposit

CAUTION: Do NOT designate the amounts sent in with your offer to cover the initial payment and application fee as "deposits." Doing so will result in the return of your offer without appeal rights.

If you are paying **more than** the initial payment with your offer and you want any part of that payment treated as a deposit, check the box below and insert the amount.

☐ My payment of $ _____ includes the $186 application fee and $ _____ for my first month's payment. I am requesting the additional amount of $ _____ be held as a deposit.

If your offer is rejected, returned, or withdrawn please check one of the boxes below and let us know what you would like us to do with your deposit.

☐ Return it to you (Initial here _____) ☐ Apply it to your tax debt (Initial here _____)

Your deposit will be returned to you, unless you indicated in the above check box that you want it applied to your tax debt.

Section 6 — Source of Funds, Making Your Payment, Filing Requirements, and Tax Payment Requirements

Source of Funds

Tell us where you will obtain the funds to pay your offer. You may consider borrowing from friends and/or family, taking out a loan, or selling assets

_____
_____
_____

Making Your Payment

Include separate checks for the payment and application fee.

Make checks payable to the "United States Treasury" and attach to the front of your Form 656, Offer in Compromise. All payments must be in U.S. dollars. **Do not send cash.** Send a separate application fee with each offer; do not combine it with any other tax payments, as this may delay processing of your offer. You may also make payments through the Electronic Federal Tax Payment System (EFTPS). Your offer will be returned to you if the application fee and the required payment are not included, or if your check is returned for insufficient funds.

Filing Requirements

☐ I have filed all required tax returns and have included a complete copy of any tax return filed within 60 days prior to this offer submission

☐ I was not required to file a tax return for the following years _____

Note: Do not include original tax returns with your offer. You must either electronically file your tax return or mail it to the appropriate IRS processing office before sending in your offer.

Tax Payment Requirements *(check all that apply)*

☐ I have made all required estimated tax payments for the current tax year

☐ I am not required to make any estimated tax payments for the current tax year

☐ I have made all required federal tax deposits for the current quarter

☐ I am not required to make any federal tax deposits for the current quarter

Catalog Number 16728N www.irs.gov Form **656** (Rev. 8-2019)

Section 7 — Offer Terms

By submitting this offer, I have read, understand and agree to the following terms and conditions:

Terms, Conditions, and Legal Agreement

a) I request that the IRS accept the offer amount listed in this offer application as payment of my outstanding tax debt (including interest, penalties, and any additional amounts required by law) as of the date listed on this form. I authorize the IRS to amend Section 1 and/or Section 2 if I failed to list any of my assessed tax debt or tax debt assessed before acceptance of my offer. By submitting a joint offer, both signers grant approval to the Internal Revenue Service to disclose the existence of any separate liabilities owed.

b) I also authorize the IRS to amend Section 1 and/or Section 2 by removing any tax years on which there is currently no outstanding liability. I understand that my offer will be accepted, by law, unless IRS notifies me otherwise, in writing, within 24 months of the date my offer was received by IRS. I also understand that if any tax debt that is included in the offer is in dispute in any judicial proceeding it/they will not be included in determining the expiration of the 24-month period.

IRS will keep my payments, fees, and some refunds.

c) I voluntarily submit the payments made on this offer and understand that they will not be returned even if I withdraw the offer or the IRS rejects or returns the offer except as otherwise provided in subpart (h) of this section (regarding "deposit" amounts) or subpart (i) of this section. Unless I designate how to apply each required payment in Section 5, the IRS will apply my payment in the best interest of the government, choosing which tax years and tax debts to pay off. The IRS will also keep my application fee unless the offer is not accepted for processing.

d) I understand that if I checked the Low-Income Certification in Section 1, then no payments are required. If I qualify for the Low-Income Certification and voluntarily submit payments, all money will be applied to my tax debt and will not be returned to me unless I designate it as a deposit. In making my deposit I do not have to designate any amounts to the application fee and my first month's payment.

e) The IRS will keep any refund, including interest, that I might be due for tax periods extending through the calendar year in which the IRS accepts my offer. I cannot designate that the refund be applied to estimated tax payments for the following year or the accepted offer amount. If I receive a refund after I submit this offer for any tax period extending through the calendar year in which the IRS accepts my offer, I will return the refund within 30 days of notification. The refund offset does not apply to offers accepted under the provisions of Effective Tax Administration or Doubt as to Collectibility with special circumstances based on public policy/equity considerations.

f) I understand that the amount I am offering may not include part or all of an expected or current tax refund, money already paid, funds attached by any collection action, or anticipated benefits from a capital or net operating loss.

g) The IRS will keep any monies it has collected prior to this offer. Under section 6331(k) the IRS may levy up to the time that the IRS official signs and acknowledges my offer as pending, which is accepted for processing and the IRS may keep any proceeds arising from such a levy. No levy will be issued on individual shared responsibility payments. However, if the IRS served a continuous levy on wages, salary, or certain federal payments under sections 6331(e) or (h), then the IRS could choose to either retain or release the levy.

h) The IRS will keep any payments that I make related to this offer. I agree that any funds submitted with this offer will be treated as a payment unless I checked the box to treat any amount more than the required initial payment as a deposit. For other than Low-Income taxpayers, only amounts that exceed the mandatory payments can be treated as a deposit. A Low-Income taxpayer who has checked the deposit box is not required to make payments with the offer. I also agree that any funds submitted with periodic payments made after the submission of this offer and prior to the acceptance, rejection, or return of this offer will be treated as payments, unless I identify the amount more than the required payment as a deposit on the check submitted with the corresponding periodic payment. A deposit will be returned if the offer is rejected, returned, or withdrawn. I understand that the IRS will not pay interest on any deposit. If the IRS attempts to return a deposit once and it comes back as undeliverable then the IRS will apply the funds to my tax liability.

i) If my offer is accepted and my final payment is more than the agreed amount by $50 or less, the IRS will not return the difference, but will apply the entire payment to my tax debt. If my final payment exceeds the agreed amount by more than $50, the IRS will return the excess payment to me.

Pending status of an offer and right to appeal

j) Once an authorized IRS official signs this form, my offer is considered pending as of that signature date and it remains pending until the IRS accepts, rejects, returns, or I withdraw my offer. An offer is also considered pending for 30 days after any rejection of my offer by the IRS, and during the time that any rejection of my offer is being considered by the Appeals Office. An offer will be considered withdrawn when the IRS receives my written notification of withdrawal by personal delivery or certified mail or when I inform the IRS of my withdrawal by other means and the IRS acknowledges in writing my intent to withdraw the offer.

k) I waive the right to an Appeals hearing if I do not request a hearing in writing within 30 days of the date the IRS notifies me of the decision to reject the offer.

Section 7 (Continued) — Offer Terms

I must comply with my future tax obligations and understand I remain liable for the full amount of my tax debt until all terms and conditions of this offer have been met.

l) I will comply with all provisions of the internal revenue laws, including requirements to timely file tax returns and timely pay taxes for the five year period beginning with the date of acceptance of this offer and ending through the fifth year, including any extensions to file and pay. I agree to promptly pay any liabilities assessed after acceptance of this offer for tax years ending prior to acceptance of this offer that were not otherwise identified in Section 1 or Section 2 of this agreement. I also understand that during the five year period I cannot request an installment agreement for unpaid taxes incurred before or after the accepted offer. If this is an offer being submitted for joint tax debt, and one of us does not comply with future obligations, only the non-compliant taxpayer will be in default of this agreement. An accepted offer will not be defaulted solely due to the assessment of an individual shared responsibility payment.

m) I agree that I will remain liable for the full amount of the tax liability, accrued penalties and interest, until I have met all of the terms and conditions of this offer. Penalty and interest will continue to accrue until all payment terms of the offer have been met. If I file for bankruptcy before the terms and conditions of the offer are met, I agree that the IRS may file a claim for the full amount of the tax liability, accrued penalties and interest, and that any claim the IRS files in the bankruptcy proceeding will be a tax claim.

n) Once the IRS accepts my offer in writing, I have no right to challenge the tax debt(s) in court or by filing a refund claim or refund suit for any liability or period listed in Section 1 or Section 2, even if the IRS defaults the offer.

I understand what will happen if I fail to meet the terms of my offer (e.g., default).

o) If I fail to meet any of the terms of this offer, the IRS may revoke the certificate of release of federal tax lien and file a new notice of federal tax lien; levy or sue me to collect any amount ranging from one or more missed payments to the original amount of the tax debt (less payments made) plus penalties and interest that have accrued from the time the underlying tax liability arose. The IRS will continue to add interest, as required by section 6601 of the Internal Revenue Code, on the amount the IRS determines is due after default. Shared responsibility payments are excluded from levy.

I agree to waive time limits provided by law.

p) To have my offer considered, I agree to the extension of the time limit provided by law to assess my tax debt (statutory period of assessment). I agree that the date by which the IRS must assess my tax debt will now be the date by which my debt must currently be assessed plus the period of time my offer is pending plus one additional year if the IRS rejects, returns, or terminates my offer or I withdraw it. (Paragraph (j) of this section defines pending and withdrawal.) I understand that I have the right not to waive the statutory period of assessment or to limit the waiver to a certain length or certain periods or issues. I understand, however, that the IRS may not consider my offer if I refuse to waive the statutory period of assessment or if I provide only a limited waiver. I also understand that the statutory period for collecting my tax debt will be suspended during the time my offer is pending with the IRS, for 30 days after any rejection of my offer by the IRS, and during the time that any rejection of my offer is being considered by the Appeals Office.

I understand the IRS may file a Notice of Federal Tax Lien on my property.

q) The IRS may file a Notice of Federal Tax Lien during consideration of the offer or for offers that will be paid over time. If the offer is accepted, the tax lien will be released within 30 days of when the payment terms have been satisfied and the payment has been verified. The time it takes to transfer funds to the IRS from commercial institutions varies based on the form of payment. The IRS will not file a Notice of Federal Tax Lien on any individual shared responsibility debt.

Correction Agreement

r) I authorize the IRS, to correct any typographical or clerical errors or make minor modifications to my/our Form 656 that I signed in connection to this offer.

I authorize the IRS to contact relevant third parties in order to process my offer.

s) By authorizing the IRS to contact third parties, I understand that I will not be notified of which third parties the IRS contacts as part of the offer application process, including tax periods that have not been assessed, as stated in §7602 (c) of the Internal Revenue Code. In addition, I authorize the IRS to request a consumer report on me from a credit bureau.

I am submitting an offer as an individual for a joint liability.

t) I understand if the liability sought to be compromised is the joint and individual liability of myself and my co-obligor(s) and I am submitting this offer to compromise my individual liability only, then if this offer is accepted, it does not release or discharge my co-obligor(s) from liability. The United States still reserves all rights of collection against the co-obligor(s).

I understand the IRS Shared Responsibility Payment (SRP).

u) If your offer includes any shared responsibility payment (SRP) amount that you owe for not having minimum essential health coverage for you and, if applicable, your dependents per Internal Revenue Code Section 5000A - Individual shared responsibility payment, it is not subject to penalties (except applicable bad check penalty) or to lien and levy enforcement actions. However, interest will continue to accrue until you pay the total SRP balance due. We may apply your federal tax refunds to the SRP amount that you owe until it is paid in full.

I understand the IRS is required to make certain information public.

v) The IRS is required to make certain information, such as taxpayer name, city/state/zip, liability amount, and offer terms, available for public inspection and review for one year after the date of offer acceptance.

Section 8 — Signatures

Under penalties of perjury, I declare that I have examined this offer, including accompanying schedules and statements, and to the best of my knowledge and belief, it is true, correct and complete.

▶ Signature of Taxpayer/Corporation Name | Phone number | Today's date (mm/dd/yyyy)

☐ By checking this box you are authorizing the IRS to contact you at the telephone number listed above and leave detailed messages concerning this offer on your voice mail or answering machine.

▶ Signature of Spouse/Authorized Corporate Officer | Phone number | Today's date (mm/dd/yyyy)

☐ By checking this box you are authorizing the IRS to contact you at the telephone number listed above and leave detailed messages concerning this offer on your voice mail or answering machine.

Section 9 — Paid Preparer Use Only

Signature of Preparer | Phone number | Today's date (mm/dd/yyyy)

☐ By checking this box you are authorizing the IRS to contact you at the telephone number listed above and leave detailed messages concerning this offer on your voice mail or answering machine.

Name of Paid Preparer | Preparer's CAF no. or PTIN

Firm's name (or yours if self-employed), address, and ZIP code

---

If you would like to have someone represent you during the offer investigation, attach a valid, signed Form 2848 with this application or a copy of a previously filed form. Form 2848 allows for representation and receipt of confidential information. You should also include the current tax year on the form, in the list of applicable years or periods.

Form 8821 allows a third party to receive confidential information but they cannot represent you before the IRS in a Collection matter. If you would like a third party to receive confidential information on your behalf attach a copy if previously filed and include the current tax year on the form.

IRS Use Only. I accept the waiver of the statutory period of limitations on assessment for the Internal Revenue Service, as described in Section 7(p).

Signature of Authorized Internal Revenue Service Official | Title | Date (mm/dd/yyyy)

Privacy Act Statement

We ask for the information on this form to carry out the internal revenue laws of the United States. Our authority to request this information is section § 7801 of the Internal Revenue Code.

Our purpose for requesting the information is to determine if it is in the best interests of the IRS to accept an offer. You are not required to make an offer; however, if you choose to do so, you must provide all of the taxpayer information requested. Failure to provide all of the information may prevent us from processing your request.

If you are a paid preparer and you prepared the Form 656 for the taxpayer submitting an offer, we request that you complete and sign Section 9 on Form 656, and provide identifying information. Providing this information is voluntary. This information will be used to administer and enforce the internal revenue laws of the United States and may be used to regulate practice before the Internal Revenue Service for those persons subject to Treasury Department Circular No. 230, Regulations Governing the Practice of Attorneys, Certified Public Accountants, Enrolled Agents, Enrolled Actuaries, and Appraisers before the Internal Revenue Service. Information on this form may be disclosed to the Department of Justice for civil and criminal litigation. We may also disclose this information to cities, states and the District of Columbia for use in administering their tax laws and to combat terrorism. Providing false or fraudulent information on this form may subject you to criminal prosecution and penalties.

APPLICATION CHECKLIST

Review the entire application using the Application Checklist below. Include this checklist with your application.

Forms 433-A (OIC), 433-B (OIC), and 656

- [ ] Did you complete all fields and sign all forms
- [ ] Did you make an offer amount that is equal to the offer amount calculated on the Form 433-A (OIC) or Form 433-B (OIC)? If not, did you describe the special circumstances that are leading you to offer less than the minimum in the "Explanation of Circumstances" Section 3 of Form 656, and did you provide supporting documentation of the special circumstances
- [ ] Have you filed all required tax returns and received a bill or notice of balance due
- [ ] Did you include a complete copy of any tax return filed within 60 days prior to this offer submission
- [ ] Did you select a payment option on Form 656
- [ ] Did you sign and attach the Form 433-A (OIC), if applicable
- [ ] Did you sign and attach the Form 433-B (OIC), if applicable
- [ ] Did you sign and attach the Form 656
- [ ] If you are making an offer that includes business and individual tax debts, did you prepare a separate Form 656 package (including separate financial statements, supporting documentation, application fee, and initial payment)

Supporting documentation and additional forms

- [ ] Did you include photocopies of all required supporting documentation
- [ ] If you want a third party to represent you and receive confidential information during the offer process, did you include a Form 2848? If you want a third party to only receive confidential information on your behalf did you include valid Form 8821? Does it include the current tax year
- [ ] Did you provide a letter of testamentary or other verification of person(s) authorized to act on behalf of the estate or deceased individual

Payment

- [ ] Did you include a check or money order made payable to the "United States Treasury" for the initial payment? (Waived if you meet Low-Income Certification guidelines—see Form 656)
- [ ] Did you include a separate check or money order made payable to the "United States Treasury" for the $186 application fee? (Waived if you meet Low-Income Certification guidelines—see Form 656)

Mail your application package to the appropriate IRS facility

Mail the Form 656, 433-A (OIC) and/or 433-B (OIC), and related financial document(s) to the appropriate IRS processing office for your state. You may wish to send it by Certified Mail so you have a record of the date it was mailed.

If you reside in:

AL, AR, FL, GA, HI, ID, KY, LA, MS, NC, NM, NV, OK, OR, TN, TX, WA, WI

AK, AZ, CA, CO, CT, DE, IA, IL, IN, KS, MA, MD, ME, MI, MN, MO, MT, ND, NE, NH, NJ, NY, OH, PA, RI, SC, SD, UT, VT, VA, WY, WV; DC, PR, or a foreign address

Mail your application to:

Memphis IRS Center COIC Unit
P.O. Box 30803, AMC
Memphis, TN 38130-0803
1-844-398-5025

Brookhaven IRS Center COIC Unit
P.O. Box 9007
Holtsville, NY 11742-9007
1-844-805-4980

Form **656-B** (Rev. 8-2019)   Catalog Number 52133W   www.irs.gov   Department of the Treasury - **Internal Revenue Service**

Department of the Treasury **Internal Revenue Service** **OPERATING DIVISION**	Date: 06/04/2016 Person to contact: Employee ID number Contact telephone number: Contact fax number: Taxpayer ID number: (last 4 digits):

Dear:

Our records show that you haven't deposited federal employment taxes as required by law (Treasury Regulation Section 31.6302). **If you do not bring your account current with the required deposits within 30 days of the date of this letter, we will consider stricter civil or criminal enforcement procedures.**

We may:

- **File a Notice of Federal Tax Lien (NFTL) to protect the government's interest**

By filing this notice, we are making a legal claim to your property as security for the payment of your tax debt. An NFTL is a public notice to your creditors that we have a claim against all your property, including property you acquire after we file the lien. An NFTL can have a negative effect on your credit rating. We may also seize (levy) your property. A levy is a legal seizure of property to satisfy a tax debt.

- **Assess a trust fund recovery penalty under Internal Revenue Code Section 6672 for the unpaid trust fund taxes**

We can assess a trust fund recovery penalty against anyone who is responsible for, and willfully fails to, collect, account for, or pay to the IRS income and employment taxes the law requires to be withheld. Willfulness exists if a person allows payment of net wages when the employer has insufficient funds to pay the taxes or uses withheld taxes for other purposes. Willfulness also exists if a person who knows of a previous failure to pay taxes allows payments to others (including payment of additional wages) rather than using available funds to pay the tax delinquency.

- **Refer the matter to the Department of Justice (DOJ) to institute a civil suit or to seek criminal prosecution**

In a civil suit, the DOJ can seek an injunction that requires the employer to comply with the federal employment tax laws and prohibits the employer from paying any amounts until the employer pays the correct amounts to the IRS. The DOJ may also ask the court to appoint a receiver to take control of the business to ensure tax compliance.

Letter 903 (Rev. 3-2016)
Catalog Number 10737Q

The DOJ can also pursue criminal charges based on the willful failure to report and pay over withheld taxes (Section 7202 of the Internal Revenue Code). Willfulness is evident if an employer paid net wages and didn't leave enough funds to make the required tax payments or used withheld trust fund taxes for other purposes. **Convictions may result in imprisonment and other penalties. Other criminal statutes may also apply.**

I encourage you to comply with the federal employment tax deposit rules and to file your returns on time. I am enclosing Notice 931, *Deposit Requirements for Employment Taxes, which explains the deposit rules.*

Thank you for your cooperation.

                                              Sincerely,

                                              [Name]
                                              [Title]

Enclosure:
Notice 931

Letter 903 (Rev. 3-2016)
Catalog Number 10737Q

UNITED STATES DISTRICT COURT FOR THE
DISTRICT OF MINNESOTA

UNITED STATES OF AMERICA,)
)
        Plaintiff,)   17-cv-104(DSD/DTS)
)
v.)
)
NURSE STAFFING SOLUTIONS)
HOME CARE and DAWDA SOWE,)
)
        Defendants.)

Permanent Injunction and Judgment

The United States seeks a permanent injunction against defendants Nurse Staffing Solutions Home Care and Dawda Sowe under 26 U.S.C. § 7402 requiring defendants to timely file employment tax returns and to pay employment tax when due. The United States also seeks a money judgment for unpaid taxes due. For good-cause shown, the United States' motion for default judgment is granted.

THEREFORE, **IT IS HEREBY ORDERED** that:

1. Nurse Staffing Solutions Home Care and Dawda Sowe, and their representatives, agents, servants, employees, and anyone in active concert or participation with them, are prohibited from failing to withhold and pay over to the IRS all employment taxes, including federal income, FICA, and FUTA taxes, required by law.

2. Nurse Staffing Solutions Home Care and Dawda Sowe shall timely pay all federal employment and unemployment taxes that become due after the date of the injunction.

3. Nurse Staffing Solutions Home Care and Dawda Sowe shall sign and deliver, no later than seven (7) days after the end of the month, affidavits to Revenue Officer Christine Braziel at 6200 Shingle Creek Parkway, Suite 610, Brooklyn Center, MN 55430 or, upon written notice by the IRS, to some other person or location designated by the IRS stating that the requisite deposits of withheld income tax, withheld FICA tax, and employer FICA tax have been made in a timely manner.

4. Nurse Staffing Solutions Home Care and Dawda Sowe shall timely file all employment (Form 941) and unemployment (Form 940) tax returns and Forms 1120 coming due after the date of the injunction.

5. Nurse Staffing Solutions Home Care and Dawda Sowe shall timely provide, no later than seven (7) days after the close of a quarter, a quarterly statement of income and expenses to Revenue Officer Braziel, or, upon written notice by the IRS, some other person designated by the IRS at such other location as the IRS may deem appropriate.

6. Nurse Staffing Solutions Home Care and Dawda Sowe shall not assign any property or make any payments after this injunction is issued until the employment tax and withholding liabilities, accruing after issuance of the injunction, are first paid to the IRS.

7. Sowe shall notify Revenue Officer Braziel, or upon written notice by the IRS, any other person designated by the IRS, of any new, related, or associated business that Sowe may come to manage or own in the next five (5) years, within thirty (30) days of Sowe obtaining ownership or commencing management.

8. The provisions of this injunction shall apply to any new, related, or associated business that Sowe may come to manage or own in the next five (5) years.

9. Judgment is entered in favor of the United States and against Nurse Staffing Solutions Home Care for its failure to pay federal employment (Form 941), unemployment (Form 940), and corporate (1120) taxes for the periods and amounts set forth below, plus interest and statutory additions accruing after July 1, 2017, until judgment is paid:

Tax Form	Tax Period	Assessment Date	Assessed Tax/Penalty	Balance as of July 1, 2017
941	03/31/2008	06/04/2012	$56,996.06	$60,834.90
941	06/30/2008	06/04/2012	$56,329.03	$60,122.92
941	09/30/2008	06/04/2012	$55,707.75	$59,459.84
941	12/31/2008	06/04/2012	$55,057.94	$58,766.24
941	03/31/2009	06/04/2012	$68,905.41	$73,546.38
941	06/30/2009	06/04/2012	$43,923.36	$48,137.44
941	09/30/2009	06/04/2012	$67,761.76	$72,325.71
941	12/31/2009	06/04/2012	$67,198.18	$71,724.16
941	03/31/2010	02/15/2016	$52,841.72	$55,756.08
941	06/30/2010	02/15/2016	$65,971.11	$69,410.18
941	09/30/2010	06/13/2016	$56,835.62	$59,041.31
941	12/31/2010	05/16/2016	$61,770.77	$64,610.87
941	3/31/2011	02/16/2016	$44,412.80	$46,728.04
941	6/30/2011	04/25/2016	$45,510.92	$47,531.48
941	9/30/2011	02/15/2016	$40,946.10	$42,971.86
941	12/31/2011	07/11/2016	$44,479.46	$46,272.10
941	3/31/2012	02/15/2016	$40,160.99	$42,871.14
941	6/30/2012	02/15/2016	$43,531.45	$46,552.49
941	9/30/2012	02/15/2016	$36,769.14	$39,652.46
941	12/31/2012	02/15/2016	$36,227.04	$39,404/27
941	3/31/2013	02/15/2016	$58,522.01	$64,213.93
941	6/30/2013	05/02/2016	$50,033.04	$54,471.08

941	9/30/2013	05/02/2016	$62,463.88	$68,619.88
941	12/31/2013	02/15/2016	$47,279.63	$54,027.78
941	03/31/2014	02/15/2016	$52,813.47	$60,130.71
941	06/30/2014	02/15/2016	$42,208.50	$48,527.10
941	09/30/2014	02/15/2016	$45,010.97	$51,969.74
941	12/31/2014	02/15/2016	$41,091.92	$47,514.58
941	03/31/2015	02/15/2016	$49,437.45	$57,249.95
941	06/30/2015	02/15/2016	$35,501.44	$41,175.72
941	09/30/2015	02/15/2016	$29,922.71	$35,111.36
941	03/31/2016	07/11/2016	$28,198.73	$32,376.19
941	06/30/2016	10/03/2016	$23,984.20	$26,203.10
940	12/31/2008	08/04/2012	$42,969.87	$45,855.24
940	12/31/2009	08/04/2012	$59,567.88	$63,569.26
940	12/31/2012	02/22/2016	$27,418.47	$29,806.16
940	12/31/2016	05/15/2017	$1,869.09	$1,903.72
1120	12/31/2009	02/08/2016	$54,120.51	$57,146.08
1120	12/31/2012	02/08/2016	$79,943.43	$88,333.66
1120	12/31/2014	02/08/2016	$25,632.39	$29,223.73
			Total:	$2,063,154.89

LET JUDGMENT BE ENTERED ACCORDINGLY.

Dated: August 8, 2017

s/David S. Doty
David S. Doty, Judge
United States District Court

Form **4180**
(August 2012)

Department of the Treasury - Internal Revenue Service

Report of Interview with Individual Relative to Trust Fund Recovery Penalty or Personal Liability for Excise Taxes

Instructions: The interviewer *must* prepare this form either in person or via telephone.
Do not leave any information blank. Enter "N/A" if an item is not applicable.

Section I - Person Interviewed

1. Name

2. Social Security Number *(SSN)*

3. Address *(street, city, state, ZIP code)*

4. Home telephone number
( )

5. Work telephone number
( )

6. Name of Business and Employer Identification Number *(EIN)*

7. Did you use a third-party payer, such as a payroll service?
☐ Yes *(If yes complete Section VI A)*
☐ No

8. What was your job title and how were you associated with the business? *(Describe your duties and responsibilities and dates of employment.)* If person being interviewed is a payroll service provider or a professional employer organization, complete Section VI B

Section II - Responsibilities

1. State whether you performed any of the duties / functions listed below for the business and the time periods during which you performed these duties.

Did you...	Yes	No	Dates From	To
a. Determine financial policy for the business?	☐	☐		
b. Direct or authorize payments of bills/creditors?	☐	☐		
c. Prepare, review, sign, or authorize transmit payroll tax returns?	☐	☐		
d. Have knowledge withheld taxes were not paid?	☐	☐		
e. Authorize payroll?	☐	☐		
f. Authorize or make Federal Tax Deposits?	☐	☐		
g. Authorize the assignment of any EFTPS or electronic banking PINS/passwords?	☐	☐		

h. Could other individuals do any of the above? *(Complete Section IV and V)* ☐ ☐

Name	Contact Number

i. Have signature authority or PIN assignment on business bank accounts?

Bank Name(s)	Account Number(s)

Section III - Signatures

I declare that I have examined the information given in this interview and to the best of my knowledge and belief, it is true, correct, and complete.

Signature of person interviewed

Date

Signature of Interviewer

Date

Date copy of completed interview form given to person interviewed ▶

Taxpayer Statement on Page 4: ☐ Yes ☐ No   Interview Continued on subsequent pages? ☐ Yes ☐ No

Interview Handouts *("X" if given or explain why not in case history.)*

☐ **Notice 609**, Privacy Act Notice   ☐ **Notice 784**, Could You be Personally Liable for Certain Unpaid Federal Taxes?

Catalog Number 22710P   www.irs.gov   Form **4180** (Rev. 8-2012)

EXHIBIT 17

Page 2

Section IV - Business Information

1. List corporate positions below, identifying the persons who occupied them and their dates of service.

Position (e.g. president, director)	Name	Address	Dates

2. Did/does the business use the Electronic Federal Tax Payment System (EFTPS) to make Federal Tax Deposits (FTD's) or payments?
   - [ ] No
   - [ ] Yes   If yes, to whom are the PINS or passwords assigned

3. Other than the EFTPS, does the business do any other banking electronically?
   - [ ] No
   - [ ] Yes   Where _____

   To whom are the PINs/passwords assigned

4. Does the business file Form 941 electronically?
   - [ ] No   Who is authorized to sign Form 941 _____
   - [ ] Yes   Who files the returns electronically _____

Section V - Knowledge / Willfulness

1. During the time the delinquent taxes were increasing, or at any time thereafter, were any financial obligations of the business paid? *(such as rent, mortgage, utilities, vehicle or equipment loans, or payments to vendors)*
   - [ ] No
   - [ ] Yes   Which obligations were paid?

   Who authorized them to be paid?

2. Were all or a portion of the payrolls met?
   - [ ] No
   - [ ] Yes

   Who authorized

3. Did any person or organization provide funds to pay net corporate payroll?
   - [ ] No
   - [ ] Yes *(explain in detail and provide name)*

4. When and how did you first become aware of the unpaid taxes?

5. What actions did you attempt to see that the taxes were paid?

6. Were discussions ever held by stockholders, officers, or other interested parties regarding nonpayment of the taxes?
   - [ ] No
   - [ ] Yes

   Identify who attended, dates, any decisions reached, and whether any documentation is available.

7. Who handled IRS contacts such as phone calls, correspondence, or visits by IRS personnel?

   When did these contacts take place, and what were the results of these contacts?

Catalog Number 22710P www.irs.gov Form **4180** (Rev. 8-2012)

Section VI - Payroll Service Provider (PSP) or Professional Employer Organization (PEO)

A - Third-Party Payer Arrangements
(complete this section only if you are interviewing a taxpayer who used a third-party payer)

1. Who signed the service contract or entered into the agreement for services with the third-party payer?

2. Who in the business handled the contacts with the third-party payer?

3. Who was your contact at the third-party payer?

4. How were funds to be made available for the third-party payer to pay the taxes?

   Name of Bank(s) and Account number(s) from which funds were to be transferred.

5. What actions did you take to verify the third-party payer was filing returns, or making required payments?

6. Were funds available for the third-party payer to use for payment of the taxes?
   ☐ Yes ☐ No

   If yes, explain in detail how and when the money was transferred to the third-party.

7. Were you aware that the third-party payer was not making the required payments?
   ☐ Yes ☐ No

8. Did you receive IRS notices indicating that the employment tax returns were not filed, or that the employment taxes were not paid?
   ☐ Yes ☐ No

B - Third-Party Payer Companies
(complete this section only if you are interviewing a Third-Party Payroll Service Payer)

1. Who in your organization handled the contacts with the client?

2. Who was your contact at the client business?

3. Who at the client business signed the service contract or entered into the agreement for services?

4. Who had control over the payments of the client's employment taxes?

5. How were funds to be made available from the client business to pay the taxes?

Bank Name(s)	Account Number(s)

6. Were there funds actually available for you to make the tax payments?
   ☐ Yes ☐ No

   If yes, explain in detail how and when the money was transferred to the third-party.

   If no, what actions did you take to attempt to collect the funds from the client?

Section VII - Personal Liability for Excise Tax Cases
(Complete only if Business is required to file Excise Tax Returns)

1. Are you aware of any required excise tax returns which have not been filed?
   ☐ No ☐ Yes *(list periods)*

2. With respect to excise taxes, were the patrons or customers informed that the tax was included in the sales price?
   ☐ No ☐ Yes

3. If the liability is one of the "collected" taxes *(transportation of persons or property and communications)*, was the tax collected?
   ☐ No ☐ Yes

4. Were you aware, during the period tax accrued, that the law required collection of the tax?
   ☐ No ☐ Yes

Catalog Number 22710P | www.irs.gov | Form **4180** (Rev. 8-2012)

Additional Information

Section VIII - Signatures

I declare that I have examined the information given in this interview and to the best of my knowledge and belief, it is true, correct, and complete.

Signature of person interviewed	Date
Signature of Interviewer	Date
Date copy of completed interview form given to person interviewed ▶	

Interview Handouts *("X" if given or explain why not in case history.)*

☐ **Notice 609**, Privacy Act Notice   ☐ **Notice 784**, Could You be Personally Liable for Certain Unpaid Federal Taxes?

Internal Revenue Service　　　　　　　　　　**Department of the Treasury**

Date:

Number of this Letter:

Person to Contact:

Employee Number:

IRS Contact Address:

IRS Telephone Number:

Employer Identification Number:

Business Name and Address:

Dear

Our efforts to collect the federal employment or excise taxes due from the business named above have not resulted in full payment of the liability. We therefore propose to assess a penalty against you as a person required to collect, account for, and pay over withhold taxes for the above business.

Under the provisions of Internal Revenue Code section 6672, individuals who were required to collect, account for, and pay over these taxes for the business may be personally liable for a penalty if the business doesn't pay the taxes. These taxes, described in the enclosed Form 2751, consist of employment taxes you withheld (or should have withheld) from the employees' wages (and didn't pay) or excise taxes you collected (or should have collected) from patrons (and didn't pay), and are commonly referred to as "trust fund taxes."

The penalty we propose to assess against you is a personal liability called the Trust Fund Recovery Penalty. It is equal to the unpaid trust fund taxes which the business still owes the government. If you agree with this penalty for each tax period shown, please sign Part 1 of the enclosed Form 2751 and return it to us in the enclosed envelope.

If you don't agree, have additional information to support your case, and wish to try to resolve the matter informally, contact the person named at the top of this letter within ten days from the date of this letter.

You also have the right to appeal or protest this action. To preserve your appeal rights you need to mail us your written appeal within 60 days from the date of this letter (75 days if this letter is addressed to you outside the United States). The instructions below explain how to make the request.

Letter 1153 (DO) (Rev. 3-2002)
Catalog Number: 40545C

APPEALS

You may appeal your case to the local Appeals Office. Send your written appeal to the attention of the Person to Contact at the address shown at the top of this letter. The dollar amount of the proposed liability for each specific tax period you are protesting affects the form your appeal should take.

For each period you are protesting, if the proposed penalty amount is:	You should:
$25,000 or less	Send a letter listing the issues you disagree with and explain why you disagree. (Small Case Request).
More than $25,000	Submit a formal Written Protest.

One protest will suffice for all the periods listed on the enclosed Form 2751, however if any one of those periods is more than $25,000, a formal protest must be filed. Include any additional information that you want the Settlement Officer/Appeals Officer to consider. You may still appeal without additional information, but including it at this stage will help us to process your request promptly.

A SMALL CASE REQUEST should include:

1. A copy of this letter, or your name, address, social security number, and any information that will help us locate your file;

2. A statement that you want an Appeal's conference;

3. A list of the issues you disagree with and an explanation of why you disagree. Usually, penalty cases like this one involve issues of responsibility and willfulness. Willfulness means that an action was intentional, deliberate or voluntary and not an accident or mistake. Therefore, your statement should include a clear explanation of your duties and responsibilities; and specifically, your duty and authority to collect, account for, and pay the trust fund taxes. Should you disagree with how we calculated the penalty, your statement should identify the dates and amounts of payments that you believe we didn't consider and or/ any computation errors that you believe we made.

Please submit two copies of your Small Case Request.

A formal **WRITTEN PROTEST should** include the items below. Pay particular attention to item 6 and the note that follows it.

Letter 1153 (DO) (Rev. 3-2002)
Catalog Number: 40545C

1. Your name, address, and social security number;

2. A statement that you want a conference;

3. A copy of this letter, or the date and number of this letter;

4. The tax periods involved (see Form 2751);

5. A list of the findings you disagree with;

6. A statement of fact, signed under penalties of perjury, that explains why you disagree and why you believe you shouldn't be charged with the penalty. Include specific dates, names, amounts, and locations which support your position. Usually, penalty cases like this one involve issues of responsibility and willfulness. Willfulness means that an action was intentional, deliberate or voluntary and not an accident or mistake. Therefore, your statement should include a clear explanation of your duties and responsibilities; and specifically, your duty and authority to collect, account for, and pay the trust fund taxes. Should you disagree with how we calculated the penalty, your statement should identify the dates and amounts of payments that you believe we didn't consider and/or any computation errors you believe we made;

NOTE:

To declare that the statement in item 6 is true under penalties of perjury, you must add the following to your statement and sign it:

"Under penalties of perjury, I declare that I have examined the facts presented in this statement and any accompanying information, and, to the best of my knowledge and belief, they are true, correct, and complete."

7. If you rely on a law or other authority to support your arguments, explain what it is and how it applies.

REPRESENTATION

You may represent yourself at your conference or have someone who is qualified to practice before the Internal Revenue Service represent you. This may be your attorney, a certified public accountant, or another individual enrolled to practice before the IRS. If your representative attends a conference without you, he or she must file a power of attorney or tax information authorization before receiving or inspecting confidential tax information. Form 2848, Power of Attorney and Declaration of Representative, or Form 8821, Tax Information Authorization, may be used for this purpose. Both forms are available from any IRS office. A properly written power of attorney or authorization is acceptable.

If your representative prepares and signs the protest for you, he or she must substitute a declaration stating:

1. That he or she submitted the protest and accompanying documents, and

2. Whether he or she knows personally that the facts stated in the protest and accompanying documents are true and correct.

CLAIMS FOR REFUND AND CONSIDERATION BY THE COURTS

CONSIDERATION BY THE COURTS

If you and the IRS still disagree after your conference, we will send you a bill. However, by following the procedures outlined below, you may take your case to the United States Court of Federal Claims or to your United States District Court. These courts have no connection with the IRS.

Before you can file a claim with these courts, you must pay a portion of the tax liability and file a claim for refund with the IRS, as described below.

SPECIAL BOND TO DELAY IRS COLLECTION ACTIONS FOR ANY PERIOD AS SOON AS A CLAIM FOR REFUND IS FILED

To request a delay in collection of the penalty by the IRS for any period as soon as you file a claim for refund for that period, you must do the following within 30 days of the date of the official notice of assessment and demand (the first bill) for that period:

1. Pay the tax for one employee for each period (quarter) of liability that you wish to contest, if we've based the amount of the penalty on unpaid employment taxes; or pay the tax for one transaction for each period that you wish to contest, if we've based the amount of the penalty on unpaid excise tax.

2. File a claim for a refund of the amount(s) you paid using Form(s) 843, Claim for Refund and Request for Abatement.

3. Post a bond with the IRS for one and one half times the amount of the penalty that is left after you have made the payment in Item 1.

If the IRS denies your claim when you have posted this bond, you then have 30 days to file suit in your United States District Court or the United States Court of Federal Claims before the IRS may apply the bond to your trust fund recovery penalty and the interest accruing on this debt.

Letter 1153 (DO) (Rev. 3-2002)
Catalog Number: 40545C

CLAIM FOR REFUND WITH NO SPECIAL BOND

If you do not file a special bond with a prompt claim for refund, as described above, you may still file a claim for refund following above action items 1 and 2, except these action items do not have to be taken in the first 30 days after the date of the official notice of assessment and demand for the period.

If IRS has not acted on your claim within 6 months from the date you filed it, you can file a suit for refund. You can also file a suit for refund within 2 years after IRS has disallowed your claim.

You should be aware that if IRS finds that the collection of this penalty is in jeopardy, we may take immediate action to collect it without regard to the 60-day period for submitting a protest mentioned above.

For further information about filing a suit you may contact the Clerk of your District Court or the Clerk of the United States Court of Federal Claims, 717 Madison Place, NW, Washington, D.C. 20005.

If we do not hear from you within 60 days from the date of this letter (or 75 days if this letter is addressed to you outside the United States), we will assess the penalty and begin collection action.

Sincerely yours,

Revenue Officer

Enclosures:
Form 2751
Publication 1
Envelope

Letter 1153 (DO) (Rev. 3-2002)
Catalog Number: 40545C

Department of the Treasury-Internal Revenue Service

Form 2751 (Rev. 7-2002)
Proposed Assessment of Trust Fund Recovery Penalty
(Sec. 6672, Internal Revenue Code, or corresponding provisions of prior internal revenue laws)

Report of Business Taxpayer's Unpaid Tax Liability

Name and address of business

BUSINESS NAME
STREET ADDRESS
CITY, STATE, ZIP

Tax Return Form Number	Tax Period Ended	Date Return Filed	Date Tax Assessed	Identifying Number	Amount Outstanding	Penalty
941	12/31/2016	05/18/2017	07/10/2017	xx-xxx-1111	$31,928.62	$25,939
941	03/31/2017	05/18/2017	07/10/2017	xx-xxx-1111	$56,143.81	$34,929
Totals:					**$88,072.43**	**$60,86**

Agreement to Assessment and Collection of Trust Fund Recovery Penalty

Name, address, and social security number of person responsible

Responsible person's name
xxx-xx-1111
Street Adress
City, State Zip

I consent to the assessment and collection of the penalty shown for each period, which is equal either to the amount of federal employment taxes withheld employees' wages or to the amount of federal excise taxes collected from patrons or members, and which was not paid over to the Government by the bus named above. I waive the 60 day restriction on notice and demand set forth in Internal Revenue Code Section 6672(b).

Signature of person responsible | Date

Part 1— Please sign and return this copy to Internal Revenue Service   Catalog No. 21955U   www.irs.gov   Form 2751 (Rev. 7-2

EXHIBIT 19

November ___, 2018

Internal Revenue Service
ATTN: _____
Street Address
City, State Zip

RE: Taxpayer Name
        Street Address
        City, State Zip
        SSN: _____

Dear _____:

My power of attorney (Form 2848) to represent the taxpayer in this matter is included.

Reference is made to the September ___, 2018 letter that proposed an assessment for unpaid trust funds in regard to the above named taxpayer for _____ Inc., a copy of which is attached. This is to protest the proposed assessment and to request a conference with the Appeals Division. The following information is submitted in support of this appeal.

I.   **CONFERENCE**

      The taxpayer wants to appeal the determination of the Internal Revenue Service, and requests a hearing before the Regional Office of Appeals in the East Hartford, Connecticut Appeals office.

II.   **NAME AND ADDRESS**

      Taxpayer Name
      Street Address
      City, State Zip
      SSN: _____

III.   **DATE AND SYMBOLS FROM LETTER**

      September 20, 2018
      Letter 1153 (DO)(Rev. 3-2002)

EXHIBIT 20

IV. TAX PERIODS

12/31/2008
03/31/2009

V. ITEMIZED SCHEDULE OF APPEAL ITEMS

The determination that the taxpayer is a responsible person as defined in IRC § 6672 for the unpaid trust funds for the tax periods listed above in the amount of $296,096.67.

VI. STATEMENT OF FACTS

The taxpayer worked as Vice President of Operations at _____, Inc., ("NAME"). The NAME was in the construction business, and the taxpayer was responsible for managing the job site operations under the general supervision and direction of _____. The taxpayer's specific duties included supervising of all job personnel, reviewing of job budgets, scheduling, attending job meetings, and consulting with the Company's agents and employees as required.

Mr. NAME was responsible for the finances. Mr. NAME ran operations in the office, and only he signed payroll checks and other documents as the sole shareholder. The taxpayer was given an officer's title, but he had no financial responsibilities in the Companies. The taxpayer was given signature rights but in ten years never signed a single check, legal document, or tax document. A stamp of his signature was made, but to his knowledge the stamp was never used. Ms. _____, who was in charge of payroll function for the years of 1983 to 2007, affirms that the taxpayer had nothing to do with nor signed a single check. A copy of her affidavit is attached.

VII. LAW AND AUTHORITIES

The issue is whether the taxpayer meets the definition of a "responsible person" who willfully failed to have the payroll taxes paid over to the government IRC § 6672.

IRC § 6672 states the following:

Any person *required to collect, truthfully account for, and pay over* any tax imposed by this title who *willfully* fails to collect such tax, or truthfully account for and pay over such tax, or willfully attempts in any manner to evade or defeat any such tax or the payment thereof, shall, in addition to other penalties provided by law, be liable to a penalty equal to the total amount of the tax evaded, or not collected, or not accounted for and paid over.

In other words, pursuant to IRC § 6672 and Regulation § 301.6672-1, the Trust Fund Recovery penalty is only imposed on individuals who:
1. Were required to collect, account for and pay over the taxes, and

2. Willfully failed to do so.

Based upon the foregoing, the taxpayer, though an officer with authority, lacked the functional responsibility for the payroll taxes of the Companies. He was never involved with the payroll function and in 10 years never signed a check or return for the Companies. It was not until after the taxpayer left the Companies that he learned from the government that taxes were owed. Prior to that he had no knowledge nor access to the financial information of the company, and was never made aware by anyone that the company had failed to pay its payroll taxes or even had a money issue. Given that the taxpayer was never involved in the Companies' taxes and did not have knowledge of the payroll tax problem, he therefore lacked the requisite willfulness required under IRC § 6672. The taxpayer therefore should not be held responsible for the companies unpaid payroll taxes.

This protest was prepared by the undersigned based upon direct involvement of TAXPAYER. To the best of my knowledge and understanding all of the statements of facts contained in the protest are true and correct.

Very truly yours,

Eric L. Green, Esq.

Enclosures
c: **Taxpayer**

February 28, 2020

<u>VIA FAX: 877-807-9215</u>
IRS FOIA Request
HQ FOIA
Stop 211
PO Box 621506
Atlanta, GA 30362-3006

  Re: **Taxpayer:** _____
     Current Address: _____
     SSN: _____

Dear Sir or Madam:

This is a request under the Freedom of Information Act.

1. **Name and Address**

    <u>Requestor:</u>
    Representative's Name
    Reps Street Address
    Rep City, State and Zip

    <u>Client:</u>
    Taxpayer's Name
    Taxpayer's Street Address
    Taxpayer's City, State and Zip

2. **Description of the Requested Records**

    The undersigned represents TAXPAYER NAME (the "Requestor"). We respectfully request copies of the taxpayers' administrative file regarding his civil penalties under IRC § 6672 for the quarters 6/30/2015 through and including 12/31/2016.

3. **Proof of Identity**

    As proof of identity, I am including a photocopy of my driver's license and a copy of my Power of Attorney and Declaration of Representative (Form 2848).

4. **Commitment to Pay Any Fees Which May Apply**

The undersigned is willing to pay for fees associated with this request. If the request shall exceed $100, the undersigned requests to be notified.

5.   Compelling Need for Speedy Response

We are in the middle of an Appeal of these civil penalties and require the information to properly present our case.

I declare that the above stated information is true and accurate to the best of my knowledge under the penalty of perjury.

Please call me with any questions.

Very truly yours,

Your Name

State of Connecticut   )
)   ss. _____
County of New Haven   )

AFFIDAVIT

I, _____, of New Haven, Connecticut hereby aver as follows:

1. That I am over eighteen years of age and believe in the obligations of an oath;

2. I was an employee of _____, Inc. ("Company") during the period of 1984 through its dissolution in 2007.

3. My role was Supervisor in-charge of payroll for the Company.

4. During Mr. TAXPAYER's time as a Vice-President at the Company he never signed a payroll check.

5. Mr. TAXPAYER never signed any tax returns or payroll-related documents

6. Mr. TAXPAYER was not involved in the payroll process at all.

7. The only person who signed payroll checks and determined which vendors to pay and not pay during my time with the company was the owner, Mr. _____.

8. I am aware this affidavit is being submitted to the Internal Revenue Service for their consideration of a material tax matter.

Subscribed and sworn to, under penalty of perjury, this _____ day of November, 2018.

_____
WITNESSES NAME

Dated at _____, Connecticut, this _____ day of November, 2018.

_____
Notary Public

EXHIBIT 22

Form 656-L

Offer in Compromise

(Doubt as to Liability)

CONTENTS

- What you need to know 2
- Important information 3
- Form 656-L 5

IRS contact information

If you have questions regarding qualifications for an offer in compromise, please call our toll-free number at 1-800-829-1040. You can get forms and publications by calling 1-800-TAX-FORM (1-800-829-3676), by visiting your local IRS office, or at www.irs.gov.

Taxpayer resources

The Taxpayer Advocate Service (TAS) is an independent organization within the Internal Revenue Service that helps taxpayers and protects taxpayer rights. TAS helps taxpayers whose problems with the IRS are causing financial difficulties, who've tried but haven't been able to resolve their problems with the IRS, or believe an IRS system or procedure isn't working as it should. And the service is free. Your local advocate's number is in your local directory and at www.taxpayeradvocate.irs.gov. You can also call TAS at 1-877-777-4778. For more information about TAS and your rights under the Taxpayer Bill of Rights, go to www.taxpayeradvocate.irs.gov. The Taxpayer Advocate is your voice at the IRS.

Low Income Taxpayer Clinics (LITCs) are independent from the IRS. LITCs serve individuals whose income is below a certain level and who need to resolve a tax problem with the IRS. LITCs provide professional representation before the IRS or in court on audits, appeals, tax collection disputes, and other issues for free or for a small fee. For more information and to find an LITC near you, see the LITC page at www.taxpayeradvocate.irs.gov/litcmap or IRS Publication 4134, Low Income Taxpayer Clinic List. This Publication is also available online at www.irs.gov or by calling the IRS toll-free at 1-800-829-3676.

Catalog Number 47516R www.irs.gov Form **656-L** (Rev. 1-2018)

INSTRUCTIONS FOR FORM 656-L, OFFER IN COMPROMISE (DOUBT AS TO LIABILITY)

What you need to know

Your Rights as a Taxpayer

Each and every taxpayer has a set of fundamental rights they should be aware of when dealing with the IRS. Explore your rights and our obligations to protect them. For more information on your rights as a taxpayer, http://www.irs.gov/Taxpayer-Bill-of-Rights.

What is a Doubt as to Liability offer?

Doubt as to liability exists where there is a genuine dispute as to the existence or amount of the correct tax debt under the law. If you have a legitimate doubt that you owe part or all of the tax debt, you will need to complete a Form 656-L, *Offer in Compromise (Doubt as to Liability)*.

Doubt as to liability cannot be disputed or considered if the tax debt has been established by a final court decision or judgment concerning the existence or amount of the assessed tax debt or if the assessed tax debt is based on current law.

Submitting an offer application does not guarantee that the IRS will accept your offer. It begins a process of evaluation and verification by the IRS.

If you have supplied information to the Internal Revenue Service or are responding to a notice you received relating to the same matter for which you are submitting your offer, you should resolve the outstanding issues prior to filing the offer. If your issue is being worked by another area, for example you have requested audit reconsideration to resolve whether you are liable for the tax, then an offer should not be filed until the issue is resolved. Failure to follow-up and resolve an issue may lead to the IRS returning the offer without further consideration.

A doubt as to liability offer will only be considered for the tax period(s) in question.

Note: If you agree that you owe the tax but cannot afford to pay, DO NOT FILE a Form 656-L. See below "What if I agree with the tax debt but cannot afford to pay in full?", for additional information.

If you file the wrong type of offer, your offer will be returned without further consideration.

What documentation or support is needed?

You must provide a written statement explaining why the tax debt or portion of the tax debt is incorrect. In addition, you should provide supporting documentation or evidence that will help the IRS identify the reason(s) you doubt the accuracy of the tax debt. If you are unable to reconstruct your books and records, you can provide an explanation that supports reasonable doubt justifying a reduction to a portion or all of your tax debt.

Note: Failing to provide a written statement explaining why the tax debt or a portion of the debt is incorrect will cause your offer to be returned without further consideration.

How much should I offer?

In order to qualify, you must make an offer that is $1 or more and should be based on what you believe the correct amount of tax should be. If you believe you do not owe any tax, you should pursue alternative solutions listed below. See "What alternatives do I have to sending in an Offer in Compromise (Doubt as to Liability)?", for additional information.

Note: Do not include any payment(s) with the Form 656-L. No deposit or application fee is required for a doubt as to liability offer.

IMPORTANT INFORMATION

What alternatives do I have to sending in an Offer in Compromise (Doubt as to Liability)?

When you disagree with the accuracy of a tax debt, depending on the situation and the type of tax, the IRS has other available remedies. If your tax debt is other than a Trust Fund Recovery Penalty (TFRP) or Personal Liability Excise Tax (PLET), you should pursue the options below first before submitting an offer.

Note: If you wish to obtain any of the tax products listed below, visit www.irs.gov/forms-pubs, or call (800) 829-3676.

If you think your tax liability is incorrect because:	Then:
of an audit	see Publication 3598, *The Audit Reconsideration Process*
IRS created a tax return for you because you did not file one	submit your correct signed, original tax return for processing to the appropriate processing center
items were not reported correctly on your Form 1040, *U.S. Individual Income Tax Return* or 1120, *U.S. Corporation Income Tax Return* or because IRS made an adjustment on your return	see the instructions for Form 1040X, *Amended U.S. Individual Income Tax Return* or Form 1120-X, *Amended U.S. Corporation Income Tax Return* which ever form is applicable
items were not reported properly on a tax return, other than Forms 1040, *U.S. Individual Income Tax Return* or 1120, *U.S. Corporation Income Tax Return*, or because IRS made an adjustment on your return	see the instructions for Form 843, *Claim for Refund and Request for Abatement*
you have reasonable cause to remove or reduce penalties IRS charged	see Notice 746, *Information About Your Notice, Penalty and Interest*
you believe additional interest IRS charged you was due to IRS errors or delays	see the instructions for Form 843, *Claim For Refund and Request for Abatement*
you believe you were not a responsible person of the business and have been assessed the trust fund portion of employment taxes or personal liability excise tax affiliated with a business reported on Form 720, *Quarterly Federal Excise Tax Return*	you have the option to file Form 656-L or see the instructions for Form 843, *Claim For Refund and Request for Abatement*
you believe you should be considered an "innocent spouse" for a joint income tax return	see Publication 971, *Innocent Spouse Relief*
you believe you should be considered an "injured spouse" for a joint income tax return	See Form 8379, *Injured Spouse Allocation* **Note: A claim for injured spouse will not be considered under doubt as to liability.**
you dispute your worker classification	See Form SS-8, *Worker Classification Determination* **Note: An SS-8 dispute will not be considered under doubt as to liability.**

Examples of when you should submit a Doubt as to Liability Offer	You should only submit a doubt as to liability offer if you are unable to dispute the amount of tax the IRS claims you owe during the time allowed by the Internal Revenue Code or IRS guidelines.

Possible reasons for submitting a doubt as to liability offer in compromise include the following: the examiner made a mistake interpreting the tax law; the examiner failed to consider the evidence presented; new evidence is available to support a change to the assessment. Below are some examples of when it may be appropriate to submit an offer based on doubt as to liability.

Example 1: You were audited by the IRS. When this happened, you moved and did not get the notification, or you suffered a disaster (such as books and records were destroyed in a fire or other natural disaster) causing you to miss the meeting with the auditor. The IRS disallowed all expenses and now you have a tax debt. You discover the problem when you try to borrow some money and find that there is a federal tax lien filed. You are unable to reconstruct your books and records, but you can provide an explanation that supports reasonable doubt justifying a reduction to a portion or all of your tax debt.

Example 2: You filed your tax return reporting stock options as valued by your employer, which created a large tax liability including Alternative Minimum Tax (AMT). You paid part of the tax debt, but could not pay the full amount owed. You later discovered that the stocks were not worth as much as you originally reported. This was due to fraudulent acts by the broker and/or your employer. You filed a claim for a refund based on the reduced value of stock options. IRS told you that the full amount of the tax debt had to be paid before they could consider your claim and denied your claim for refund. |
| **What if I agree with the tax debt but cannot afford to pay in full?** | *A doubt as to collectibility* offer, is when you agree that you owe the taxes but you cannot pay your tax debt in full. To be considered for a doubt as to collectibility offer you must make an appropriate offer based on what the IRS considers your true ability to pay. To request consideration under doubt as to collectibility, do not use this form. You must complete a **Form 656, Offer in Compromise**, found in Form 656-B, *Offer in Compromise Booklet*. You may get a Form 656-B by calling the toll free number 1-800-829-1040, by visiting a local IRS office, or at www.irs.gov. For additional assistance, use the online Offer In Compromise Pre-Qualifier tool at http://irs.treasury.gov/oic_pre_qualifier/.

IMPORTANT NOTE

You cannot submit an offer based on doubt as to liability (Form 656-L) and a separate offer based on doubt as to collectibility (Form 656) at the same time.

It is in your best interest to resolve any disagreements about the validity of the tax debt before filing an offer based on doubt as to collectibility. **If you send both kinds of offers at the same time, the doubt as to collectability offer will be returned without further consideration. However, when the IRS returns the doubt as to collectability offer to you, it will not return the application fee or any payment you made with the offer, but will apply any payment to your liability.** |
| **Where do I send my application?** | You should mail the completed package to:

Brookhaven Internal Revenue Service

COIC Unit
P.O. Box 9008
Stop 681-D
Holtsville, NY 11742-9008 |

Page 5

Form **656-L**
(January 2018)

Department of the Treasury - Internal Revenue Service

Offer in Compromise *(Doubt as to Liability)*

OMB Number
1545-1686

IRS Received Date

▶ **To: Commissioner of Internal Revenue Service**

In the following agreement, the pronoun "we" may be assumed in place of "I" when there are joint liabilities and both parties are signing this agreement.
I submit this offer to compromise the tax liabilities plus any interest, penalties, additions to tax, and additional amounts required by law for the tax type and period(s) marked below:

Section 1 — Individual Information (Form 1040 filers)

Your First Name, Middle Initial, Last Name

Social Security Number (SSN)
- -

If a Joint Offer: Spouse's First Name, Middle Initial, Last Name

Social Security Number (SSN)
- -

Your Physical Home Address *(Street, City, State, ZIP Code)*

Your Mailing Address *(if different from your Physical Home Address or Post Office Box Number)*

Is this a new address?
☐ Yes ☐ No

If yes, would you like us to update our records to this address?
☐ Yes ☐ No

Employer Identification Number *(For self-employed individuals only)*
-

Individual Tax Periods

☐ **1040** U.S. Individual Income Tax Return [List all year(s); for example 2009, 2010, etc.]

☐ **941** Employer's Quarterly Federal Tax Return [List all quarterly period(s); for example 03/31/2010, 06/30/2010, 09/30/2010, etc.]

☐ **940** Employer's Annual Federal Unemployment (FUTA) Tax Return [List all year(s); for example 2010, 2011, etc.]

☐ **Trust Fund Recovery Penalty** as a responsible person of *(enter business name)* _____ ,
for failure to pay withholding and Federal Insurance Contributions Act taxes (Social Security taxes), for period(s) ending [List all quarterly period(s); for example 03/31/2009, 06/30/2009, etc.]

☐ **Other Federal Tax(es)** [specify type(s) and period(s)]

Section 2 — Business Information (Form 1120, 1065, etc., filers)

Business Name

Business Physical Address *(Street, City, State, ZIP Code)*

Business Mailing Address *(Street, City, State, ZIP Code)*

Employer Identification Number *(EIN)*
-

Name and Title of Primary Contact

Telephone Number
( ) -

Business Tax Periods

☐ **1120** U.S. Corporate Income Tax Return [List all year(s); for example 1120 2010, 1120 2013, etc.]

☐ **941** Employer's Quarterly Federal Tax Return [List all quarterly period(s); for example 03/31/2010, 06/30/2010, 09/30/2010, etc.]

☐ **940** Employer's Annual Federal Unemployment (FUTA) Tax Return [List all year(s); for example 2010, 2011, etc.]

☐ **Other Federal Tax(es)** [specify type(s) and period(s)]

Note: If you need more space, use a separate sheet of paper and title it "Attachment to Form 656-L Dated _____." Sign and date the attachment following the listing of the tax periods.

Catalog Number 47516R www.irs.gov Form **656-L** (Rev. 1-2018)

Page 6

Section 3 — Amount of the Offer

I offer to pay $ _____

Must be $1 or more and payable within 90 days of the notification of acceptance, unless an alternative payment term is approved at the time the offer is accepted. **Do not send any payment with this form.** If you do not offer at least $1, your offer will be returned without consideration.

Section 4 — Terms

By submitting this offer, I have read, understand and agree to the following terms and conditions:

Terms, Conditions, and Legal Agreement

a) The IRS will apply payments made under the terms of this offer in the best interest of the government.

IRS will keep my payments and fees

b) I voluntarily submit all payments made on this offer.

c) The IRS will keep all payments and credits made, received, or applied to the total original tax debt before I send in the offer or while it is under consideration, including any refunds from tax returns and/or credits from tax years prior to the year in which the offer was accepted.

d) The IRS may levy under section 6331(a) up to the time that the IRS official signs and acknowledges my offer as pending, which is accepted for processing, and the IRS may keep any proceeds arising from such a levy.

e) If the Doubt as to Liability offer determines that I do not owe the taxes, or the IRS ultimately over-collected the compromised tax liability, the IRS will return the over-collected amount to me, unless such refund is legally prohibited by statute.

f) If the IRS served a continuous levy on wages, salary, or certain federal payments under sections 6331(e) or (h), then the IRS could choose to either retain or release the levy. No levy may be made during the time an offer in compromise is pending.

I agree to the time extensions allowed by law

g) To have my offer considered, I agree to the extension of time limit provided by law to assess my tax debt (statutory period of assessment). I agree that the date by which the IRS must assess my tax debt will now be the date by which my debt must currently be assessed plus the period of time my offer is pending plus one additional year if the IRS rejects, returns, or terminates my offer, or I withdraw it. [Paragraph (l) of this section defines pending and withdrawal]. I understand I have the right not to waive the statutory period of assessment or to limit the waiver to a certain length or certain periods or issues. I understand, however, the IRS may not consider my offer if I decline to waive the statutory period of assessment or if I provide only a limited waiver. I also understand the statutory period for collecting my tax debt will be suspended during the time my offer is pending with the IRS, for 30 days after any rejection of my offer by the IRS, and during the time any rejection of my offer is being considered by the Appeals Office.

I understand I remain responsible for the full amount of the tax liability

h) The IRS cannot collect more than the full amount of the tax debt under this offer.

i) I understand I remain responsible for the full amount of the tax debt, unless and until the IRS partially or fully abates the tax, or accepts the offer in writing and I have met all the terms and conditions of the offer. The IRS will not remove the original amount of the tax debt from its records until I have met all the terms of the offer.

j) I understand the tax I offer to compromise is and will remain a tax debt until I meet all the terms and conditions of this offer. If I file bankruptcy before the terms and conditions of this offer are completed, any claim the IRS files in bankruptcy proceedings will be a tax claim.

k) Once the IRS accepts the offer in writing, I have no right to contest, in court or otherwise, the amount of the tax debt.

Pending status of an offer and right to appeal

l) The offer is pending starting with the date an authorized IRS official signs this form. The offer remains pending until an authorized IRS official accepts, rejects, returns, or acknowledges withdrawal of the offer in writing. If I appeal an IRS rejection decision on the offer, the IRS will continue to treat the offer as pending until the Appeals Office accepts or rejects the offer in writing. If an offer is rejected, no levy may be made during the 30 days of rejection. If I do not file a protest within 30 days of the date the IRS notifies me of the right to protest the decision, I waive the right to a hearing before the Appeals Office about the offer.

I understand if IRS fails to make a decision in 24-months my offer will be accepted

m) I understand under Internal Revenue Code (IRC) § 7122(f), my offer will be accepted, by law, unless IRS notifies me otherwise, in writing, within 24 months of the date my offer was initially received.

I understand what will happen if I fail to meet the terms of my offer (e.g. default)

n) If I fail to meet any of the terms of this offer, the IRS may levy or sue me to collect any amount ranging from the unpaid balance of the offer to the original amount of the tax debt (less payments made) plus penalties and interest that have accrued from the time the underlying tax liability arose. The IRS will continue to add interest, as required by Section § 6601 of the Internal Revenue Code, on the amount of the IRS determines is due after default.

I understand the IRS may file a Notice of Federal Tax Lien on my/our property

o) The IRS may file a Notice of Federal Tax Lien to protect the Government's interest during the offer investigation. The tax lien will be released 30 days after the payment terms have been satisfied and the payment has been verified. If the offer is accepted, the tax lien will be released within 30 days of when the payment terms have been satisfied and the payment has been verified. The time it takes to verify the payment varies based on the form of payment.

Catalog Number 47516R — www.irs.gov — Form **656-L** (Rev. 1-2018)

Section 4	Terms *(continued)*
I authorize the IRS to contact relevant third parties in order to process my/our offer	p) I understand that IRS employees may contact third parties in order to respond to this request, and I authorize the IRS to make such contacts. Further, in connection with this request, by authorizing the IRS to contact third parties, I understand that I will not receive notice of third parties contacted as is otherwise required by IRC § 7602(c).

Section 5 — Explanation of Circumstances

THIS SECTION MUST BE COMPLETED.

Explain why you believe the tax is incorrect. Reminder: if your explanation indicates you cannot afford to pay, do not file a Form 656-L. Refer to page 4 "What if I agree with the tax debt but cannot afford to pay in full?", for additional information. **Note: You may attach additional sheets if necessary. Please include your name and SSN and/or EIN on all additional sheets or supporting documentation.**

_____
_____
_____
_____
_____
_____
_____
_____
_____
_____
_____
_____

Section 6 — Signature(s)

Taxpayer Attestation: If I submit this offer on a substitute form, I affirm this form is a verbatim duplicate of the official Form 656-L, and I agree to be bound by all the terms and conditions set forth in the official Form 656-L. Under penalties of perjury, I declare that I have examined this offer, including accompanying schedules and statements, and to the best of my knowledge and belief, it is true, correct and complete.

▶ Signature of Taxpayer/Corporation Name | Daytime Telephone Number ( ) - | Today's date *(mm/dd/yyyy)*

☐ The IRS may contact you by telephone about this offer. By checking this box, you authorize the IRS to leave detailed messages concerning your offer on your voice mail or answering machine.

▶ Signature of Spouse/Authorized Corporate Officer | Today's date *(mm/dd/yyyy)*

☐ The IRS may contact you by telephone about this offer. By checking this box, you authorize the IRS to leave detailed messages concerning your offer on your voice mail or answering machine.

Section 7 — Application Prepared by Someone Other than the Taxpayer

If this application was prepared by someone other than you (the taxpayer), please fill in that person's name and address below.

Name

Address *(Street, City, State, ZIP Code)* | Daytime Telephone Number ( ) -

Section 8 — Paid Preparer Use Only

Signature of Preparer

☐ The IRS may contact you by telephone about this offer. By checking this box, you authorize the IRS to leave detailed messages concerning your offer on your voice mail or answering machine.

Name of Preparer | Today's date *(mm/dd/yyyy)* | Preparer's CAF no. or PTIN

Firm's Name, Address, and ZIP Code | Daytime Telephone Number ( ) -

If you would like to have someone represent you during the offer investigation, include a valid, signed Form 2848 or 8821 with this application, or a copy of a previously filed form.

IRS Use Only		
I accept the waiver of the statutory period of limitations on assessment for the Internal Revenue Service, as described in Section 4(g).		
Signature of Authorized IRS Official	Title	Today's date *(mm/dd/yyyy)*

Privacy Act Statement

We ask for the information on this form to carry out the internal revenue laws of the United States. Our authority to request this information is contained in Section 7801 of the Internal Revenue Code.

Our purpose for requesting the information is to determine if it is in the best interests of the IRS to accept an offer. You are not required to make an offer; however, if you choose to do so, you must provide all of the information requested. Failure to provide all of the information may prevent us from processing your request.

If you are a paid preparer and you prepared the Form 656-L for the taxpayer submitting an offer, we request that you complete and sign Section 8 on the Form 656-L, and provide identifying information. Providing this information is voluntary. This information will be used to administer and enforce the internal revenue laws of the United States and may be used to regulate practice before the Internal Revenue Service for those persons subject to Treasury Department Circular No. 230, Regulations Governing the Practice of Attorneys, Certified Public Accountants, Enrolled Agents, Enrolled Actuaries, and Appraisers before the Internal Revenue Service. Information on this form may be disclosed to the Department of Justice for civil and criminal litigation.

We may also disclose this information to cities, states and the District of Columbia for use in administering their tax laws and to combat terrorism. Providing false or fraudulent information on this form may subject you to criminal prosecution and penalties.

APPLICATION CHECKLIST

☐ Did you include supporting documentation and an explanation as to why you doubt you owe the tax?

☐ Did you complete all fields on the Form 656-L?

☐ Did you make an offer amount that is $1 or more?

Note: The amount of your offer should be based on what you believe the correct amount of the tax debt should be. However, you must offer at least $1. If you do not want to offer $1 or more, you should pursue the alternative solutions provided under "What alternatives do I have to sending in an Offer in Compromise (Doubt as to Liability)?" found on page 3.

☐ If someone other than you completed the Form 656-L, did that person sign it?

☐ Did you sign and include the Form 656-L?

☐ If you want a third party to represent you during the offer process, did you include a Form 2848 or Form 8821 unless one is already on file?

Note: There is no application fee or deposit required for a Doubt as to Liability offer. Do not send any payments with this offer.

Mail your package to:

Brookhaven Internal Revenue Service
COIC Unit
P.O. Box 9008
Stop 681-D
Holtsville, NY 11742-9008

Form 843
(Rev. August 2011)
Department of the Treasury
Internal Revenue Service

Claim for Refund and Request for Abatement

▶ See separate instructions.

OMB No. 1545-0024

Use Form 843 if your claim or request involves:
- (a) a refund of one of the taxes (other than income taxes or an employer's claim for FICA tax, RRTA tax, or income tax withholding) or a fee, shown on line 3,
- (b) an abatement of FUTA tax or certain excise taxes, or
- (c) a refund or abatement of interest, penalties, or additions to tax for one of the reasons shown on line 5a.

Do not use Form 843 if your claim or request involves:
- (a) an overpayment of income taxes or an employer's claim for FICA tax, RRTA tax, or income tax withholding (use the appropriate amended tax return),
- (b) a refund of excise taxes based on the nontaxable use or sale of fuels, or
- (c) an overpayment of excise taxes reported on Form(s) 11-C, 720, 730, or 2290.

Name(s)	Your social security number
Address (number, street, and room or suite no.)	Spouse's social security number
City or town, state, and ZIP code	Employer identification number (EIN)
Name and address shown on return if different from above	Daytime telephone number

1 Period. Prepare a separate Form 843 for each tax period or fee year.
From   to

2 Amount to be refunded or abated:
$

3 Type of tax or fee. Indicate the type of tax or fee to be refunded or abated or to which the interest, penalty, or addition to tax is related.
☐ Employment   ☐ Estate   ☐ Gift   ☐ Excise   ☐ Income   ☐ Fee

4 Type of penalty. If the claim or request involves a penalty, enter the Internal Revenue Code section on which the penalty is based (see instructions). IRC section:

5a Interest, penalties, and additions to tax. Check the box that indicates your reason for the request for refund or abatement. (If none apply, go to line 6.)
☐ Interest was assessed as a result of IRS errors or delays.
☐ A penalty or addition to tax was the result of erroneous written advice from the IRS.
☐ Reasonable cause or other reason allowed under the law (other than erroneous written advice) can be shown for not assessing a penalty or addition to tax.

b Date(s) of payment(s) ▶

6 Original return. Indicate the type of fee or return, if any, filed to which the tax, interest, penalty, or addition to tax relates.
☐ 706   ☐ 709   ☐ 940   ☐ 941   ☐ 943   ☐ 945
☐ 990-PF   ☐ 1040   ☐ 1120   ☐ 4720   ☐ Other (specify) ▶

7 Explanation. Explain why you believe this claim or request should be allowed and show the computation of the amount shown on line 2. If you need more space, attach additional sheets.

Signature. If you are filing Form 843 to request a refund or abatement relating to a joint return, both you and your spouse must sign the claim. Claims filed by corporations must be signed by a corporate officer authorized to sign, and the officer's title must be shown.

Under penalties of perjury, I declare that I have examined this claim, including accompanying schedules and statements, and, to the best of my knowledge and belief, it is true, correct, and complete. Declaration of preparer (other than taxpayer) is based on all information of which preparer has any knowledge.

Signature (Title, if applicable. Claims by corporations must be signed by an officer.)   Date

Signature (spouse, if joint return)   Date

Paid Preparer Use Only	Print/Type preparer's name	Preparer's signature	Date	Check ☐ if self-employed	PTIN
	Firm's name ▶			Firm's EIN ▶	
	Firm's address ▶			Phone no.	

For Privacy Act and Paperwork Reduction Act Notice, see separate instructions.   Cat. No. 10180R   Form **843** (Rev. 8-2011)

EXHIBIT 24

UNITED STATES DISTRICT COURT
DISTRICT OF CONNECTICUT

TAXPAYER	:	CIVIL ACTION NO.
Plaintiff	:	
v.	:	
UNITED STATES OF AMERICA	:	
Defendant	:	APRIL 1, 20__

COMPLAINT AND JURY DEMAND

The plaintiff, TAXPAYER NAME (the "Plaintiff"), hereby brings the following complaint upon information and belief as follows:

PARTIES

1. The plaintiff, TAXPAYER NAME (the "Plaintiff"), is a resident of the State of Connecticut with a place of residence at STREET, CITY, CT 06___.

2. The defendant, United States of America ("USA"), is the proper party in interest for seeking refund of monies paid to the Internal Revenue Service (the "IRS").

JURISDICTION AND VENUE

3. This Court has subject matter jurisdiction over this matter pursuant to 28 U.S.C. § 1346(a)(1), 26 U.S.C. §§ 6532(a), 6672(d), 7402 and 7422.

4. This Court has personal jurisdiction and venue over this matter as the Plaintiff is a resident of the State of Connecticut. The USA is amenable to service of process pursuant to Fed. R. Civ. P. 4(i).

COUNT ONE: Claim for Refund Pursuant to 26 U.S.C. § 7422

1-4. The Plaintiff incorporates paragraphs 1 through 4 of the Complaint as the corresponding paragraphs to this Count as if fully stated herein.

5. For many years NAME OF CORPORATION, Inc. ("CORP"), was a successful electrical contracting firm.

6. At all times relevant hereto, BOOKEEPER NAME ("BOOKKEEPER"), was a resident of the State of Connecticut with a last known place of address at 33 Lindale Street # 89, Stamford CT 06902. Until June 2008 BOOKKEEPER was employed by CORP as its bookkeeper.

7. At all times relevant hereto, the defendant, DEFANDANT ("DEFENDANT"), was a resident of the State of Connecticut with a last known place of address at 64 West Hill Circle, Stamford CT 06902. DEFENDANT was a fifty (50%) owner of CORP and the corporate treasurer.

8. CORP is owned fifty (50%) percent each by the Plaintiff and DEFENDANT.

9. During the construction and housing boom of 2002-2007, CORP's work load grew significantly and, as such, retained additional employees and expanded its operations.

10. Most of CORP's employees were union members.

11. During the second half of 2007 CORP began to experience issues with on-going projects, including increased material costs and increased default rates by its customers.

12. During the beginning of 2008 the Plaintiff injected more than $140,000.00 of his personal funds into CORP to ensure bills, including federal tax payments, were paid.

13. However, unbeknownst to the Plaintiff, CORP's bookkeeper, BOOKKEEPER, failed to make employment tax deposits even though he was specifically instructed to do so, and reminded on a weekly basis, by the Plaintiff.

14. During all times relevant hereto, every Monday morning the Plaintiff questioned BOOKKEEPER as to whether the tax deposit payment concerning the prior week's payroll had

been made. BOOKKEEPER always acknowledge the reminders and indicated that appropriate tax deposits were being made to the IRS.

15. Despite the repeated admonitions by the Plaintiff to BOOKKEEPER', and BOOKKEEPER assurances that he was making federal tax deposits, BOOKKEEPER in fact failed to actually make the tax deposits.

16. Indeed, during the times relevant hereto, the Plaintiff had invested and/or lent his own personal funds to CORP to ensure that CORP had sufficient cash on hand to make federal tax deposits. Thus, despite BOOKKEEPER' explicit instruction from the Plaintiff and his assurances that federal tax deposits were being made, BOOKKEEPER redirected the funds injected into CORP by the Plaintiff for other purposes for which it was not intended.

17. On account of, inter alia, BOOKKEEPER' conduct filed for Chapter 11 bankruptcy on June 6, 2008.

18. On or about December 15, 2008, REVENUE OFFICER'S NAME, Revenue Officer, issued a proposed assessment of a Trust Fund Recovery Penalty pursuant to 26 U.S.C. § 6672 against the Plaintiff for the first quarter and second quarter of 2008. (A copy of the Proposed Assessment is attached hereto as Exhibit A.)

19. The Plaintiff timely appealed the proposed assessment, which was denied, and the proposed assessment became final in the amount of: (a) $69,471.09, Assessed Balance for March 31, 2008; and (b) $54,718.32, Assessed Balance for June 30, 2008 for a total of $124,189.41 (the "Trust Fund Recovery Penalty Assessment"), plus accrued interest.

20. On October 14, 2009 the Plaintiff paid a portion of the tax due for each assessed period and requested a refund thereon. See, Steele v. United States, 280 F.2d 89 (8th Cir. 1960);

IRM 5.7.6.6 (2). A copy of the payments made to the IRS and Refund Requests are attached hereto as <u>Exhibit B</u>.

21. On March 3, 2010 said refund requests were denied. A copy of the denial letter is attached hereto as <u>Exhibit C</u>.

22. Pursuant to 26 U.S.C. § 6672, Congress has only authorized the IRS to assess and collect a "trust fund recovery penalty" against taxpayers who are both "responsible persons" and who "willfully" failed to collect, account for and pay over the "trust fund" taxes of a corporate employer.

23. At all times relevant in this matter, from January through April 2008, the Plaintiff did not act "willfully" as that terms is defined by 26 U.S.C. § 6672.

24. The IRS' assessment of the Trust Fund Recovery Penalty Assessment against the Plaintiff was improper, excessive, erroneous and illegal.

25. The Plaintiff is entitled to a refund of all payments made to the USA on account of the IRS' improper assessment of a Trust Fund Recovery Penalty Assessment. Further, the Plaintiff is entitled to a determination that he is not liable for the Trust Fund Recovery Penalty Assessment against him.

WHEREFORE the Plaintiff prays that the following relief enter:

1. A declaration that he is not liable for the Trust Fund Recovery Penalty assessed against him;

2. A declaration and/or injunction prohibiting the IRS from enforcing and/or collecting the Trust Fund Recovery Penalty assessed against him;

3. Refund of amounts paid on account of said Trust Fund Recovery Penalty;

4. Attorneys fees and costs; and

5. Such other relief as the court may deem just and proper.

THE PLAINTIFF: TAXPAYER'S NAME

By: _____

THE PLAINTIFF DEMANDS TRIAL BY JURY

Revenue Procedures, Rev. Proc. 2002-26, Internal Revenue Service, (Apr. 15, 2002)

Click to open document in a browser

Rev. Proc. 2002-26, I.R.B. 2002-15, 746, April 15, 2002.

Superseding: Rev. Rul. 73-304, Rev. Rul. 73-305, Rev. Rul. 79-284, Rev. Rul. 79-304

[Code Secs. 6601 and 6651]

Deficiencies: Taxes, penalties and interest: Underpayments: Partial payment: Allocation of: Computation.–

The IRS has updated and restated its position regarding the way in which it applies a partial payment of tax, penalty and interest for one or more taxable periods. The new guidelines apply to all taxes under the Internal Revenue Code with the exception of alcohol, tobacco, and firearms taxes and the harbor maintenance tax. If the taxpayer voluntarily remits payment and provides specific written instructions as to the application of the payment, the IRS will apply the payment in accordance with the instructions. If the taxpayer does not supply written instructions as to the application of a payment, the IRS will apply the payment to periods in the order of priority that the IRS determines will serve its best interest. Back references: ¶50,615.01, ¶51,075.01 and ¶51,075.45 .

SECTION 1. PURPOSE

The purpose of this revenue procedure is to update and restate the Internal Revenue Service's position regarding the application, by the Service, of a partial payment of tax, penalty, and interest for one or more taxable periods. This revenue procedure supersedes Rev. Rul. 73-304 (1973-2 C.B. 42); Rev. Rul. 73-305 (1973-2 C.B. 43); and Rev. Rul. 79-284 (1979-2 C.B. 83).

SECTION 2. SCOPE

This revenue procedure applies to all taxes under the Internal Revenue Code, except alcohol, tobacco, and firearms taxes and the harbor maintenance tax. For purposes of this revenue procedure, the term "penalty" includes any additional amount, addition to tax, or assessable penalty.

SECTION 3. PROCEDURE

.01 If additional taxes, penalty, and interest for one or more taxable periods have been assessed against a taxpayer (or have been mutuallyagreed to as to the amount and liability but are unassessed) at the time the taxpayer voluntarily tenders a partial payment that is accepted by the Service and the taxpayer provides specific written directions as to the application of the payment, the Service will apply the payment in accordance with those directions.

.02 If additional taxes, penalty, and interest for one or more taxable periods have been assessed against a taxpayer (or have been mutually agreed to as to the amount and liability but are unassessed) at the time the taxpayer voluntarily tenders a partial payment that is accepted by the Service and the taxpayer does not provide specific written directions as to the application of payment, the Service will apply the payment to periods in the order of priority that the Service determines will serve its best interest. The payment will be applied to satisfy the liability for successive periods in descending order of priority until the payment is absorbed. If the amount applied to a period is less than the liability for the period, the amount will be applied to tax, penalty, and interest, in that order, until the amount is absorbed.

.03 Payments made pursuant to the terms of offers in compromise (or offers in compromise and collateral agreements) that have been accepted by the Government in compromise of outstanding tax liabilities, in accordance with §7122 of the Internal Revenue Code, will be applied as follows:

(1) If an offer in compromise and collateral agreement have been accepted by the Government in compromise of an outstanding liability and the offer in compromise and collateral agreement provide for the allocation of payments made pursuant thereto, payments made pursuant to the agreements will be applied by the Service in accordance with the terms of the agreements.

(2) In all other cases, the Service will apply payments, whether paid in installments or in a lump sum and whether paid pursuant to the offer or a collateral agreement, to periods in the order of priority that the Service determines will serve its best interest. The payment will be applied to satisfy the liability for successive periods in descending order of priority until the payment is absorbed. If the amount applied to a period is less than the liability for the period, the amount will be applied to tax, penalty, and interest, in that order, until the amount is absorbed.

.04 If any part of a payment is applied to interest under the rules set forth in this revenue procedure, the amount applied to interest is treated for purposes of §163 of the Code as interest paid in the year in which the payment is made. Under §163, interest paid or accrued in a taxable year may be deducted in calculating taxable income for the year except to the extent such interest is personal interest as defined in §163(h) and §1.163-9T(b)(2) of the Income Tax Regulations or is otherwise disallowed under applicable provisions of the Internal Revenue Code and Income Tax Regulations.

SECTION 4. EFFECT ON OTHER DOCUMENTS

Rev. Rul. 73-304, Rev. Rul. 73-305, and Rev. Rul. 79-284 are hereby superseded.

SECTION 5. DRAFTING INFORMATION

The principal author of this revenue procedure is Inga Plucinski of the Office of Associate Chief Counsel (Procedure and Administration), Administrative Provisions and Judicial Practice. For further information regarding this revenue procedure, contact Emly Berndt at (202) 622-4940 (not a toll-free call).

January 3, 2020

VIA FEDERAL EXPRESS
Department of Treasury
Internal Revenue Service
Attn: REVENUE OFFICER NAME
Street Address
City, State Zip

      Re: **TAXPAYER NAME, SSN: xxx-xx-xxxx**
              Directed Payment of Trust Fund Portion of Employment Taxes
              Employer: COMPANY NAME, Inc., EIN XX-XXXXXXX

Dear REVENUE OFFICER NAME:

      This office represents TAXPAYERS NAME and COMPANY NAME, Inc. Enclosed please find a check in the amount of $499,261.57 (check # _____) payable to the U.S. Treasury. Pursuant to Rev. Proc. 2002-26, 2002-15 IRB 746, 2002-1 CB 746 and IRM 5.1.2.3 and 26 C.F.R. 301.7701-2(c)(2)(iv), this payment constitutes a voluntary payment and should be applied to reduce any trust fund recovery penalty and/or trust fund portions of employment taxes for which TAXPAYERS NAME is personally liable.

      If for any reason the Internal Revenue Service intends and/or expects to apply the enclosed payment *not* in accordance with this letter of direction, the U.S. Treasury is *not* authorized to deposit the enclosed check and it should be returned to me.

      Please call me should you have any questions.

                            Very truly yours,

                            REP NAME

EXHIBIT 27

Form **14135** (June 2010)	Department of the Treasury — Internal Revenue Service **Application for Certificate of Discharge of Property from Federal Tax Lien**	OMB No. 1545-2174

Complete the entire application. Enter NA *(not applicable)*, when appropriate. Attachments and exhibits should be included as necessary. Additional information may be requested of you or a third party to clarify the details of the transaction(s).

1. Taxpayer Information *(Individual or Business named on the notice of lien)*:

Name *(Individual First, Middle Initial, Last)* or *(Business)* as it appears on lien	Primary Social Security Number *(last 4 digits only)*
Name Continuation *(Individual First, Middle Initial, Last)* or *(Business d/b/a)*	Secondary Social Security Number *(last 4 digits only)*
Address *(Number, Street, P.O. Box)*	Employer Identification Number

City	State	ZIP Code
Telephone Number *(with area code)*	Fax Number *(with area code)*	

2. Applicant Information: ☐ Check if also the Taxpayer *(If not the taxpayer, attach copy of lien. See Sec.10)*

Name *(First, Middle Initial, Last)*	Relationship to taxpayer
Address *(Number, Street, P.O. Box)*	

City	State	ZIP Code
Telephone Number *(with area code)*	Fax Number *(with area code)*	

3. Purchase/Transferee/New Owner   ☐ Check if also the Applicant

	Relationship to taxpayer

4. Attorney/Representative Information   Attached: Form 8821 or Power of Attorney Form 2848   ☐ Yes   ☐ No

Name *(First, Middle Initial, Last)*	Interest Represented *(e.g. taxpayer, lender, etc.)*
Address *(Number, Street, P.O. Box)*	

City	State	ZIP Code
Telephone Number *(with area code)*	Fax Number *(with area code)*	

5. Lender/Finance Company Information - or *(Settlement/Escrow Company* for applications under Section 6325(b)(3) only)

Company Name	Contact Name	Contact Phone Number

Catalog Number 54727S   www.irs.gov   Form **14135** (Rev. 06-2010)

EXHIBIT 28

6. Monetary Information

Proposed sales price	
Expected proceeds to be paid to the United States in exchange for the certificate of discharge (Enter NA if no proceeds are anticipated)	

7. Basis for Discharge:
Check the box below that best addresses what you would like the United States to consider in your application for discharge. (Publication 783 has additional descriptions of the Internal Revenue Code sections listed below.)

☐ 6325(b)(1)   Value of property remaining attached by the lien(s) is at least double the liability of the federal tax lien(s) plus other encumbrances senior to the lien(s)

☐ 6325(b)(2)(A)   The United States receives an amount not less than the value of the United States' interest.
                   (**Note**: If you are applying under 6325(b)(2)(A) and are the property owner but not the taxpayer, see also section 16.)

☐ 6325(b)(2)(B)   Interest of the United States in the property to be discharged has no value.

☐ 6325(b)(3)   Proceeds from property sale held in escrow subject to the liens and claims of the United States.

☐ 6325(b)(4)   Deposit made or bond furnished in an amount equal to the value of the United States' interest.
                   (**Note**: This selection provides a remedy under 7426(a)(4) for return of deposit but is exclusively for a property owner not named as the taxpayer on the lien)

8. Description of property (for example, 3 bedroom rental house; 2002 Cessna twin engine airplane, serial number AT919000000000X00; etc.):

Address of real property (If this is personal property, list the address where the property is located):
Address (Number, Street, P.O. Box)

City	State	ZIP Code

FOR REAL ESTATE: a legible copy of the deed or title showing the legal description is required	☐ Attached	☐ NA
FOR Discharge Requests under Section 6325(b)(1): copy of deed(s) or title(s) for property remaining subject to the Federal Tax Lien is required	☐ Attached	☐ NA

9. Appraisal and Valuations

REQUIRED APPRAISAL Professional appraisal completed by a disinterested third party	☐ Attached
PLUS ONE OF THE FOLLOWING ADDITIONAL VALUATIONS:	
County valuation of property (real property)	☐ Attached
Informal valuation of property by disinterested third party	☐ Attached
Proposed selling price (for property being sold at auction)	☐ Attached
Other: _____	☐ Attached

AND for applications under Section 6325(b)(1), valuation information (of the type described above in this section) must also be provided for property remaining subject to the lien.

10. Copy of Federal Tax Lien(s) *(Complete if applicant and taxpayer differ)* ☐ Attached ☐ No

OR list the lien number(s) found near the top right corner on the lien document(s) *(if known)*

11. Copy of the sales contract/purchase agreement *(if available)* ☐ Attached ☐ No

OR

Describe how and when the taxpayer will be divested of his/her interest in the property:

12. Copy of a current title report ☐ Attached ☐ No

OR

List encumbrances senior to the Federal Tax Lien. Include name and address of holder; description of encumbrance, e.g., mortgage, state lien, etc.; date of agreement; original loan amount and interest rate; amount due at time of application; and family relationship, if applicable *(Attach additional sheets as needed)*:

13. Copy of proposed closing statement *(aka HUD-1)* ☐ Attached ☐ No

OR

Itemize all proposed costs, commissions, and expenses of any transfer or sale associated with property *(Attach additional sheets as needed)*:

14. Additional information that may have a bearing on this request, such as pending litigation, explanations of unusual situations, etc., is attached for consideration ☐ Attached ☐ No

15. Escrow Agreement *(For applications under IRC 6325(b)(3))* ☐ Attached ☐ No
Escrow agreement must specify type of account, name and depositary for account, conditions under which payment will be made, cost of escrow, name and address of any party identified as part of escrow agreement, and signatures of all parties involved including Advisory Group Manager. Terms for agreement must be reached before discharge approved.

16. WAIVER *(For applications made by third parties under IRC 6325(b)(2))*
If you are applying as an owner of the property and you are not the taxpayer, to have this application considered under section 6325(b)(2), you must waive the rights that would be available if the application were made under section 6325(b)(4). If you choose not to waive these rights, the application will be treated as one made under 6325(b)(4) and any payment will be treated like a deposit under that section. Please check the appropriate box.

I understand that an application and payment made under section 6325(b)(2) does not provide the judicial remedy available under section 7426(a)(4). In making such an application / payment, I waive the option to have the payment treated as a deposit under section 6325(b)(4) and the right to request a return of funds and to bring an action under section 7426(a)(4). ☐ Waive ☐ No

17. Declaration
Under penalties of perjury, I declare that I have examined this application, including any accompanying schedules, exhibits, affidavits, and statements and to the best of my knowledge and belief it is true, correct and complete.

_____ _____
Signature/Title   Date

_____ _____
Signature/Title   Date

UNITED STATES DISTRICT COURT

DISTRICT OF OREGON

PORTLAND DIVISION

UNITED STATES OF AMERICA,

v.

GARY B. BERTONI,

Defendant.

Case No. 3:15-CR-00410-HZ

INDICTMENT

26 U.S.C. § 7202

THE GRAND JURY CHARGES:

Introductory Allegations
Parties and Entities

1. At all times relevant to this Indictment, Gary B. BERTONI was a resident of Lake Oswego, Oregon.

2. At all times relevant to this Indictment, Bertoni & Associates, LLC (hereinafter "LAW FIRM") was a limited liability corporation doing business in Portland, Oregon, which is within the District of Oregon.

3. In or about November 2007 defendant BERTONI created LAW FIRM, a sole member limited liability corporation in the State of Oregon.

4. From November 2007 to at least July 2012, BERTONI was the sole member and general manager of LAW FIRM and had significant control of LAW FIRM.

5. As the sole member and general manager of LAW FIRM, BERTONI exercised significant control over LAW FIRM business affairs and finances, controlled all LAW FIRM bank accounts, possessed the authority to hire and fire employees, made decisions as to the disbursement of funds and payment of creditors, and possessed check-signing authority.

Employment Tax Withholding

6. At all times relevant to this Indictment, LAW FIRM withheld taxes from its employees' paychecks, including federal income taxes, and Medicare and social security taxes (often referred to as Federal Insurance Contribution Act or "FICA" taxes). These taxes will be referred to in this Indictment collectively as "payroll taxes."

7. At all times relevant to this Indictment, LAW FIRM was required to make deposits of the payroll taxes to the Internal Revenue Service on a periodic basis. In addition, LAW FIRM was required to file, at the end of the month following the end of each calendar quarter, an Employer's Quarterly Federal Income Tax Return (Form 941), setting forth the total amount of wages and other compensation subject to withholding, the total amount of income tax withheld, the total amount of social security and Medicare taxes due, and the total tax deposits. For example, the Form 941 for the 2nd quarter of 2009 was due on or before July 31, 2009, because the 2nd calendar quarter ended on June 30, 2009.

8. As the sole owner and general manager of LAW FIRM, defendant BERTONI was a "responsible person," that is, he had the corporate responsibility to collect, truthfully account for, and pay over LAW FIRM's payroll taxes.

9. Throughout the calendar years 2009 through 2011, LAW FIRM withheld tax payments from its employees' paychecks. Beginning in approximately the first quarter of 2009,

however, LAW FIRM failed to pay over fully to the IRS those payroll taxes withheld from the total taxable wages of its employees as they became due.

10. During the calendar years 2009, 2010, and 2011, LAW FIRM further failed to timely file quarterly employment tax returns (Forms 941) with the Internal Revenue Service.

11. During the period of January 2009 through at least July 2012, defendant BERTONI caused LAW FIRM to make thousands of dollars of expenditures for defendant's personal benefit while, at the same time, failing to pay over to the Internal Revenue Service payroll tax withheld from LAW FIRM employees' paychecks and, further, failing to remit monies withheld from LAW FIRM employees' paychecks for various employee benefits, including health insurance and retirement account contributions. For example, BERTONI caused LAW FIRM to make payments to BERTONI's personal bank accounts totaling more than $300,000 during the 2009, 2010, and 2011 calendar years.

12. Altogether, during the ten calendar quarters alleged in Counts 1-10 of this Indictment, LAW FIRM failed to account for and pay over approximately $184,791 in payroll taxes.

Counts 1-10
Failure to Pay Over Employment Tax
(26 U.S.C. § 7202)

13. The Grand Jury hereby repeats and re-alleges paragraphs 1 – 12 of this Indictment as if fully set forth here.

14. Beginning on or about July 31, 2009, and continuing up to and including on or about October 31, 2011, in the District of Oregon, the defendant, BERTONI, a responsible person of LAW FIRM, did willfully fail to truthfully account for, collect, and pay over to the United States, namely the Internal Revenue Service, the federal income taxes and Federal

Insurance Contributions Act ("FICA") taxes withheld and due and owing to the United States on behalf of LAW FIRM and its employees, in the amounts set forth in the table below, for each of the following quarters set forth in the table below, with each calendar quarter constituting a separate count of this Indictment:

Count	Quarter		Quarterly Due Date	Approx. Tax Due
1	2009	2nd	Jul. 31, 2009	$18,414
2	2009	3rd	Oct. 31, 2009	$20,658
3	2009	4th	Jan. 31, 2010	$19,261
4	2010	1st	Apr. 30, 2010	$18,831
5	2010	2nd	Jul. 31, 2010	$19,079
6	2010	3rd	Oct. 31, 2010	$17,421
7	2010	4th	Jan. 31, 2011	$17,579
8	2011	1st	Apr. 30, 2011	$17,640
9	2011	2nd	Jul. 31, 2011	$17,270
10	2011	3rd	Oct. 31, 2011	$18,636

//

//

//

//

//

//

INDICTMENT
United States v. Gary B. Bertoni

15. Each of these counts is a separate violation of Title 26, United States Code, Section 7202.

DATED this 18th day of November, 2015.

A TRUE BILL.

_____
OFFICIATING FOREPERSON

Presented By:
CAROLINE D. CIRAOLO
Acting Assistant Attorney General

_____
STUART A. WEXLER
QUINN P. HARRINGTON
Trial Attorneys
United States Department of Justice
Tax Division

INDICTMENT
United States v. Gary B. Bertoni

CPSIA information can be obtained
at www.ICGtesting.com
Printed in the USA
JSRBC010501100620
6115JS00009BA/5